ECCO Travels

THE MATE'S SHADOW FROZE TO THE DECK

FOLLOWING
THE
EQUATOR

A Journey Around the World

MARK TWAIN

Vol. II · Illustrated

THE ECCO PRESS

Originally published by P.F. Collier & Son Company, New York
Published in 1993 by The Ecco Press
100 West Broad Street, Hopewell, NJ 08525
Published simultaneously in Canada by
Penguin Books Canada Ltd., Ontario
Printed in the United States of America
Designed by Nick Mazzella

Library of Congress Cataloging-in-Publication Data
  (Revised for vol. 2)

Twain, Mark 1835–1910.
  Following the equator.

  (Ecco travels)
  Originally published: New York: P.F. Collins, 1897.
  1. Twain, Mark, 1835–1910—Journeys.   2. Voyages and
travels.   I. Title.   II. Series
G440.T95T93   1992   910.4'1   91-34826
ISBN 0-88001-280-3 (v. 1: paper)
ISBN 0-88001-297-8 (v. 2)

The text of this book is set in Bembo.

Contents

CONTENTS

FOLLOWING
THE
EQUATOR

Chapter I

To succeed in the other trades, capacity must be shown; in the law, concealment of it will do.
—Pudd'nhead Wilson's New Calendar.

To succeed in the other trades, capacity must be shown;
in the law, concealment of it will do.
          —Pudd'nhead Wilson's New Calendar.

*M*ONDAY, *December 23 1895* Sailed from Sydney for Ceylon in the P. & O. steamer *Oceana*. A Lascar crew mans this ship—the first I have seen. White cotton petticoat and pants; barefoot; red shawl for belt; straw cap, brimless, on head, with red scarf wound around it; complexion a rich dark brown; short straight black hair; whiskers fine and silky; lustrous and intensely black. Mild, good faces; willing and obedient people; capable, too; but are said to go into hopeless panics when there is danger. They are from Bombay and the coast thereabouts. . . . Left some of the trunks in Sydney, to be shipped to South Africa by a vessel advertised to sail three months hence. The proverb says: "Separate not yourself from your baggage." . . . This *Oceana* is a stately big ship, luxuriously appointed. She has spacious promenade decks. Large rooms; a surpassingly comfortable ship. The officers' library is well selected; a ship's library is not usually that. . . . For meals, the bugle-call, man–of–war fashion; a pleasant change

from the terrible gong. . . . Three big cats—very friendly
loafers; they wander all over the ship; the white one follows
the chief steward around like a dog. There is also a basket of
kittens. One of these cats goes ashore, in port, in England,
Australia, and India, to see how his various families are getting along, and is seen no more till the ship is ready to sail.
No one knows how he finds out the sailing-date, but no
doubt he comes down to the dock every day and takes a
look, and when he sees baggage and passengers flocking in,
recognizes that it is time to get aboard. This is what the sailors
believe. . . . The Chief Engineer has been in the China and
India trade thirty-three years, and has had but three Christ-
mases at home in that time. . . . Conversational items at
dinner: "Mocha! sold all over the world! It is not true. In fact,
very few foreigners except the Emperor of Russia have ever
seen a grain of it, or ever will, while they live." Another man
said: "There is no sale in Australia for Australian wine. But
it goes to France and comes back with a French label on it,
and then they buy it." I have heard that the most of the
French-labeled claret in New York is made in California. And
I remember what Professor S. told me once about Veuve
Clicquot—if that was the wine, and I think it was. He was
the guest of a great wine merchant whose town was quite
near that vineyard, and this merchant asked him if very much
V.C. was drunk in America.

"Oh, yes," said S., "a great abundance of it."

"Is it easy to be had?"

"Oh, yes—easy as water. All first and second class hotels
have it."

"What do you pay for it?"

"It depends on the style of the hotel—from fifteen to
twenty-five francs a bottle."

"Oh, fortunate country! Why, it's worth one hundred
francs right here on the ground."

"No."

"Yes."

"Do you mean that we are drinking a bogus Veuve Clicquot over there?"

"Yes—and there was never a bottle of the genuine in America since Columbus's time. That wine all comes from a little bit of a patch of ground which isn't big enough to raise many bottles; and all of it that is produced goes every year to one person—the Emperor of Russia. He takes the whole crop in advance, be it big or little."

January 4, 1896. Christmas in Melbourne, New Year's Day in Adelaide, and saw most of the friends again in both places. . . . Lying here at anchor all day—Albany (King George's Sound), Western Australia. It is a perfectly land-locked harbor, or roadstead—spacious to look at, but not deep water. Desolate-looking rocks and scarred hills. Plenty of ships arriving now, rushing to the new gold-fields. The papers are full of wonderful tales of the sort always to be heard in connection with new gold diggings. A sample: a youth staked out a claim and tried to sell half for five pounds; no takers; he stuck to it fourteen days, starving, then struck it rich and sold out for ten thousand pounds. . . . About sunset, strong breeze blowing, got up the anchor. We were in a small deep puddle, with a narrow channel leading out of it, minutely buoyed, to the sea. I stayed on deck to see how we were going to manage it with such a big ship and such a strong wind. On the bridge our giant captain, in uniform; at his side a little pilot in elaborately gold-laced uniform; on the forecastle a white mate and quartermaster or two, and a brilliant crowd of lascars standing by for business. Our stern was pointing straight at the head of the channel; so we must turn entirely around in the puddle—and the wind blowing as described. It was done, and beautifully. It was done by help of a jib. We stirred up much mud, but did not touch the bottom. We turned right around in our tracks—a seeming impossibility. We had several casts of quarter-less 5, and one cast of half 4—27 feet; we were drawing 26 astern. By the time we were entirely around and *pointed*, the first buoy was not more than a hundred yards in front of us. It was a fine piece of work, and I was the only passenger that saw it. However, the others got their dinner; the P. & O. Company got mine. . . . More cats developed. Smythe says it is a British law that they must be carried; and he instanced a case of a ship not allowed to sail till she sent for a couple. The bill came, too: "Debtor, to two cats, twenty shillings." . . . News comes that within this week Siam has acknowledged herself to be, in effect, a French province. It seems plain that all savage and semi-civilized countries are going to be grabbed. . . . A vulture on board; bald, red, queer-shaped head, featherless red places here and there on his body, intense great black eyes set in featherless rims of inflamed flesh; dissipated look; a businesslike style, a selfish, conscienceless, murderous aspect—the very look of a professional assassin, and yet a bird which does no murder. What was the use of getting him up in that tragic style for so innocent a trade as his? For this one isn't the sort that wars upon the living, his diet is offal—and the more out of date it is the better he likes it. Nature should give him a suit of rusty black; then he would be all right, for he would look like an undertaker and would harmonize with his business; whereas the way he is now he is horribly out of true.

January 5. At nine this morning we passed Cape Leeuwin (lioness) and ceased from our long due-west course along the southern shore of Australia. Turning this extreme southwestern corner, we now take a long straight slant nearly N.W., without a break, for Ceylon. As we speed northward it will grow hotter very fast—but it isn't chilly, now. . . . The vulture is from the public menagerie at Adelaide—a great and interesting collection. It was there that we saw the baby tiger solemnly spreading its mouth and trying to roar like its majestic mother. It swaggered, scowling, back and forth on its short legs just as it had seen her do on her long ones, and now and then snarling viciously, exposing its teeth, with a threatening lift of its upper lip and bristling mustache; and when it thought it was impressing the visitors, it would spread its mouth wide and do that screechy cry which it meant for a roar, but which did not deceive. It took itself quite seriously, and was lovably comical. And there was a hyena—an ugly creature; as ugly as the tiger-kitty was pretty. It repeatedly arched its back and delivered itself of *such* a human cry; a startling resemblance; a cry which was just that of a grown person badly hurt. In the dark one would assuredly go to its assistance—and be disappointed. . . . Many friends of Australasian Federation on board. They feel sure that the good day is not far off, now. But there seems to be a party that would go further—have Australasia cut loose from the British Empire and set up housekeeping on her own hook. It seems an unwise idea. They point to the United States, but it seems to me that the cases lack a good deal of being alike. Australasia governs herself wholly—there is no interference; and her commerce and manufactures are not oppressed in any way. If our case had been the same we should not have gone out when we did.

January 13. Unspeakably hot. The equator is arriving again. We are within eight degrees of it. Ceylon present. Dear me, it is beautiful! And most sumptuously tropical, as to character of foliage and opulence of it. "What though the spicy breezes blow soft o'er Ceylon's isle"—an eloquent line, an incomparable line; it says little, but conveys whole libraries of sentiment, and Oriental charm and mystery, and tropic deliciousness—a line that quivers and tingles with a thousand unexpressed and inexpressible things, things that haunt one and find no articulate voice. . . . Colombo, the capital. An Oriental town, most manifestly; and fascinating. . . . In this palatial ship the passengers dress for dinner. The ladies' toilettes make a fine display of color, and this is in keeping with the elegance of the vessel's furnishings and the flooding brilliancies of the electric light. On the stormy Atlantic one never sees a man in evening dress, except at the rarest intervals; and then there is only one, not two; and he shows up but once on a voyage—the night before the ship makes port—the night when they have the "concert" and do the amateur wailings and recitations. He is the tenor, as a rule. . . . There has been a deal of cricket-playing on board; it seems a queer game for a ship, but they inclose the promenade deck with nettings and keep the ball from flying overboard, and the sport goes very well, and is properly violent and exciting. . . . We must part from this vessel here.

January 14. Hotel Bristol. Servant Brompy. Alert, gentle, smiling, winning young brown creature as ever was. Beautiful shining black hair combed back like a woman's, and knotted at the back of his head—tortoise-shell comb in it, sign that he is a Singhalese; slender, shapely form; jacket; under it is a beltless and flowing white cotton gown—from neck straight to heel; he and his outfit quite unmasculine. It was an embarrassment to undress before him.

We drove to the market, using the Japanese jinrikisha—our first acquaintanceship with it. It is a light cart, with a native to draw it. He makes good speed for half an hour, but it is hard work for him; he is too slight for it. After the half-hour there is no more pleasure for you; your attention is all on the man, just as it would be on a tired horse, and necessarily your sympathy is there, too. There's a plenty of these 'rikishas, and the tariff is incredibly cheap.

I was in Cairo years ago. That was Oriental, but there was a lack. When you are in Florida or New Orleans you are in the South—that is granted; but you are not in *the* South; you are in a modified South, a tempered South. Cairo was a tempered Orient—an Orient with an indefinite something wanting. That feeling was not present in Ceylon. Ceylon was Oriental in the last measure of completeness—utterly Oriental; also utterly tropical; and indeed to one's unreasoning spiritual sense the two things belong together. All the requisites were present. The costumes were right; the black and brown exposures, unconscious of immodesty, were right; the juggler was there, with his basket, his snakes, his mongoose, and his arrangements for growing a tree from seed to foliage and ripe fruitage before one's eyes; in sight were plants and flowers familiar to one on books but in no other way—celebrated, desirable, strange, but in production restricted to the hot belt of the equator; and out a little way in the country were the proper deadly snakes, and fierce beasts of prey, and the wild elephant and the monkey. And there was that swoon in the air which one associates with the tropics, and that smother of heat, heavy with odors of unknown flowers, and that sudden invasion of purple gloom fissured with lightnings—then the tumult of crashing thunder and the downpour—and presently all sunny and smiling again; all these things were there; the conditions were complete, nothing was lacking. And away off in the deeps of the jungle and in the remotenesses of the mountains were the ruined cities and moldering temples, mysterious relics of the pomps of a forgotten time and a vanished race—and this was as it should be, also, for nothing is quite satisfyingly Oriental that lacks the somber and impressive qualities of mystery and antiquity.

The drive through the town and out to the Gallè Face by the seashore, what a dream it was of tropical splendors of bloom and blossom, and Oriental conflagrations of costume! The walking groups of men, women, boys, girls, babies— each individual was a flame, each group a house afire for color. And such stunning colors, such intensely vivid colors, such rich and exquisite minglings and fusings of rainbows and lightnings! And all harmonious, all in perfect taste; never a discordant note; never a color on any person swearing at another color on him or failing to harmonize faultlessly with the colors of any group the wearer might join. The stuffs were silk—thin, soft, delicate, clinging; and, as a rule, each piece a solid color: a splendid green, a splendid blue, a splendid yellow, a splendid purple, a splendid ruby, deep and rich with smoldering fires—they swept continuously by in crowds and legions and multitudes, glowing, flashing, burning, radiant; and every five seconds came a burst of blinding red that made a body catch his breath, and filled his heart with joy. And then, the unimaginable grace of those costumes! Sometimes a woman's whole dress was but a scarf wound about her person and her head, sometimes a man's was but a turban and a careless rag or two—in both cases generous areas of polished dark skin showing—but always the arrangement compelled the homage of the eye and made the heart sing for gladness.

I can see it to this day, that radiant panorama, that wilderness of rich color, that incomparable dissolving-view of harmonious tints, and lithe half-covered forms, and beautiful brown faces, and gracious and graceful gestures and attitudes and movements, free, unstudied, barren of stiffness and restraint, and—

Just then, into this dream of fairyland and paradise a grating dissonance was injected. Out of a missionary school came marching, two and two, sixteen prim and pious little Christian black girls, Europeanly clothed—dressed, to the last detail, as they would have been dressed on a summer Sunday in an English or American village. Those clothes— oh, they were unspeakably ugly! Ugly, barbarous, destitute of taste, destitute of grace, repulsive as a shroud. I looked at my womenfolk's clothes—just full-grown duplicates of the outrages disguising those poor little abused creatures—and was ashamed to be seen in the street with them. Then I looked at my own clothes, and was ashamed to be seen in the street with myself.

However, we must put up with our clothes as they are— they have their reason for existing. They are on us to expose us—to advertise what we wear them to conceal. They are a sign; a sign of insincerity; a sign of suppressed vanity; a pretense that we despise gorgeous colors and the graces of harmony and form; and we put them on to propagate that lie and back it up. But we do not deceive our neighbor; and when we step into Ceylon we realize that we have not even deceived ourselves. We do love brilliant colors and graceful costumes; and at home we will turn out in a storm to see them when the procession goes by—and envy the wearers. We go to the theater to look at them and grieve that we can't be clothed like that. We go to the King's ball, when we get a chance, and are glad of a sight of the splendid uniforms and the glittering orders. When we are granted permission to attend an imperial drawing-room we shut ourselves up in private and parade around in the theatrical court-dress by the hour, and admire ourselves in the glass, and are utterly happy; and every member of every governor's staff in democratic America does the same with his grand new uniform—and if he is not watched he will get himself photographed in it, too. When I see the Lord Mayor's footman I am dissatisfied with my lot. Yes, our clothes are a lie, and have been nothing short of that these hundred years. They are insincere, they are the ugly and appropriate outward exposure of an inward sham and a moral decay.

The last little brown boy I chanced to notice in the

crowds and swarms of Colombo had nothing on but a twine string around his waist, but in my memory the frank honesty of his costume still stands out in pleasant contrast with the odious flummery in which the little Sunday-school dowdies were masquerading.

Chapter II

Prosperity is the best protector of principle.
—Pudd'nhead Wilson's New Calendar.

*E*VENING—*14th*. Sailed in the *Rosetta*. This is a poor old ship, and ought to be insured and sunk. As in the *Oceana,* just so here: everybody dresses for dinner; they make it a sort of pious duty. These fine and formal costumes are a rather conspicuous contrast to the poverty and shabbiness of the surroundings. . . . If you want a slice of a lime at four-o'clock tea, you must sign an order on the bar. Limes cost fourteen cents a barrel.

January 18. We have been running up the Arabian Sea, latterly. Closing up on Bombay now, and due to arrive this evening.

January 20. Bombay! A bewitching place, a bewildering place, an enchanting place—the Arabian Nights come again! It is a vast city; contains about a million inhabitants. Natives, they are, with a slight sprinkling of white people—not enough to have the slightest modifying effect upon the massed dark complexion of the public. It is winter here, yet the weather is the divine weather of June, and the foliage is the fresh and heavenly foliage of June. There is a rank of noble great shade trees across the way from the hotel, and under them sit groups of picturesque natives of both sexes; and the juggler is his turban is there with his snakes and his magic; and all day long the cabs and the multitudinous varieties of costumes flock by. It does not seem as if one could ever get tired of watching this moving show, this shining and shifting spectacle. . . . In the great bazar the pack and jam of natives was marvelous, the sea of rich-colored turbans and draperies an inspiring sight, and the quaint and showy Indian architecture was just the right setting for it. Toward sunset another show; this is the drive around the seashore to Malabar Point, where Lord Sandhurst, the Governor of the Bombay Presidency, lives. Parsee palaces all along the first part of the drive; and past them all the world is driving; the private carriages of wealthy Englishmen and natives of rank are manned by a driver and three footmen in stunning oriental liveries—two of these turbaned statues standing up behind, as fine as monuments. Sometimes even the public carriages have this superabundant crew, slightly modified—one to drive, one to sit by and see it done, and one to stand up behind and yell—yell when there is anybody in the way, and for practice when there isn't. It all helps to keep up the liveliness and augment the general sense of swiftness and energy and confusion and pow-wow.

In the region of Scandal Point—felicitous name—where there are handy rocks to sit on and a noble view of the sea on the one hand, and on the other the passing and repassing whirl and tumult of gay carriages, are great groups of comfortably off Parsee women—perfect flower-beds of brilliant color, a fascinating spectacle. Tramp, tramp, tramping along the road, in singles, couples, groups, and gangs, you have the working-man and the working-woman—but not clothed

like ours. Usually the man is a nobly built great athlete, with
not a rag on but his loin-handkerchief; his color a deep dark
brown, his skin satin, his rounded muscles knobbing it as if
it had eggs under it. Usually the woman is a slender and
shapely creature, as erect as a lightning-rod, and she has but
one thing on—a bright-colored piece of stuff which is wound
about her head and her body down nearly half-way to her
knees, and which clings like her own skin. Her legs and feet
are bare, and so are her arms, except for her fanciful bunches
of loose silver rings on her ankles and on her arms. She has
jewelry bunched on the side of her nose also, and showy
cluster-rings on her toes. When she undresses for bed she
takes off her jewelry, I suppose. If she took off anything more
she would catch cold. As a rule, she has a large shiny brass
water-jar of graceful shape on her head, and one of her naked
arms curves up and the hand holds it there. She is so straight,
so erect, and she steps with such style, and such easy grace
and dignity; and her curved arm and her brazen jar are such
a help to the picture—indeed, our working-women cannot
begin with her as a road decoration.

It is all color, bewitching color, enchanting color—everywhere—all around—all the way around the curving great
opaline bay clear to Government House, where the turbaned
big native *chuprassies* stand grouped in state at the door in
their robes of fiery red, and do most properly and stunningly
finish up the splendid show and make it theatrically complete.
I wish I were a *chuprassy*.

This is indeed India; the land of dreams and romance, of
fabulous wealth and fabulous poverty, of splendor and rags,
of palaces and hovels, of famine and pestilence, of genii and
giants and Aladdin lamps, of tigers and elephants, the cobra
and the jungle, the country of a hundred nations and a hundred tongues, of a thousand religions and two million gods,
cradle of the human race, birthplace of human speech, mother

of history, grandmother of legend, great-grandmother of tradition, whose yesterdays bear date with the moldering antiquities of the rest of the nations—the one sole country under the sun that is endowed with an imperishable interest for alien prince and alien peasant, for lettered and ignorant, wise and fool, rich and poor, bond and free, the one land that *all* men desire to see, and having seen once, by even a glimpse, would not give that glimpse for the shows of all the rest of the globe combined.

Even now, after the lapse of a year, the delirium of those days in Bombay has not left me, and I hope never will. It was all new, no detail of it hackneyed. And India did not wait for morning, it began at the hotel—straight away. The lobbies and halls were full of turbaned and fez'd and embroidered, cap'd, and barefooted, and cotton-clad dark natives, some of them rushing about, others at rest squatting, or sitting on the ground; some of them chattering with energy, others still and dreamy; in the dining-room every man's own private native servant standing behind his chair, and dressed for a part in the Arabian Nights.

Our rooms were high up, on the front. A white man— he was a burly German—went up with us, and brought three natives along to see to arranging things. About fourteen others followed in procession, with the hand-baggage; each carried an article—and only one; a bag, in some cases, in other cases less. One strong native carried my overcoat, another a parasol, another a box of cigars, another a novel, and the last man in the procession had no load but a fan. It was all done with earnestness and sincerity, there was not a smile in the procession from the head of it to the tail of it. Each man waited patiently, tranquilly, in no sort of hurry, till one of us found time to give him a copper, then he bent his head reverently, touched his forehead with his fingers, and went

EACH CARRIED ONE ARTICLE

his way. They seemed a soft and gentle race, and there was something both winning and touching about their demeanor.

There was a vast glazed door which opened upon the balcony. It needed closing, or cleaning, or something, and a native got down on his knees and went to work at it. He seemed to be doing it well enough, but perhaps he wasn't, for the burly German put on a look that betrayed dissatisfaction, then without *explaining* what was wrong, gave the native a brisk cuff on the jaw and *then* told him where the defect was. It seemed such a shame to do that before us all. The native took it with meekness, saying nothing, and not showing in his face or manner any resentment. I had not seen the like of this for fifty years. It carried me back to my boyhood, and flashed upon me the forgotten fact that this was the *usual* way of explaining one's desires to a slave. I was able to remember that the method seemed right and natural to me in those days, I being born to it and unaware that elsewhere there were other methods; but I was also able to remember that those unresented cuffings made me sorry for the victim and ashamed for the punisher. My father was a refined and kindly gentleman, very grave, rather austere, of rigid probity, a sternly just and upright man, albeit he attended no church and never spoke of religious matters, and had no part nor lot in the pious joys of his Presbyterian family, nor ever seemed to suffer from this deprivation. He laid his hand upon me in punishment only twice in his life, and then not heavily; once for telling him a lie—which surprised me, and showed me how unsuspicious he was, for that was not my maiden effort. He punished me those two times only, and never any other member of the family at all; yet every now and then he cuffed our harmless slave-boy, Lewis, for trifling little blunders and awkwardnesses. My father had passed his life among the slaves from his cradle up, and his cuffings proceeded from the custom of the time, not from his nature. When I was ten years old I saw a man fling a lump of iron-ore at a slave-man in anger, for merely doing something awkwardly—as if that were a crime. It bounded from the man's skull, and the man fell and never spoke again. He was dead in an hour. I knew the man had a right to kill his slave if he wanted to, and yet it seemed a pitiful thing and somehow wrong, though why wrong I was not deep enough to explain if I had been asked to do it. Nobody in the village approved of that murder, but of course no one said much about it.

It is curious—the space annihilating power of thought. For just one second, all that goes to make the *me* in me was in a Missourian village, on the other side of the globe, vividly seeing again these forgotten pictures of fifty years ago, and wholly unconscious of all things but just those; and in the next second I was back in Bombay, and that kneeling native's smitten cheek was not done tingling yet! Back to boyhood—fifty years; back to age again, another fifty; and a flight equal to the circumference of the globe—all in two seconds by the watch!

Some natives—I don't remember how many—went into my bedroom, now, and put things to rights and arranged the mosquito-bar, and I went to bed to nurse my cough. It was about nine in the evening. What a state of things! For three hours the yelling and shouting of natives in the hall continued, along with the velvety patter of their swift bare feet—what a racket it was! They were yelling orders and messages down three flights. Why, in the matter of noise it amounted to a riot, an insurrection, a revolution. And then there were other noises mixed up with these and at intervals tremendously accenting them—roofs falling in, I judged, windows smashing, persons being murdered, crows squawking, and deriding, and cursing, canaries screeching, monkeys jabbering, macaws blaspheming, and every now and then fiendish bursts of laughter and explosions of dynamite. By midnight I had suffered all the different kinds of shocks there are, and knew that I could never more be disturbed by them, either isolated or in combination. Then came peace—stillness deep and solemn—and lasted till five.

Then it all broke loose again. And who restarted it? The Bird of Birds—the Indian crow. I came to know him well, by and by, and be infatuated with him. I suppose he is the hardest lot that wears feathers. Yes, and the cheerfulest, and the best satisfied with himself. He never arrived at what he is by any careless process, or any sudden one; he is a work of art, and "art is long"; he is the product of immemorial ages, and of deep calculation; one can't make a bird like that in a day. He has been reincarnated more times than Shiva; and he has kept a sample of each incarnation, and fused it into his constitution. In the course of his evolutionary promotions, his sublime march toward ultimate perfection, he has been a gambler, a low comedian, a dissolute priest, a fussy woman, a blackguard, a scoffer, a liar, a thief, a spy, an informer, a trading politician, a swindler, a professional hypocrite, a patriot for cash, a reformer, a lecturer, a lawyer, a conspirator, a rebel, a royalist, a democrat, a practicer and propagator of irreverence, a meddler, an intruder, a busybody, an infidel, and a wallower in sin for the mere love of it. The strange result, the incredible result, of this patient accumulation of all damnable traits is, that he does not know what care is, he does not know what sorrow is, he does not know what remorse is; his life is one long thundering ecstasy of happiness, and he will go to his death untroubled, knowing that he will soon turn up again as an author or something, and be even more intolerably capable and comfortable than ever he was before.

In his straddling wide forward-step, and his springy sidewise series of hops, and his impudent air, and his cunning way of canting his head to one side upon occasion, he reminds one of the American blackbird. But the sharp resemblances stop there. He is much bigger than the blackbird; and he lacks the blackbird's trim and slender and beautiful build and shapely beak; and of course his sober garb of gray and rusty black is a poor and humble thing compared with the splendid luster of the blackbird's metallic sables and shifting and flashing bronze glories. The blackbird is a perfect gentleman, in deportment and attire, and is not noisy, I believe, except when holding religious services and political conventions in a tree; but this Indian sham Quaker is just a rowdy, and is always noisy when awake—always chaffing, scolding, scoffing, laughing, ripping, and cursing, and carrying on about something or other. I never saw such a bird for delivering opinions. Nothing escapes him; he notices everything that happens, and brings out his opinion about it, particularly if it is a matter that is none of his business. And it is never a mild opinion, but always violent—violent and profane—the presence of ladies does not affect him. His opinions are not the outcome of reflection, for he never thinks about anything, but heaves out the opinion that is on top in his mind, and which is often an opinion about some quite different thing and does not fit the case. But that is his way; his main idea is to get out an opinion, and if he stopped to think he would lose chances.

I suppose he has no enemies among men. The whites and Mohammedans never seemed to molest him; and the Hindus, because of their religion, never take the life of any creature, but spare even the snakes and tigers and fleas and rats. If I sat on one end of the balcony, the crows would gather on the railing at the other end and talk about me; and edge closer, little by little, till I could almost reach them; and they would sit there, in the most unabashed way, and talk about my clothes, and my hair, and my complexion, and probable character and vocation and politics, and how I came to be in India, and what I had been doing, and how many days I had got for it, and how I had happened to go unhanged so long, and when would it probably come off, and might there be more of my sort where I came from, and when would *they* be hanged—and so on, and so on, until I could not longer endure the embarrassment of it; then I would shoo them away, and they would circle around in the air a little while, laughing and deriding and mocking, and presently settle on the rail and do it all over again.

They were very sociable when there was anything to eat—oppressively so. With a little encouragement they would come in and light on the table and help me eat my breakfast; and once when I was in the other room and they found themselves alone, they carried off everything they could lift; and they were particular to choose things which they could make no use of after they got them. In India their number is beyond estimate, and their noise is in proportion. I suppose they cost the country more than the government does; yet that is not a light matter. Still, they pay; their company pays; it would sadden the land to take their cheerful voice out of it.

Chapter III

By trying we can easily learn to endure adversity. Another man's, I mean.
          —Pudd'nhead Wilson's New Calender.

YOU soon find your long-ago dreams of India rising in a sort of vague and luscious moonlight above the horizon-rim of your opaque consciousness, and softly lighting up a thousand forgotten details which were parts of a vision that had once been vivid to you when you were a boy, and steeped your spirit in tales of the East. The barbaric gorgeousnesses, for instance; and the princely titles, the sumptuous titles, the sounding titles—how good they taste in the mouth! The Nizam of Hyderabad; the Maharajah of Travancore; the Nabob of Jubbulpore; the Begum of Bhopal; the Nawab of Mysore; the Ranee of Gulnare; the Ahkoond of Swat; the Rao of Rohilkund; the Gaikwar of Baroda. Indeed, it is a country that runs richly to name. The great god Vishnu has 108—108 special ones—108 peculiarly holy ones—names just for Sunday use only. I learned the whole of Vishnu's 108 by heart once, but they wouldn't stay; I don't remember any of them now but John W.

And the romances connected with those princely native houses—to this day they are always turning up, just as in the old, old times. They were sweating out a romance in an English court in Bombay a while before we were there. In this case a native prince, sixteen and a half years old, who had been enjoying his titles and dignities and estates unmolested for fourteen years, is suddenly haled into court on the charge that he is rightfully no prince at all, but a pauper peasant; that the real prince died when two and one-half years old; that the death was concealed, and a peasant child smuggled into the royal cradle, and that this present incumbent was that smuggled substitute. This is the very material that so many oriental tales have been made of.

The case of that great prince, the Gaikwar of Baroda, is a reversal of the theme. When that throne fell vacant, no heir could be found for some time, but at last one was found in the person of a peasant child who was making mud pies in a village street, and having an innocent good time. But his pedigree was straight; he was the true prince, and he has reigned ever since, with none to dispute his right.

Lately there was another hunt for an heir to another princely house, and one was found who was circumstanced about as the Gaikwar had been. His fathers were traced back, in humble life, along a branch of the ancestral tree to the point where it joined the stem fourteen generations ago, and his heirship was thereby squarely established. The tracing was done by means of the records of one of the great Hindu shrines, where princes on pilgrimage record their names and the date of their visit. This is to keep the prince's religious account straight, and his spiritual person safe; but the record has the added value of keeping the pedigree authentic, too.

When I think of Bombay now, at this distance of time, I seem to have a kaleidoscope at my eye; and I hear the clash of the glass bits as the splendid figures change, and fall apart, and flash into new forms, figure after figure, and with the birth of each new form I feel my skin crinkle and my nerve-web tingle with a new thrill of wonder and delight. These remembered pictures float past me in a sequence of contrasts; following the same order always, and always whirling by and disappearing with the swiftness of a dream, leaving me with the sense that the actuality was the experience of an hour, at most, whereas it really covered days, I think.

The series begins with the hiring of a "bearer"—native man-servant—a person who should be selected with some care, because as long as he is in your employ he will be about as near to you as your clothes.

In India your day may be said to begin with the "bearer's" knock on the bedroom door, accompanied by a formula of words—a formula which is intended to mean that the bath is ready. It doesn't really seem to mean anything at all. But that is because you are not used to "bearer" English. You will presently understand.

Where he gets his English is his own secret. There is nothing like it elsewhere in the earth; or even in paradise, perhaps, but the other place is probably full of it. You hire him as soon as you touch Indian soil; for no matter what your sex is, you cannot do without him. He is messenger, valet, chambermaid, table-waiter, lady's maid, courier—he is everything. He carries a coarse linen clothes-bag and a quilt; he sleeps on the stone floor outside your chamber door, and gets his meals you do not know where nor when; you only know that he is not fed on the premises, either when you are in a hotel or when you are a guest in a private house. His wages are large—from an Indian point of view—and he feeds and clothes himself out of them. We had three of him in two and a half months. The first one's rate was thirty rupees a month—that is to say, twenty-seven cents a day; the rate of the others, Rs. 40 (40 rupees) a month. A princely sum; for the native switchman on a railway and the native servant in a private family get only Rs. 7 per month, and the farm-hand only four. The two former feed and clothe themselves and their families on their $1.90 per month; but I cannot believe that the farm-hand has to feed himself on his $1.08. I think the farm probably feeds him, and that the whole of his wages, except a trifle for the priest, goes to the support of his family. That is, to the feeding of his family; for they live in a mud hut, hand-made, and, doubtless, rent-free, and they wear no clothes; at least, nothing more than a rag. And not much of a rag at that, in the case of the males. However, these are handsome times for the farm-hand; he was not always the child of luxury that he is now. The Chief Commissioner of the Central Provinces, in a recent official utterance wherein he was rebuking a native deputation for complaining of hard times, reminded them that they could easily remember when a farm-hand's wages were only half a rupee (former value) a month—that is to say, less than a cent a day; nearly $2.90 a year. If such a wage-earner had a good deal of a family—and they all have that, for God is very good to these poor natives in some ways—he would save a profit of fifteen cents, clean and clear, out of his year's toil; I mean a frugal, thrifty person would, not one given to display and ostentation. And if he owed $13.50 and took good care of his health, he could pay it off in ninety years. Then he could hold up his head and look his creditors in the face again.

Think of these facts and what they mean. India does not consist of cities. There are no cities in India—to speak of. Its stupendous population consists of farm-laborers. India is one vast farm—one almost interminable stretch of fields with mud fences between. Think of the above facts; and consider what an incredible aggregate of poverty they place before you.

The first Bearer that applied waited below and sent up

his recommendations. That was the first morning in Bombay. We read them over; carefully, cautiously, thoughtfully. There was not a fault to find with them—except one; they were all from Americans. Is that a slur? If it is, it is a deserved one. In my experience, an American's recommendation of a servant is not usually valuable. We are too good-natured a race; we hate to say the unpleasant thing; we shrink from speaking the unkind truth about a poor fellow whose bread depends upon our verdict; so we speak of his good points only, thus not scrupling to tell a lie—a *silent* lie—for in not mentioning his bad ones we as good as say he hasn't any. The only difference that I know of between a silent lie and a spoken one is, that the silent lie is a less respectable one than the other. And it can deceive, whereas the other can't—as a rule. We not only tell the silent lie as to a servant's faults, but we sin in another way: we overpraise his merits; for when it comes to writing recommendations of servants we are a nation of gushers. And we have not the Frenchman's excuse. In France you *must* give the departing servant a good recommendation; and you *must* conceal his faults; you have no choice. If you mention his faults for the protection of the next candidate for his services, he can sue you for damages; and the court will award them, too; and, moreover, the judge will give you a sharp dressing-down from the bench for trying to destroy a poor man's character and rob him of his bread. I do not state this on my own authority, I got it from a French physician of fame and repute—a man who was born in Paris, and had practised there all his life. And he said that he spoke not merely from common knowledge, but from exasperating personal experience.

As I was saying, the Bearer's recommendations were all from American tourists; and St. Peter would have admitted him to the fields of the blest on them—I mean if he is as unfamiliar with our people and our ways as I suppose he is.

According to these recommendations, Manuel X was supreme in all the arts connected with his complex trade; and these manifold arts were mentioned—and praised—in detail. His English was spoken of in terms of warm admiration—admiration verging upon rapture. I took pleased note of that, and hoped that some of it might be true.

We had to have some one right away; so the family went down-stairs and took him a week on trial; then sent him up to me and departed on their affairs. I was shut up in my quarters with a bronchial cough, and glad to have something fresh to look at, something new to play with. Manuel filled the bill; Manuel was very welcome. He was toward fifty years old, tall, slender, with a slight stoop—an artificial stoop, a deferential stoop, a stoop rigidified by long habit—with face of European mold; short hair, intensely black; gentle black eyes, timid black eyes, indeed; complexion very dark, nearly black in fact; face smooth-shaven. He was bareheaded and barefooted, and was never otherwise while his week with us lasted; his clothing was European, cheap, flimsy, and showed much wear.

He stood before me and inclined his head (and body) in the pathetic Indian way, touching his forehead with the finger-ends of his right hand, in salute. I said:

"Manuel, you are evidently Indian, but you seem to have a Spanish name when you put it all together. How is that?"

A perplexed look gathered in his face; it was plain that he had not understood—but he didn't let on. He spoke back placidly:

"Name, Manuel. Yes, master."

"I know; but how did you *get* the name?"

"Oh, yes, I suppose. Think happen so. Father same name, not mother."

I saw that I must simplify my language and spread my words apart, if I would be understood by this English scholar.

"Well—then—how—did—your—father—get—*his*—name?"

"Oh, he"—brightening a little—"he Christian—Portygee; live in Goa; I born Goa; mother not Portygee, mother native—high-caste Brahman—Coolin Brahman; highest caste; no other so high caste. I high-caste Brahman, too. Christian, too, same like father; high-caste Christian Brahman, master—Salvation Army."

All this haltingly, and with difficulty. Then he had an inspiration, and began to pour out a flood of words that I could make nothing of; so I said:

"There—don't do that. I can't understand Hindustani."

"Not Hindustani, master—English. Always I speaking English sometimes when I talking everyday all the time at you."

"Very well, stick to that; that is intelligible. It is not up to my hopes, it is not up to the promise of the recommendations, still it is English, and I understand it. Don't elaborate it; I don't like elaborations when they are crippled by uncertainty of touch."

"Master?"

"Oh, never mind; it was only a random thought; I didn't expect you to understand it. How did you get your English; is it an acquirement, or just a gift of God?"

After some hesitation—piously:

"Yes, he very good. Christian god very good; Hindu god very good, too. Two million Hindu god, one Christian god—make two million and one. All mine; two million and one god. I got a plenty. Sometime I pray all time at those, keep it up, go all time every day; give something at shrine, all good for me, make me better man; good for me, good for my family, dam good."

Then he had another inspiration, and went rambling off into fervent confusions and incoherencies, and I had to stop him again. I thought we had talked enough, so I told him to

go to the bathroom and clean it up and remove the slops—
this to get rid of him. He went away, seeming to understand,
and got out some of my clothes and began to brush them. I
repeated my desire several times, simplifying and resimpli-
fying it, and at last he got the idea. Then he went away and
put a coolie at the work, and explained that he would lose
caste if he did it himself; it would be pollution, by the law of
his caste, and it would cost him a deal of fuss and trouble to
purify himself and accomplish his rehabilitation. He said that
that kind of work was strictly forbidden to persons of caste,
and as strictly restricted to the very bottom layer of Hindu
society—the despised *Sudra* (the toiler, the laborer). He was
right; and apparently the poor Sudra has been content with
his strange lot, his insulting distinction, for ages and ages—
clear back to the beginning of things, so to speak. Buckle
says that his name—laborer—is a term of contempt; that it
is ordained by the Institutes of Menu (900 B.C.) that *if a Sudra
sit on a level with his superior he shall be exiled or branded*[1] . . . ;
if he speak contemptuously of his superior or insult him *he
shall suffer death; if he listen to the reading of the sacred books he
shall have burning oil poured in his ears;* if he memorize passages
from them *he shall be killed;* if he marry his daughter to a
Brahman *the husband shall go to hell for defiling himself by contact
with a woman so infinitely his inferior;* and that it is *forbidden to
a Sudra to acquire wealth.* "The bulk of the population of India," says Buckle,[2] "is the Sudras—the *workers, the farmers,
the creators of wealth.*"

Manuel was a failure, poor old fellow. His age was
against him. He was desperately slow and phenomenally for-
getful. When he went three blocks on an errand he would be
gone two hours, and then forget what it was he went for.

---

[1] Without going into particulars, I will remark that, as a rule, they wear no clothing
that would conceal the brand.—M.T.
[2] Population to-day, 300,000,000.

When he packed a trunk it took him forever, and the trunk's contents were an unimaginable chaos when he got done. He couldn't wait satisfactorily at table—a prime defect, for if you haven't your own servant in an Indian hotel you are likely to have a slow time of it and go away hungry. We couldn't understand his English; he couldn't understand ours; and when we found that he couldn't understand his own, it seemed time for us to part. I had to discharge him; there was no help for it. But I did it as kindly as I could, and as gently. We must part, said I, but I hoped we should meet again in a better world. It was not true, but it was only a little thing to say, and saved his feelings and cost me nothing.

But now that he was gone, and was off my mind and heart, my spirits began to rise at once, and I was soon feeling brisk and ready to go out and have adventures. Then his newly hired successor flitted in, touched his forehead, and began to fly around here, there, and everywhere, on his velvet feet, and in five minutes he had everything in the room "ship-shape and Bristol fashion," as the sailors say, and was standing at the salute, waiting for orders. Dear me, what a rustler he was after the slumbrous way of Manuel, poor old slug! All my heart, all my affection, all my admiration, went out spontaneously to this frisky little forked black thing, this compact and compressed incarnation of energy and force and promptness and celerity and confidence, this smart, smily, engaging, shiny-eyed little devil, feruled on his upper end by a gleaming fire-coal of a fez with a red-hot tassel dangling from it. I said, with deep satisfaction:

"You'll suit. What is your name?"

He reeled it mellowly off.

"Let me see if I can make a selection out of it—for business uses, I mean; we will keep the rest for Sundays. Give it to me in instalments."

He did it. But there did not seem to be any short ones,

except Mousa—which suggested mouse. It was out of character; it was too soft, too quiet, too conservative; it didn't fit his splendid style. I considered, and said:

"Mousa is short enough, but I don't quite like it. It seems colorless—inharmonious—inadequate; and I am sensitive to such things. How do you think Satan would do?"

"Yes, master. Satan do wair good."

It was his way of saying "very good."

There was a rap at the door. Satan covered the ground with a single skip; there was a word or two of Hindustani, then he disappeared. Three minutes later he was before me again, militarily erect, and waiting for me to speak first.

"What is it, Satan?"

"God want to see you."

"*Who?*"

"God. I show him up, master?"

"Why, this is so unusual, that—that—well, you see—indeed I am so unprepared—I don't quite know what I *do* mean. Dear me, can't you explain? Don't you see that this is a most ex—"

"Here his card, master."

Wasn't it curious—and amazing, and tremendous, and all that? Such a personage going around calling on such as I, and sending up his card, like a mortal—sending it up by Satan. It was a bewildering collision of the impossibles. But this was the land of the Arabian Nights, this was India! and what is it that cannot happen in India?

We had the interview. Satan was right—the Visitor was indeed a God in the conviction of his multitudinous followers, and was worshipped by them in sincerity and humble adoration. They are troubled by no doubts as to his divine origin and office. They believe in him, they pray to him, they make offerings to him, they beg of him remission of sins; to them his person, together with everything connected with it, is sacred; from his barber they buy the parings of his nails and set them in gold, and wear them as precious amulets.

I tried to seem tranquilly conversational and at rest, but I was not. Would you have been? I was in a suppressed frenzy of excitement and curiosity and glad wonder. I could not keep my eyes off him. I was looking upon a *god*, an actual god, a recognized and accepted god; and every detail of his person and his dress had a consuming interest for me. And the thought went floating through my head, "He is worshiped— think of it—he is not a recipient of the pale homage called compliment, wherewith the highest human clay must make shift to be satisfied, but of an infinitely richer spiritual food: adoration, worship!—men and women lay their cares and their griefs and their broken hearts at his feet; and he gives them his peace, and they go away healed."

And just then the Awful Visitor said, in the simplest way:

"There is a feature of the philosophy of Huck Finn which"—and went luminously on with the construction of a compact and nicely discriminated literary verdict.

It *is* a land of surprises—India! I had had my ambitions— I had hoped, and almost expected, to be read by kings and presidents and emperors—but I had never looked so high as That. It would be false modesty to pretend that I was not inordinately pleased. I was. I was much more pleased than I should have been with a compliment from a man.

He remained half an hour, and I found him a most courteous and charming gentleman. The godship has been in his family a good while, but I do not know how long. He is a Mohammedan deity; by earthly rank he is a prince; not an Indian but a Persian prince. He is a direct descendant of the Prophet's line. He is comely; also young—for a god; not forty, perhaps not above thirty-five years old. He wears his immense honors with tranquil grace, and with a dignity proper to his awful calling. He speaks English with the ease and purity of a person born to it. I think I am not overstating this. He was the only god I had ever seen, and I was very favorably impressed. When he rose to say good-by, the door swung open and I caught the flash of a red fez, and heard these words, reverently said:

"Satan see God out?"

"Yes." And these mismated Beings passed from view— Satan in the lead and The Other following after.

Chapter IV

Few of us can stand prosperity. Another man's, I mean.
—Pudd'nhead Wilson's New Calendar.

THE next picture in my mind is Government House, on Malabar Point, with the wide sea view from the windows and broad balconies; abode of his Excellency the Governor of the Bombay Presidency—a residence which is European in everything but the native guards and servants, and is a home and a palace of state harmoniously combined.

That was England, the English power, the English civilization, the modern civilization—with the quiet elegancies and quiet colors and quiet tastes and quiet dignity that are the outcome of the modern cultivation. And following it came a picture of the ancient civilization of India—an hour in the mansion of a native prince: Kumar Schri Samatsinhji Bahadur of the Palitana State.

The young lad, his heir, was with the prince; also, the lad's sister, a wee brown sprite, very pretty, very serious, very winning, delicately molded, costumed like the daintiest butterfly, a dear little fairy-land princess, gravely willing to be friendly with the strangers, but in the beginning preferring to hold her father's hand until she could take stock of them and determine how far they were to be trusted. She must have been eight years old; so in the natural (Indian) order of things she would be a bride in three or four years from now, and then this free contact with the sun and the air and the other belongings of outdoor nature and comradeship with visiting male folk would end, and she would shut herself up in the zenana for life, like her mother, and by inherited habit of mind would be happy in that seclusion and not look upon it as an irksome restraint and a weary captivity.

The game which the prince amuses his leisure with—however, never mind it, I should never be able to describe it intelligibly. I tried to get an idea of it while my wife and daughter visited the princess in the zenana, a lady of charming graces and a fluent speaker of English, but I did not make it out. It is a complicated game, and I believe it is said that nobody can learn to play it well but an Indian. And I was not able to learn how to wind a turban. It seemed a simple art and easy; but that was a deception. It is a piece of thin, delicate stuff a foot wide or more, and forty or fifty feet long; and the exhibitor of the art takes one end of it in his two hands, and winds it in and out intricately about his head, twisting it as he goes, and in a minute or two the thing is finished, and is neat and symmetrical and fits as snugly as a mold.

We were interested in the wardrobe and the jewels, and in the silverware, and its grace of shape and beauty and delicacy of ornamentation. The silverware is kept locked up, except at meal-times, and none but the chief butler and the prince have keys to the safe. I did not clearly understand why, but it was not for the protection of the silver. It was either to protect the prince from the contamination which his caste would suffer if the vessels were touched by low-caste hands, or it was to protect his highness from poison. Possibly it was both. I believe a salaried taster has to taste everything before the prince ventures it—an ancient and judicious custom in the East, which has thinned out the tasters a good deal, for of course it is the cook that puts the poison in. If I were an Indian prince I would not go to the expense of a taster, I would eat with the cook.

Ceremonials are always interesting; and I noted that the Indian good-morning is a ceremonial, whereas ours doesn't amount to that. In salutation the son reverently touches the father's forehead with a small silver implement tipped with vermilion paste which leaves a red spot there, and in return the son receives the father's blessing. Our good-morning is well enough for the rowdy West, perhaps, but would be too brusque for the soft and ceremonious East.

After being properly necklaced, according to custom, with great garlands made of yellow flowers, and provided with betel-nut to chew, this pleasant visit closed, and we passed thence to a scene of a different sort: from this glow of color and this sunny life to those grim receptacles of the Parsee dead, the Towers of Silence. There is something stately about that name, and an impressiveness which sinks deep; the hush of death is in it. We have the Grave, the Tomb, the Mausoleum, God's Acre, the Cemetery; and association has made them eloquent with solemn meaning; but we have no name that is so majestic as that one, or lingers upon the ear with such deep and haunting pathos.

On lofty ground, in the midst of a paradise of tropical foliage and flowers, remote from the world and its turmoil and noise, they stood—the Towers of Silence; and away below were spread the wide groves of cocoa-palms, then the city, mile on mile, then the ocean with its fleets of creeping ships—all steeped in a stillness as deep as the hush that hallowed this high place of the dead. The vultures were there. They stood close together in a great circle all around the rim of a massive low tower—waiting; stood as motionless as sculptured ornaments, and indeed almost deceived one into the belief that that was what they were. Presently there was a slight stir among the score of persons present, and all moved reverently out of the path and ceased from talking. A funeral procession entered the great gate, marching two and two, and moved silently by, toward the Tower. The corpse lay in a shallow shell, and was under cover of a white cloth, but was otherwise naked. The bearers of the body were separated by an interval of thirty feet from the mourners. They, and also the mourners, were draped all in pure white, and each couple of mourners was figuratively bound together by a piece of white rope or a handkerchief—though they merely held the ends of it in their hands. Behind the procession followed a dog, which was led in a leash. When the mourners had reached the neighborhood of the Tower—neither they nor any other human being but the bearers of the dead must approach within thirty feet of it—they turned and went back to one of the prayer-houses within the gates, to pray for the spirit of their dead. The bearers unlocked the Tower's sole door and disappeared from view within. In a little while they came out bringing the bier and the white covering-cloth, and locked the door again. Then the ring of vultures rose, flapping their wings, and swooped down into the Tower to devour the body. Nothing was left of it but a clean-picked skeleton when they flocked out again a few minutes afterward.

The principle which underlies and orders everything connected with a Parsee funeral is Purity. By the tenets of the Zoroastrian religion, the elements, Earth, Fire, and Water, are sacred, and must not be contaminated by contact with a dead body. Hence corpses must not be burned, neither must they be buried. None may touch the dead or enter the Towers where they repose except certain men who are officially appointed for that purpose. They receive high pay, but theirs is a dismal life, for they must live apart from their species, because their commerce with the dead defiles them, and any who should associate with them would share their defilement. When they come out of the Tower the clothes they are wearing are exchanged for others, in a building within the grounds, and the ones which they have taken off are left behind, for they are contaminated, and must never be used again or suffered to go outside the grounds. These bearers come to every funeral in new garments. So far as is known, no human being, other than an official corpse-bearer—save one—has ever entered a Tower of Silence after its consecration. Just a hundred years ago a European rushed in behind the bearers and fed his brutal curiosity with a glimpse of the forbidden mysteries of the place. This shabby savage's name is not given; his quality is also concealed. These two details, taken in connection with the fact that for his extraordinary offense the only punishment he got from the East India Company's Government was a solemn official "reprimand"—suggest the suspicion that he was a European of consequence. The same public document which contained the reprimand gave warning that future offenders of his sort, if in the company's service, would be dismissed; and if merchants, suffer revocation of license and exile to England.

The Towers are not tall, but are low in proportion to their circumference, like a gasometer. If you should fill a gasometer half-way up with solid granite masonry, then drive a wide and deep well down through the center of this mass of masonry, you would have the idea of a Tower of Silence. On the masonry surrounding the well the bodies lie, in shallow trenches which radiate like wheel-spokes from the well. The trenches slant toward the well and carry into it the rainfall. Underground drains, with charcoal filters in them, carry off this water from the bottom of the well.

When a skeleton has lain in the Tower exposed to the

rain and the flaming sun a month it is perfectly dry and clean. Then the same bearers that brought it there come gloved and take it up with tongs and throw it into the well. There it turns to dust. It is never seen again, never touched again, in the world. Other peoples separate their dead, and preserve and continue social distinctions in the grave—the skeletons of kings and statesmen and generals in temples and pantheons proper to skeletons of their degree, and the skeletons of the commonplace and the poor in places suited to their meaner estate; but the Parsees hold that all men rank alike in death—all are humble, all poor, all destitute. In sign of their poverty they are sent to their grave naked, in sign of their equality the bones of the rich, the poor, the illustrious, and the obscure are flung into the common well together. At a Parsee funeral there are no vehicles; all concerned must walk, both rich and poor, howsoever great the distance to be traversed may be. In the wells of the Five Towers of Silence is mingled the dust of all the Parsee men and women and children who have died in Bombay and its vicinity during the two centuries which have elapsed since the Mohammedan conquerors drove the Parsees out of Persia, and into that region of India. The earliest of the five towers was built by the Modi family something more than two hundred years ago, and it is now reserved to the heirs of that house; none but the dead of that blood are carried thither.

The origin of at least one of the details of a Parsee funeral is not now known—the presence of the dog. Before a corpse is borne from the house of mourning it must be uncovered and exposed to the gaze of a dog; a dog must also be led in the rear of the funeral. Mr. Nusserwanjee Byramjee, Secretary to the Parsee Punchayet, said that these formalities had once had a meaning and a reason for their institution, but that they were survivals whose origin none could now account for. Custom and tradition continue them in force, antiquity hallows them. It is thought that in ancient times in Persia the dog was a sacred animal and could guide souls to heaven; also that his eye had the power of purifying objects which had been contaminated by the touch of the dead; and that hence his presence with the funeral cortège provides an ever-applicable remedy in case of need.

The Parsees claim that their method of disposing of the dead is an effective protection of the living; that it disseminates no corruption, no impurities of any sort, no disease-germs; that no wrap, no garment which has touched the dead is allowed to touch the living afterward; that from the Towers of Silence nothing proceeds which can carry harm to the outside world. These are just claims, I think. As a sanitary measure, their system seems to be about the equivalent of cremation, and as sure. We are drifting slowly—but hopefully—toward cremation in these days. It could not be expected that this progress should be swift, but if it be steady and continuous, even if slow, that will suffice. When cremation becomes the rule we shall cease to shudder at it; we should shudder at burial if we allowed ourselves to think what goes on in the grave.

The dog was an impressive figure to me, representing as he did a mystery whose key is lost. He was humble, and apparently depressed; and he let his head droop pensively, and looked as if he might be trying to call back to his mind what it was that he had used to symbolize ages ago when he began his function. There was another impressive thing close at hand, but I was not privileged to see it. That was the sacred fire—a fire which is supposed to have been burning without interruption for more than two centuries; and so, living by the same heat that was imparted to it so long ago.

The Parsees are a remarkable community. There are only about sixty thousand in Bombay, and only about half as many as that in the rest of India; but they make up in importance what they lack in numbers. They are highly educated, energetic, enterprising, progressive, rich, and the Jew himself is not more lavish or catholic in his charities and benevolences. The Parsees build and endow hospitals, for both men and animals; and they and their womenkind keep an open purse for all great and good objects. They are a political force, and a valued support to the government. They have a pure and lofty religion, and they preserve it in its integrity and order their lives by it.

We took a final sweep of the wonderful view of plain and city and ocean, and so ended our visit to the garden and the Towers of Silence; and the last thing I noticed was another symbol—a voluntary symbol this one; it was a vulture standing on the sawed-off top of a tall and slender and branchless palm in an open space in the ground; he was perfectly motionless, and looked like a piece of sculpture on a pillar. And he had a mortuary look, too, which was in keeping with the place.

Chapter V

*There is an old-time toast which is golden for its beauty.
"When you ascend the hill of prosperity may you not
meet a friend."*
                                    —Pudd'nhead Wilson's New Calendar.

THE next picture that drifts across the field of my memory
is one which is connected with religious things. We were
taken by friends to see a Jain temple. It was small, and had
many flags or streamers flying from poles standing above its
roof; and its little battlements supported a great many small
idols or images. Up-stairs, inside, a solitary Jain was praying
or reciting aloud in the middle of the room. Our presence
did not interrupt him, nor even incommode him or modify
his fervor. Ten or twelve feet in front of him was the idol, a
small figure in a sitting posture. It had the pinkish look of a
wax doll, but lacked the doll's roundness of limb and approxi-
mation to correctness of form and justness of proportion.
Mr. Gandhi explained everything to us. He was delegate to
the Chicago Fair Congress of Religions. It was lucidly done,
in masterly English, but in time it faded from me, and now
I have nothing left of that episode but an impression: a dim

idea of a religious belief clothed in subtle intellectual forms, lofty and clean, barren of fleshly grossnesses; and with this another dim impression which connects that intellectual system somehow with that crude image, that inadequate idol—how, I do not know. Properly, they do not seem to belong together. Apparently, the idol symbolized a person who had become a saint or a god through accessions of steadily augmenting holiness acquired through a series of reincarnations and promotions extending over many ages; and was now at last a saint and qualified to vicariously receive worship and transmit it to heaven's chancellery. Was that it?

And thence we went to Mr. Premchand Roychand's bungalow, in Lovelane, Byculla, where an Indian prince was to receive a deputation of the Jain community who desired to congratulate him upon a high honor lately conferred upon him by his sovereign, Victoria, Empress of India. She had made him a knight of the order of the Star of India. It would seem that even the grandest Indian prince is glad to add the modest title "Sir" to his ancient native grandeurs, and is willing to do valuable service to win it. He will remit taxes liberally, and will spend money freely upon the betterment of the condition of his subjects, if there is a knighthood to be gotten by it. And he will also do good work and a deal of it to get a gun added to the salute allowed him by the British Government. Every year the Empress distributes knighthoods and adds guns for public services done by native princes. The salute of a small prince is three or four guns; princes of greater consequence have salutes that run higher and higher, gun by gun—oh, clear away up to eleven; possibly more, but I did not hear of any above eleven-gun princes. I was told that when a four-gun prince gets a gun added, he is pretty troublesome for a while, till the novelty wears off, for he likes the music, and keeps hunting up pretexts to get himself saluted. It may be that supremely grand folk, like the

Nizam of Hyderabad and the Gaikwar of Baroda, have more than eleven guns, but I don't know.

When we arrived at the bungalow, the large hall on the ground floor was already about full, and carriages were still flowing into the grounds. The company present made a fine show, an exhibition of human fireworks, so to speak, in the matters of costume and comminglings of brilliant color. The variety of form noticeable in the display of turbans was remarkable. We were told that the explanation of this was, that this Jain delegation was drawn from many parts of India, and that each man wore the turban that was in vogue in his own region. This diversity of turbans made a beautiful effect.

I could have wished to start a rival exhibition there, of Christian hats and clothes. I would have cleared one side of the room of its Indian splendors and repacked the space with Christians drawn from America, England, and the Colonies, dressed in the hats and habits of now, and of twenty and forty and fifty years ago. It would have been a hideous exhibition, a thoroughly devilish spectacle. Then there would have been the added disadvantage of the white complexion. It is not an unbearably unpleasant complexion when it keeps to itself, but when it comes into competition with masses of brown and black the fact is betrayed that it is endurable only because we are used to it. Nearly all black and brown skins are beautiful, but a beautiful white skin is rare. How rare, one may learn by walking down a street in Paris, New York, or London on a week-day—particularly an unfashionable street—and keeping count of the satisfactory complexions encountered in the course of a mile. Where dark complexions are massed, they make the whites look bleached out, unwholesome, and sometimes frankly ghastly. I could notice this as a boy, down South in the slavery days before the war. The splendid black-satin skin of the South African Zulus of Durban seemed to me to come very close to perfection. I can see those Zulus yet—'rikisha athletes waiting in front of the hotel for custom; handsome and intensely black creatures, moderately clothed in loose summer stuffs whose snowy whiteness made the black all the blacker by contrast. Keeping that group in my mind, I can compare those complexions with the white ones which are streaming past this London window now:

A lady. Complexion, new parchment.

Another lady. Complexion, old parchment.

Another. Pink and white, very fine.

Man. Grayish skin, with purple areas.

Man. Unwholesome fish-belly skin.

Girl. Sallow face, sprinkled with freckles.

Old woman. Face whitey-gray.

Young butcher. Face a general red flush.

Jaundiced man. Mustard yellow.

Elderly lady. Colorless skin, with two conspicuous moles.

Elderly man—a drinker. Boiled-cauliflower nose in a flabby face veined with purple crinklings.

Healthy young gentleman. Fine fresh complexion.

Sick young man. His face a ghastly white.

No end of people whose skins are dull and characterless modifications of the tint which we miscall white. Some of these faces are pimply; some exhibit other signs of diseased blood; some show scars of a tint out of harmony with the surrounding shades of color. The white man's complexion makes no concealments. It can't. It seems to have been designed as a catch-all for everything that can damage it. Ladies have to paint it, and powder it, and cosmetic it, and diet it with arsenic, and enamel it, and be always enticing it, and persuading it, and pestering it, and fussing at it, to make it beautiful; and they do not succeed. But these efforts show what they think of the natural complexion, as distributed. As distributed it needs these helps. The complexion which they

try to counterfeit is one which nature restricts to the few—
to the very few. To ninety-nine persons she gives a bad
complexion, to the hundredth a good one. The hundredth
can keep it—how long? Ten years, perhaps.

The advantage is with the Zulu, I think. He starts with
a beautiful complexion, and it will last him through. And as
for the Indian brown—firm, smooth, blemishless, pleasant
and restful to the eye, afraid of no color, harmonizing with
all colors and adding a grace to them all—I think there is no
sort of chance for the average white complexion against that
rich and perfect tint.

To return to the bungalow. The most gorgeous costumes present were worn by some children. They seemed to
blaze, so bright were the colors, and so brilliant the jewels
strung over the rich materials. These children were professional nautch-dancers, and locked like girls, but they were
boys. They got up by ones and twos and fours, and danced
and sang to an accompaniment of weird music. Their postur-
ings and gesturings were elaborate and graceful, but their
voices were stringently raspy and unpleasant, and there was
a good deal of monotony about the tune.

By and by, there was a burst of shouts and cheers outside
and the prince with his train entered in fine dramatic style. He
was a stately man, he was ideally costumed, and fairly festooned
with ropes of gems; some of the ropes were of pearls, some
were of uncut great emeralds—emeralds renowned in Bombay
for their quality and value. Their size was marvelous, and enticing to the eye, those rocks. A boy—a princeling—was with the
prince, and he also was a radiant exhibition.

The ceremonies were not tedious. The prince strode to
his throne with the port and majesty—and the sternness—of
a Julius Cæsar coming to receive and receipt for a back-
country kingdom and have it over and get out, and no fool-
ing. There was a throne for the young prince, too, and the

two sat there, side by side, with their officers grouped at either hand and most accurately and creditably reproducing the pictures which one sees in the books—pictures which people in the prince's line of business have been furnishing ever since Solomon received the Queen of Sheba and showed her his things. The chief of the Jain delegation read his paper of congratulations, then pushed it into a beautifully engraved silver cylinder, which was delivered with ceremony into the prince's hands and at once delivered by him without ceremony into the hands of an officer. I will copy the address here. It is interesting, as showing what an Indian prince's subject may have opportunity to thank him for in these days of modern English rule, as contrasted with what his ancestor would have given them opportunity to thank him for a century and a half ago—the days of freedom unhampered by English interference. A century and a half ago an address of thanks could have been put into small space. It would have thanked the prince:

1. For not slaughtering too many of his people upon mere caprice;

2. For not stripping them bare by sudden and arbitrary tax levies, and bringing famine upon them;

3. For not upon empty pretext destroying the rich and seizing their property;

4. For not killing, blinding, imprisoning, or banishing the relatives of the royal house to protect the throne from possible plots;

5. For not betraying the subject secretly, for a bribe, into the hands of bands of professional Thugs, to be murdered and robbed in the prince's back lot.

Those were rather common princely industries in the old times, but they and some others of a harsh sort ceased long ago under English rule. Better industries have taken their place, as this Address from the Jain community will show:

Your Highness,—We the undersigned members of the Jain community of Bombay have the pleasure to approach your Highness with the expression of our heartfelt congratulations on the recent conference on your Highness of the Knighthood of the Most Exalted Order of the Star of India. Ten years ago we had the pleasure and privilege of welcoming your Highness to this city under circumstances which have made a memorable epoch in the history of your State, for had it not been for a generous and reasonable spirit that your Highness displayed in the negotiations between the Palitana Durbar and the Jain community, the conciliatory spirit that animated our people could not have borne fruit. That was the first step in your Highness's administration, and it fitly elicited the praise of the Jain community, and of the Bombay Government. A decade of your Highness's administration, combined with the abilities, training, and acquirements that your Highness brought to bear upon it, has justly earned for your Highness the unique and honorable distinction—the Knighthood of the Most Exalted Order of the Star of India, which we understand your Highness is the first to enjoy among Chiefs of your Highness's rank and standing. And we assure your Highness that for this mark of honor that has been conferred on you by her Most Gracious Majesty, the Queen-Empress, we feel no less proud than your Highness. Establishment of commercial factories, schools, hospitals, etc., by your Highness in your State has marked your Highness's career during these ten years, and we trust that your Highness will be spared to rule over your people with wisdom and foresight, and foster the many reforms that your Highness has been pleased to introduce in your State. We again offer your Highness our warmest felicitations for the honor that has been conferred on you. We beg to remain your Highness's obedient servants.

Factories, schools, hospitals, reforms. The prince propagates that kind of things in the modern times, and gets knighthood and guns for it.

After the address the prince responded with snap and brevity; spoke a moment with half a dozen guests in English, and with an official or two in a native tongue; then the garlands were distributed as usual, and the function ended.

Chapter VI

Each person is born to one possession which outvalues
all his others—his last breath.
                    —Pudd'nhead Wilson's New Calendar.

TOWARD midnight, that night, there was another function. This was a Hindu wedding—no, I think it was a
betrothal ceremony. Always before, we had driven through
streets that were multitudinous and tumultuous with picturesque native life, but now there was nothing of that. We
seemed to move through a city of the dead. There was hardly
a suggestion of life in those still and vacant streets. Even the
crows were silent. But everywhere on the ground lay sleeping
natives—hundreds and hundreds. They lay stretched at full
length and tightly wrapped in blankets, heads and all. Their
attitude and their rigidity counterfeited death. The plague
was not in Bombay then, but it is devastating the city now.
The shops are deserted, now, half of the people have fled,
and of the remainder the smitten perish by shoals every day.
No doubt the city looks now in the daytime as it looked then
at night. When we had pierced deep into the native quarter
and were threading its narrow dim lanes, we had to go care-

fully, for men were stretched asleep all about, and there was hardly room to drive between them. And every now and then a swarm of rats would scamper across past the horses' feet in the vague light—the forebears of the rats that are carrying the plague from house to house in Bombay now. The shops were but sheds, little booths open to the street; and the goods had been removed, and on the counters families were sleeping, usually with an oil-lamp present. Recurrent dead-watches, it looked like.

But at last we turned a corner and saw a great glare of light ahead. It was the home of the bride, wrapped in a perfect conflagration of illuminations—mainly gas-work designs, gotten up specially for the occasion. Within was abundance of brilliancy—flames, costumes, colors, decorations, mirrors—it was another Aladdin show.

The bride was a trim and comely little thing of twelve years, dressed as we would dress a boy, though more expensively than we should do it, of course. She moved about very much at her ease, and stopped and talked with the guests and allowed her wedding jewelry to be examined. It was very fine. Particularly a rope of great diamonds, a lovely thing to look at and handle. It had a great emerald hanging to it.

The bridegroom was not present. He was having betrothal festivities of his own at his father's house. As I understood it, he and the bride were to entertain company every night and nearly all night for a week or more, then get married, if alive. Both of the children were a little elderly, as brides and grooms go, in India—twelve; they ought to have been married a year or two sooner; still to a stranger twelve seems quite young enough.

A while after midnight a couple of celebrated and high-priced nautch-girls appeared in the gorgeous place, and danced and sang. With them were men who played upon strange instruments which made uncanny noises of a sort to make one's flesh creep. One of these instruments was a pipe, and to its music the girls went through a performance which represented snake-charming. It seemed a doubtful sort of music to charm anything with, but a native gentleman assured me that snakes like it and will come out of their holes and listen to it with every evidence of refreshment and gratitude. He said that at an entertainment in his grounds once, the pipe brought out half a dozen snakes, and the music had to be stopped before they would be persuaded to go. Nobody wanted their company, for they were bold, familiar, and dangerous; but no one would kill them, of course, for it is sinful for a Hindu to kill any kind of a creature.

We withdrew from the festivities at two in the morning. Another picture, then—but it has lodged itself in my memory rather as a stage-scene than as a reality. It is of a porch and short flight of steps crowded with dark faces and ghostly white draperies flooded with the strong glare from the dazzling concentration of illuminations; and midway of the steps one conspicuous figure for accent—a turbaned giant, with a name according to his size: Rao Bahadur Baskirao Balinkanje Pitale, Vakeel to his Highness the Gaikwar of Baroda. Without him the picture would not have been complete; and if his name had been merely Smith, *he* wouldn't have answered. Close at hand on house-fronts on both sides of the narrow street were illuminations of a kind commonly employed by the natives—scores of glass tumblers (containing tapers) fastened a few inches apart all over great latticed frames, forming starry constellations which showed out vividly against their black backgrounds. As we drew away into the distance down the dim lanes the illuminations gathered together into a single mass, and glowed out of the enveloping darkness like a sun.

Then again the deep silence, the scurrying rats, the dim

forms stretched everywhere on the ground; and on either hand those open booths counterfeiting sepulchers, with counterfeit corpses sleeping motionless in the flicker of the counterfeit death-lamps. And now, a year later, when I read the cablegrams I seem to be reading of what I myself partly saw— saw before it happened—in a prophetic dream, as it were. One cablegram says, "Business in the native town is about suspended. Except the wailing and the tramp of the funerals. There is but little life or movement. The closed shops exceed in number those that remain open." Another says that 325,000 of the people have fled the city and are carrying the plague to the country. Three days later comes the news, "The population is reduced by *half*." The refugees have carried the disease to Karachi; "220 cases, 214 deaths." A day or two later, "52 fresh cases, *all* of which proved fatal."

The plague carries with it a terror which no other disease can excite; for of all diseases known to men it is the deadliest—by far the deadliest. "Fifty-two fresh cases—*all* fatal." It is the Black Death alone that slays like that. We can all imagine, after a fashion, the desolation of a plague-stricken city, and the stupor of stillness broken at intervals by distant bursts of wailing, marking the passing of funerals, here and there and yonder; but I suppose it is not possible for us to realize to ourselves the nightmare of dread and fear that possesses the living who are present in such a place and cannot get away. That half million fled from Bombay in a wild panic suggests to us something of what they were feeling, but perhaps not even they could realize what the half million were feeling whom they left stranded behind to face the stalking horror without chance of escape. Kinglake was in Cairo many years ago during an epidemic of the Black Death, and he has imagined the terrors that creep into a man's heart at such a time and follow him until they themselves breed the fatal sign in the armpit, and then the delirium with confused images, and home-dreams, and reeling billiard-tables, and then the sudden blank of death:

> To the contagionist, filled as he is with the dread of final causes, having no faith in destiny, nor in the fixed will of God, and with none of the devil-may-care indifference which might stand him instead of creeds—to such one, every rag that shivers in the breeze of a plague-stricken city has this sort of sublimity. If by any terrible ordinance he be forced to venture forth, he sees death dangling from every sleeve; and, as he creeps forward, he poises his shuddering limbs between the imminent jacket that is stabbing at his right elbow and the murderous pelisse that threatens to mow him clean down as it sweeps along on his left. But most of all he dreads that which most of all he should love—the touch of a woman's dress; for mothers and wives, hurrying forth on kindly errands from the bedsides of the dying, go slouching along through the streets more wilfully and less courteously than the men. For a while it may be that the caution of the poor Levantine may enable him to avoid contact, but sooner or later, perhaps, the dreaded chance arrives; that bundle of linen, with the dark tearful eyes at the top of it, that labors along with the voluptuous clumsiness of Grisi—she has touched the poor Levantine with the hem of her sleeve! From that dread moment his peace is gone; his mind forever hanging upon the fatal touch invites the blow which he fears; he watches for the symptoms of plague so carefully, that sooner or later they come in truth. The parched mouth is a sign—his mouth *is* parched; the throbbing brain—his brain *does* throb; the rapid pulse—he touches his own wrist (for he dares not ask counsel of any man, lest he be deserted), he touches his wrist, and feels how his frighted blood goes galloping out of his heart. There is nothing but the fatal swelling that is wanting to make his sad conviction complete; immediately, he has an odd feel under the arm—no

pain, but a little straining of the skin; he would to God it were
his fancy that were strong enough to give him that sensation;
this is the worst of all. It now seems to him that he could be
happy and contented with his parched mouth, and his
throbbing brain, and his rapid pulse, if only he could know
that there were no swelling under the left arm; but dares he
try?—in a moment of calmness and deliberation he dares not;
but when for a while he has writhed under the torture of suspense, a sudden strength of will drives him to seek and know
his fate; he touches the gland, and finds the skin sane and
sound, but under the cuticle there lies a small lump like a pistol-
bullet, that moves as he pushes it. Oh! but is this for all certainty, is this the sentence of death? Feel the gland of the other
arm. There is not the same lump exactly, yet something a little
like it. Have not some people glands naturally enlarged?—
would to heaven he were one! So he does for himself the work
of the plague, and when the Angel of Death thus courted does
in deed and in truth come, he has only to finish that which has
been so well begun; he passes his fiery hand over the brain of
the victim, and lets him rave for a season, but all chance-wise,
of people and things once dear, or of people and things indifferent. Once more the poor fellow is back at his home in fair
Provence, and sees the sun-dial that stood in his childhood's
garden—sees his mother, and the long-since-forgotten face of
that little dear sister—(he sees her, he says, on a Sunday morning, for all the church-bells are ringing); he looks up and down
through the universe, and owns it well piled with bales upon
bales of cotton, and cotton eternal—so much so—that he
feels—he knows—he swears he could make that winning haz-
ard, if the billiard-table would not slant upward, and if the cue
were a cue worth playing with; but it is not—it's a cue that
won't move—his own arm won't move—in short, there's the
devil to pay in the brain of the poor Levantine; and perhaps,
the next night but one he becomes the "life and the soul" of
some squalling jackal family, who fish him out by the foot
from his shallow and sandy grave.

Chapter VII

Hunger is the handmaid of genius.
—Pudd'nhead Wilson's New Calendar.

O NE day during our stay in Bombay there was a criminal trial of a most interesting sort, a terribly realistic chapter out of the Arabian Nights, a strange mixture of simplicities and pieties and murderous practicalities, which brought back the forgotten days of Thuggee and made them live again; in fact, even made them believable. It was a case where a young girl had been assassinated for the sake of her trifling ornaments, things not worth a laborer's day's wages in America. This thing could have been done in many other countries, but hardly with the cold business–like depravity, absence of fear, absence of caution, destitution of the sense of horror, repentance, remorse, exhibited in this case. Elsewhere the murderer would have done his crime secretly, by night, and without witnesses; his fears would have allowed him no peace while the dead body was in his neighborhood; he would not have rested until he had gotten it safe out of the way and hidden as effectually as he could hide it. But this Indian murderer does his deed in the full light of day, cares nothing for the society of witnesses, is in no way incommoded by the presence of the corpse, takes his own time about disposing of it, and the whole party are so indifferent, so phlegmatic, that they take their regular sleep as if nothing was happening and no halters hanging over them; and these five bland people close the episode with a religious service. The thing reads like a Meadows-Taylor Thug-tale of half a century ago, as may be seen by the official report of the trial:

At the Mazagon Police Court yesterday, Superintendent Nolan again charged Tookaram Suntoo Savat Baya, woman, her daughter Krishni, and Gopal Vithoo Bhanayker, before Mr. Phiroze Hoshang Dastur, Fourth Presidency Magistrate, under sections 302 and 109 of the Code, with having on the night of the 30th of December last murdered a Hindu girl named Cassi, aged twelve, by strangulation, in the room of a chawl at Jakaria Bunder, on the Sewri road, and also with aiding and abetting each other in the commission of the offense.

Mr. F. A. Little, Public Prosecutor, conducted the case on behalf of the Crown, the accused being undefended.

Mr. Little applied under the provisions of the Criminal Procedure Code to tender pardon to one of the accused, Krishni, woman, aged twenty-two, on her undertaking to make a true and full statement of facts under which the deceased girl Cassi was murdered.

The Magistrate having granted the Public Prosecutor's application, the accused Krishni went into the witness-box, and, on being examined by Mr. Little, made the following confession:—"I am a mill-hand employed at the Jubilee Mill. I recollect the day (Tuesday) on which the body of the deceased Cassi was found. Previous to that I attended the mill for half a day, and then returned home at three in the afternoon, when I saw five persons in the house, *viz*.: the first accused Tookaram, who is my paramour, my mother, the second accused, Baya, the accused Gopal, and two guests named Ramji Daji and Annaji Gungaram. Tookaram rented the room of the chawl situated at Jakaria Bunder road from its owner, Girdharilal Radhakishan, and in that room I, my paramour, Tookaram, and his younger brother, Yesso Mahadhoo, live. Since his arrival in Bombay from his native country Yesso came and lived with us. When I returned from the mill on the afternoon of that day, I saw the two guests seated on a cot in the veranda, and a few minutes after the accused Gopal came and took his seat by their side, while I and my mother were seated inside the room. Tookaram, who had gone out to fetch some *pan* and betelnuts, on his return home had brought the two guests with him. After returning home he gave them *pan supari*. While they were eating it my mother came out of the room and inquired of one of the guests, Ramji, what had happened to his foot, when he replied that he had tried many remedies, but they had done him no good. My mother then took some rice in her hand and prophesied that the disease which Ramji was suffering from would not be cured until he returned to his native country. In the mean time the deceased Cassi came from the direction of an outhouse, and stood in front on the threshold of our room with a *lota* in her hand. Tookaram then told his two guests to leave the room, and they then went up the steps toward the quarry. After the guests had gone away, Tookaram seized the deceased, who had come into the room, and he afterward put a waistband around her, and tied her to a post which supports a loft. After doing this, he pressed the girl's throat, and, having tied her mouth with the *dhotur* (now shown in court), fastened it to the post. Having killed the girl, Tookaram removed her gold head ornament and a gold *putlee*, and also took charge of her *lota*. Besides these two ornaments Cassi had on her person ear-studs, a nose-ring, some silver toe-rings, two necklaces, a pair of silver anklets and bracelets. Tookaram afterward tried to remove the silver amulets, the ear-studs, and the nose-ring; but he failed in his attempt. While he was doing so, I, my mother, and Gopal were present. After removing the two gold ornaments, he handed them over to Gopal, who was at the time standing near me. When he killed Cassi, Tookaram threatened to strangle me also if I informed any one of this. Gopal and myself were then standing at the door of our room, and we both were threatened by Tookaram. My mother, Baya, had seized the legs of the deceased at the time she was killed, and while she was being tied to the post. Cassi then made a noise. Tookaram and my mother took part in killing the girl. After the murder her body was wrapped up in a mattress and kept on the loft over the door of our room. When Cassi was strangled, the door of the room was fastened from the inside by Tookaram. This deed was committed shortly after my return home from work in the mill. Tookaram put the body of the deceased in the mattress, and, after it was left on the loft, he went to have his head shaved by a barber named Sambhoo Ragho, who lives only one door away from me. My mother and myself then remained in the possession of the information. I was slapped and threatened by my paramour, Tookaram, and that was the only reason why I did not inform any one at that time. When I told Tookaram that I would give information of the occurrence, he slapped me. The accused Gopal was asked by Tookaram to go back to his room, and he did so, taking away with him the two gold ornaments and the *lota*. Yesso Mahadhoo, a brother-in-law of Tookaram, came to the house and asked Tookaram why he was washing, the water-pipe being just opposite. Tookaram replied that he was washing his *dhotur*, as a fowl had polluted it. About six o'clock of the evening of that day my mother gave me three pice and asked me to buy a cocoanut, and I gave the money to Yesso, who went and fetched a cocoanut and some betel leaves. When Yesso and others were in the room I was bathing, and, after I finished my bath, my mother took the cocoanut and the betel leaves from Yesso, and we five went to the sea. The party consisted of Tookaram, my mother, Yesso, Tookaram's younger brother, and myself. On reaching the seashore, my mother made the offering to the sea, and prayed to be pardoned for what we had done. Before we went to the sea, some one came to inquire after the girl Cassi. The police and other people came to make these inquiries both before and after we left the house for the seashore. The police questioned my mother about the girl, and she replied that Cassi had come to her door, but had left. The next day the police questioned Tookaram, and he, too, gave a similar reply. This was said the same night when the search was made for the girl. After the offering was made to the sea, we partook of the cocoanut and returned home, when my mother gave me some food; but Tookaram did not partake of any food that night. After dinner I and my mother slept inside the room, and Tookaram slept on a cot near his brother-in-law, Yesso Mahadhoo, just outside the door. That was not the usual place where Tookaram slept. He usually slept inside the room. The body of the deceased remained on the loft when I went to sleep. The room in which we slept was locked, and I heard that my paramour, Tookaram, was restless outside. About three o'clock the following morning, Tookaram knocked at the door, when both myself and my mother opened it. He then told me to go to the steps leading to the quarry, and see if any one was about. Those steps lead to a stable, through which we go to the quarry at the back of the compound. When I got to the steps I saw no one there. Tookaram asked me if any one was there, and I replied that I could see no one about. He then took the body of the deceased from the loft, and, having wrapped it up in his *saree*, asked me to accompany him to the steps of the quarry, and I did so. The *saree* now produced here was the same. Besides the *saree*, there was also a *cholee* on the body. He then carried the body in his arms, and went up the steps, through the stable, and then to the right hand toward a *sahib's* bungalow, where Tookaram placed the body near a wall. All the time I and my mother were with him. When the body was taken down, Yesso was lying on the cot. After depositing the body under the wall, we all returned home, and soon after 5 A.M. the police again came and took Tookaram away. About an hour after they returned and took me and my mother away. We were questioned about it, when I made a statement. Two hours later I was taken to the room, and I pointed out this waistband, the *dhotur*, the mattress, and the wooden post to Superintendent Nolan and Inspectors Roberts and Rashanali, in the presence of my mother and Tookaram. Tookaram killed the girl Cassi for her ornaments, which he wanted for the girl to whom he was shortly going to be married. The body was found in the same place where it was deposited by Tookaram."

The criminal side of the native has always been picturesque, always readable. The Thuggee and one or two other particularly outrageous features of it have been suppressed by the English, but there is enough of it left to keep it darkly interesting. One finds evidence of these survivals in the newspapers. Macaulay has a light-throwing passage upon this matter in his great historical sketch of Warren Hastings, where he is describing some effects which followed the temporary paralysis of Hastings's powerful government brought about by Sir Philip Francis and his party:

The natives considered Hastings as a fallen man; and they acted after their kind. Some of our readers may have seen, in India, a cloud of crows pecking a sick vulture to death—no bad type of what happens in that country as often as fortune deserts one who has been great and dreaded. In an instant all the sycophants, who had lately been ready to lie for him, to forge for him, to poison for him, hasten to purchase the favor of his victorious enemies by accusing him. An Indian government has only to let it be understood that it wishes a particular man to be ruined, and in twenty-four hours it will be furnished with grave charges, supported by depositions so full and circumstantial that any person unaccustomed to Asiatic mendac-

ity would regard them as decisive. It is well if the signature of
the destined victim is not counterfeited at the foot of some
illegal compact, and if some treasonable paper is not slipped
into a hiding-place in his house.

That was nearly a century and a quarter ago. An article
in one of the chief journals of India (the *Pioneer*) shows that
in some respects the native of to-day is just what his ancestor
was then. Here are niceties of so subtle and delicate a sort that
they lift their breed of rascality to a place among the fine arts,
and almost entitle it to respect:

> The records of the Indian courts might certainly be relied
> upon to prove that swindlers as a class in the East come very
> close to, if they do not surpass, in brilliancy of execution and
> originality of design the most expert of their fraternity in
> Europe and America. India in especial is the home of forgery.
> There are some particular districts which are noted as marts for
> the finest specimens of the forger's handiwork. The business is
> carried on by firms who possess *stores of stamped papers to suit
> every emergency*. They habitually lay in a store of fresh stamped
> papers every year, and some of the older and more thriving
> houses can supply documents *for the past forty years, bearing the
> proper water-mark and possessing the genuine appearance of age*.
> Other districts have earned notoriety for skilled perjury, a pre-
> eminence that excites a respectful admiration when one thinks
> of *the universal prevalence of the art*, and persons desirous of
> succeeding in false suits are ready to pay handsomely to avail
> themselves of the services of these local experts as witnesses.

Various instances illustrative of the methods of those
swindlers are given. They exhibit deep cunning and total
depravity on the part of the swindler and his pals, and more
obtuseness on the part of the victim than one would expect
to find in a country where suspicion of your neighbor must

surely be one of the earliest things learned. The favorite subject is the young fool who has just come into a fortune and
is trying to see how poor a use he can put it to. I will quote
one example:

>   Sometimes another form of confidence trick is adopted,
> which is invariably successful. The particular pigeon is spot-
> ted, and, his acquaintance having been made, he is encouraged
> in every form of vice. When the friendship is thoroughly
> established, the swindler remarks to the young man that he
> has a brother who has asked him to lend him Rs.10,000. The
> swindler says he has the money and would lend it; but, as
> the borrower is his brother, he cannot charge interest. So he
> proposes that he should hand the dupe the money, and the
> latter should lend it to the swindler's brother, exacting a heavy
> pre-payment of interest, which, it is pointed out, they may
> equally enjoy in dissipation. The dupe sees no objection, and
> on the appointed day receives Rs.7,000 from the swindler,
> which he hands over to the confederate. The latter is profuse
> in his thanks, and executes a promissory note for Rs.10,000,
> payable to bearer. The swindler allows the scheme to remain
> quiescent for a time, and then suggests that, as the money has
> not been repaid and as it would be unpleasant to sue his
> brother, it would be better to sell the note in the bazar. The
> dupe hands the note over, for the money he advanced was not
> his, and, on being informed that it would be necessary to
> have his signature on the back so as to render the security
> negotiable, he signs without any hesitation. The swindler
> passes it on to confederates, and the latter employ a respectable
> firm of solicitors to ask the dupe if his signature is genuine.
> He admits it at once, and his fate is sealed. A suit is filed by a
> confederate against the dupe, two accomplices being made co-
> defendants. They admit their signatures as indorsers, and the
> one swears he bought the note for value from the dupe. The
> latter has no defense, for no court would believe the apparently

idle explanation of the manner in which he came to indorse the note.

There is only one India! It is the only country that has a monopoly of grand and imposing specialties. When another country has a remarkable thing, it cannot have it all to itself—some other country has a duplicate. But India—that is different. Its marvels are its own; the patents cannot be infringed; imitations are not possible. And think of the size of them, the majesty of them, the weird and outlandish character of the most of them!

There is the Plague, the Black Death: India invented it; India is the cradle of that mighty birth.

The Car of Juggernaut was India's invention.

So was the Suttec; and within the time of men still living eight hundred widows willingly, and, in fact, rejoicingly, burned themselves to death on the bodies of their dead husbands in a single year. Eight hundred would do it this year if the British Government would let them.

Famine is India's specialty. Elsewhere famines are inconsequential incidents—in India they are devastating cataclysms; in one case they annihilate hundreds; in the other, millions.

India has two million gods, and worships them all. In religion all other countries are paupers; India is the only millionaire.

With her everything is on a giant scale—even her poverty; no other country can show anything to compare with it. And she has been used to wealth on so vast a scale that she has to shorten to single words the expressions describing great sums. She describes one hundred thousand with one word—a *lakh;* she describes ten millions with one word—a *crore.*

In the bowels of the granite mountains she has patiently carved out dozens of vast temples, and made them glorious with sculptured colonnades and stately groups of statuary, and has adorned the eternal walls with noble paintings. She has built fortresses of such magnitude that the show-strongholds of the rest of the world are but modest little things by comparison; palaces that are wonders for rarity of materials, delicacy and beauty of workmanship, and for cost; and one tomb which men go around the globe to see. It takes eighty nations, speaking eighty languages, to people her, and they number three hundred millions.

On top of all this she is the mother and home of that wonder of wonders—*caste*—and of that mystery of mysteries, the satanic brotherhood of the Thugs.

India had the start of the whole world in the beginning of things. She had the first civilization; she had the first accumulation of material wealth; she was populous with deep thinkers and subtle intellects; she had mines, and woods, and a fruitful soil. It would seem as if she should have kept the lead, and should be to-day not the meek dependent of an alien master, but mistress of the world, and delivering law and command to every tribe and nation in it. But, in truth, there was never any possibility of such supremacy for her. If there had been but one Indian and one language—but there were eighty of them! Where there are eighty nations and several hundred governments, fighting and quarreling must be the common business of life; unity of purpose and policy are impossible; out of such elements supremacy in the world cannot come. Even caste itself could have had the defeating effect of a multiplicity of tongues, no doubt; for it separates a people into layers, and layers, and still other layers, that have no community of feeling with each other; and in such a condition of things as that, patriotism can have no healthy growth.

It was the division of the country into so many states and nations that made Thuggee possible and prosperous. It is difficult to realize the situation. But perhaps one may approximate it by imagining the states of our Union peopled by separate nations, speaking separate languages, with guards and custom-houses strung along all frontiers, plenty of interruptions for travelers and traders, interpreters able to handle all the languages very rare or non-existent, and a few wars always going on here and there and yonder as a further embarrassment to commerce and excursioning. It would make inter-communication in a measure ungeneral. India had eighty languages, and more custom-houses than cats. No clever man with the instinct of a highway robber could fail to notice what a chance for business was here offered. India was full of clever men with the highwayman instinct, and so, quite naturally, the brotherhood of the Thugs came into being to meet the long-felt want.

How long ago that was nobody knows—centuries, it is supposed. One of the chiefest wonders connected with it was the success with which it kept its secret. The English trader did business in India two hundred years and more before he ever heard of it; and yet it was assassinating its thousands all around him every year, the whole time.

Chapter VIII

The old saw says, "Let a sleeping dog lie." Right. Still,
when there is much at stake it is better to get a newspaper
to do it.

—Pudd'nhead Wilson's New calendar.

FROM DIARY:

January 28. I learned of an *official* Thug-book the other
day. I was not aware before that there was such a thing. I am
allowed the temporary use of it. We are making preparations
for travel. Mainly the preparations are purchases of bedding.
This is to be used in sleeping-berths in the trains; in private
houses sometimes; and in nine-tenths of the hotels. It is not
realizable; and yet it is true. It is a survival; an apparently
unnecessary thing which in some strange way has outlived
the conditions which once made it necessary. It comes down
from a time when the railway and the hotel did not exist;
when the occasional white traveler went horseback or by
bullock-cart, and stopped overnight in the small dak-bungalow
provided at easy distances by the government—a shelter,
merely, and nothing more. He had to carry bedding along,
or do without. The dwellings of the English residents are
spacious and comfortable and commodiously furnished, and

surely it must be an odd sight to see half a dozen guests come filing into such a place and dumping blankets and pillows here and there and everywhere. But custom makes incongruous things congruous.

One buys the bedding, with waterproof hold-all for it, at almost any shop—there is no difficulty about it.

January 30. What a spectacle the railway-station was at train-time! It was a very large station, yet when we arrived it seemed as if the whole world was present—half of it inside, the other half outside, and both halves, bearing mountainous head-loads of bedding and other freight, trying simultaneously to pass each other, in opposing floods, in one narrow door. These opposing floods were patient, gentle, long-suffering natives, with whites scattered among them at rare intervals; and wherever a white man's native servant appeared, *that* native seemed to have put aside his natural gentleness for the time and invested himself with the white man's privilege of making a way for himself by promptly shoving all intervening black things out of it. In these exhibitions of authority Satan was scandalous. He was probably a Thug in one of his former incarnations.

Inside the great station, tides upon tides of rainbow-costumed natives swept along, this way and that, in massed and bewildering confusion, eager, anxious, belated, distressed; and washed up to the long trains and flowed into them with their packs and bundles, and disappeared, followed at once by the next wash, the next wave. And here and there, in the midst of this hurly-burly, and seemingly undisturbed by it, sat great groups of natives on the bare stone floor—young, slender brown women, old gray wrinkled women, little soft brown babies, old men, young men, boys; all poor people, but all the females among them, both big and little, bejeweled with cheap and showy nose-rings, toe-rings, leglets, and armlets, these things constituting all their wealth, no doubt. These silent crowds sat there with their humble bundles and baskets and small household gear about them, and patiently waited—for what? A train that was to start at some time or other during the day or night! They hadn't timed themselves well, but that was no matter—the thing had been so ordered from on high, therefore why worry? There was plenty of time, hours and hours of it, and the thing that was to happen would happen—there was no hurrying it.

The natives traveled third class, and at marvelously cheap rates. They were packed and crammed into the cars that held each about fifty; and it was said that often a Brahman of the highest caste was thus brought into personal touch, and consequent defilement, with persons of the lowest castes— no doubt a very shocking thing if a body could understand it and properly appreciate it. Yes, a Brahman who didn't own a rupee and couldn't borrow one might have to touch elbows with a rich hereditary lord of inferior caste, inheritor of an ancient title a couple of yards long, and he would just have to stand it; for if either of the two was allowed to go in the cars where the sacred white people were, it probably wouldn't be the august poor Brahman. There was an immense string of those third-class cars, for the natives travel by hordes; and a weary hard night of it the occupants would have, no doubt.

When we reached our car, Satan and Barney had already arrived there with their train of porters carrying bedding and parasols and cigar-boxes, and were at work. We named him Barney for short; for we couldn't use his real name, there wasn't time.

It was a car that promised comfort; indeed, luxury. Yet the cost of it—well, economy could no further go; even in France; not even in Italy. It was built of the plainest and cheapest partially smoothed boards, with a coating of dull paint on them, and there was nowhere a thought of decoration. The floor was bare, but would not long remain so when the dust should begin to fly. Across one end of the compartment ran a netting for the accommodation of hand-baggage; at the other end was a door which would shut, upon compulsion, but wouldn't stay shut; it opened into a narrow little closet which had a washbowl in one end of it, and a place to put a towel, in case you had one with you—and you would be sure to have towels, because you buy them with the bedding, knowing that the railway doesn't furnish them. On each side of the car, and running fore and aft, was a broad leather-covered sofa—to sit on in the day and sleep on at night. Over each sofa hung, by straps, a wide, flat, leather-covered shelf—to sleep on. In the daytime you can hitch it up against the wall, out of the way—and then you have a big unencumbered and most comfortable room to spread out in. No car in any country is quite its equal for comfort (and privacy) I think. For usually there are but two persons in it; and even when there are four there is but little sense of impaired privacy. Our own cars at home can surpass the railway world in all details but that one: they have no coziness; there are too many people together.

At the foot of each sofa was a side-door, for entrance and exit.

Along the whole length of the sofa on each side of the car ran a row of large single-plate windows, of a blue tint— blue to soften the bitter glare of the sun and protect one's eyes from torture. These could be let down out of the way when one wanted the breeze. In the roof were two oil-lamps which gave a light strong enough to read by; each had a green-cloth attachment by which it could be covered when the light should be no longer needed.

While we talked outside with friends, Barney and Satan

placed the hand-baggage, books, fruits, and soda-bottles in the racks, and the hold-alls and heavy baggage in the closet, hung the overcoats and sun-helmets and towels on the hooks, hoisted the two bed-shelves up out of the way, then shouldered their bedding and retired to the third class.

Now then, you see what a handsome, spacious, light, airy, homelike place it was, wherein to walk up and down, or sit and write, or stretch out and read and smoke. A central door in the forward end of the compartment opened into a similar compartment. It was occupied by my wife and daughter. About nine in the evening, while we halted awhile at a station, Barney and Satan came and undid the clumsy big hold-alls, and spread the bedding on the sofas in both compartments—mattresses, sheets, gay coverlets, pillows, all complete; there are no chambermaids in India—apparently it was an office that was never heard of. Then they closed the communicating door, nimbly tidied up our place, put the night-clothing on the beds and the slippers under them, then returned to their own quarters.

January 31. It was novel and pleasant, and I stayed awake as long as I could, to enjoy it, and to read about those strange people the Thugs. In my sleep they remained with me, and tried to strangle me. The leader of the gang was that giant Hindu who was such a picture in the strong light when we were leaving those Hindu betrothal festivities at two o'clock in the morning—Rao Bahadur Baskirao Balinkanje Pitale, Vakeel to the Gaikwar of Baroda. It was he that brought me the invitation from his master to go to Baroda and lecture to that prince—and now he was misbehaving in my dreams. But all things can happen in dreams. It is, indeed, as the Sweet Singer of Michigan says—irrelevantly, of course, for the one and unfailing great quality which distinguishes her poetry from Shakespeare's and makes it precious to us is its stern and simple irrelevancy:

My heart was gay and happy,
This was ever in my mind,
There is better times a coming,
And I hope some day to find
Myself capable of composing,
It was my heart's delight
To compose on a sentimental subject
If it came in my mind just right.[1]

Baroda. Arrived at seven this morning. The dawn was just beginning to show. It was forlorn to have to turn out in a strange place at such a time, and the blinking lights in the station made it seem night still. But the gentlemen who had come to receive us were there with their servants, and they made quick work; there was no lost time. We were soon outside and moving swiftly through the soft gray light, and presently were comfortably housed—with more servants to help than we were used to, and with rather embarrassingly important officials to direct them. But it was custom; they spoke Ballarat English, their bearing was charming and hospitable, and so all went well.

Breakfast was a satisfaction. Across the lawns was visible in the distance through the open window an Indian well, with two oxen tramping leisurely up and down long inclines, drawing water; and out of the stillness came the suffering screech of the machinery—not quite musical, and yet soothingly melancholy and dreamy and reposeful—a wail of lost spirits, one might imagine. And commemorative and reminiscent, perhaps; for of course the Thugs used to throw people down that well when they were done with them.

After breakfast the day began, a sufficiently busy one. We were driven by winding roads through a vast park, with noble forests of great trees, and with tangles and jungles of

[1] *The Sentimental Song Book,* p. 49; theme, "The Author's Early Life," 19th stanza.

lovely growths of a humbler sort; and at one place three large gray apes came out and pranced across the road—a good deal of a surprise and an unpleasant one, for such creatures belong in the menagerie, and they look artificial and out of place in a wilderness.

We came to the city, by and by, and drove all through it. Intensely Indian, it was, and crumbly, and moldering, and immemorially old, to all appearance. And the houses—oh, indescribably quaint and curious they were, with their fronts an elaborate lacework of intricate and beautiful wood-carving, and now and then further adorned with rude pictures of elephants and princes and gods done in shouting colors; and all the ground floors along these cramped and narrow lanes occupied as shops—shops unbelievably small and impossibly packed with merchantable rubbish, and with nine-tenths-naked natives squatting at their work of hammering, pounding, brazing, soldering, sewing, designing, cooking, measuring out grain, grinding it, repairing idols—and then the swarm of ragged and noisy humanity under the horses' feet and everywhere, and the pervading reek and fume and smell! It was all wonderful and delightful.

Imagine a file of elephants marching through such a crevice of a street and scraping the paint off both sides of it with their hides. How big they must look, and how little they must make the houses look; and when the elephants are in their glittering court costume, what a contrast they must make with the humble and sordid surroundings. And when a mad elephant goes raging through, belting right and left with his trunk, how do these swarms of people get out of the way? I suppose it is a thing which happens now and then in the mad season (for elephants have a mad season).

I wonder how old the town is. There are patches of building—massive structures, monuments, apparently—that are so battered and worn, and seemingly so tired and so burdened with the weight of age, and so dulled and stupefied with trying to remember things they forgot before history began, that they give one the feeling that they must have been a part of original Creation. This is indeed one of the oldest of the princedoms of India, and has always been celebrated for its barbaric pomps and splendors, and for the wealth of its princes.

Chapter IX

*It takes your enemy and your friend, working together,
to hurt you to the heart; the one to slander you and the
other to get the news to you.*
— *Pudd'nhead Wilson's New Calendar.*

O UT of the town again; a long drive through open country, by winding roads among secluded villages nestling
in the inviting shade of tropic vegetation, a Sabbath stillness
everywhere, sometimes a pervading sense of solitude, but
always barefoot natives gliding by like spirits, without sound
of footfall, and others in the distance dissolving away and
vanishing like the creatures of dreams. Now and then a string
of stately camels passed by—always interesting things to look
at—and they were velvet-shod by nature, and made no noise.
Indeed, there were no noises of any sort in this paradise. Yes,
once there was one, for a moment: a file of native convicts
passed along in charge of an officer, and we caught the soft
clink of their chains. In a retired spot, resting himself under
a tree, was a holy person—a naked black fakir, thin and
skinny, and whitey-gray all over with ashes.

By and by to the elephant stables, and I took a ride; but
it was by request—I did not ask for it, and didn't want it; but

I took it, because otherwise they would have thought I was afraid, which I was. The elephant kneels down, by command—one end of him at a time—and you climb the ladder and get into the howdah, and then he gets up, one end at a time, just as a ship gets up over a wave; and after that, as he strides monstrously about, his motion is much like a ship's motion. The mahout bores into the back of his head with a great iron prod, and you wonder at his temerity and at the elephant's patience, and you think that perhaps the patience will not last; but it does, and nothing happens. The mahout talks to the elephant in a low voice all the time, and the elephant seems to understand it all and to be pleased with it; and he obeys every order in the most contented and docile way. Among these twenty-five elephants were two which were larger than any I had ever seen before, and if I had thought I could learn to not be afraid, I would have taken one of them while the police were not looking.

In the howdah-house there were many howdahs that were made of silver, one of gold, and one of old ivory, and equipped with cushions and canopies of rich and costly stuffs. The wardrobe of the elephants was there, too; vast velvet covers stiff and heavy with gold embroidery; and bells of silver and gold; and ropes of these metals for fastening the things on—harness, so to speak; and monster hoops of massive gold for the elephant to wear on his ankles when he is out in procession on business of state.

But we did not see the treasury of crown jewels, and that was a disappointment, for in mass and richness it ranks only second in India. By mistake we were taken to see the new palace instead, and we used up the last remnant of our spare time there. It was a pity, too; for the new palace is mixed modern American-European, and has not a merit except costliness. It is wholly foreign to India, and impudent and out of place. The architect has escaped. This comes of overdoing the suppression of the Thugs; they had their merits. The old palace is Oriental and charming, and in consonance with the country. The old palace would still be great if there were nothing of it but the spacious and lofty hall where the durbars are held. It is not a good place to lecture in, on account of the echoes, but it is a good place to hold durbars in and regulate the affairs of a kingdom, and that is what it is for. If I had it I would have a durbar every day, instead of once or twice a year.

The prince is an educated gentleman. His culture is European. He has been in Europe five times. People say that this is costly amusement for him, since in crossing the sea he must sometimes be obliged to drink water from vessels that are more or less public, and thus damage his caste. To get it purified again he must make pilgrimage to some renowned Hindu temples and contribute a fortune or two to them. His people are like the other Hindus, profoundly religious; and they could not be content with a master who was impure.

We failed to see the jewels, but we saw the gold cannon and the silver one—they seemed to be six-pounders. They were not designed for business, but for salutes upon rare and particularly important state occasions. An ancestor of the present Gaikwar had the silver one made, and a subsequent ancestor had the gold one made, in order to outdo him.

This sort of artillery is in keeping with the traditions of Baroda, which was of old famous for style and show. It used to entertain visiting rajahs and viceroys with tiger-fights, elephant-fights, illuminations, and elephant-processions of the most glittering and gorgeous character.

It makes the circus a pale, poor thing.

In the train, during a part of the return journey from Baroda, we had the company of a gentleman who had with him a remarkable-looking dog. I had not seen one of its kind before, as far as I could remember; though of course I might have seen one and not noticed it, for I am not acquainted with dogs, but only with cats. This dog's coat was smooth and shiny and black, and I think it had tan trimmings around the edges of the dog, and perhaps underneath. It was a long, low dog, with very short, strange legs—legs that curved inboard, something like parentheses turned the wrong way)(. Indeed, it was made on the plan of a bench for length and lowness. It seemed to be satisfied, but I thought the plan poor, and structurally weak, on account of the distance between the forward supports and those abaft. With age the dog's back was likely to sag; and it seemed to me that it would have been a stronger and more practicable dog if it had had some more legs. It had not begun to sag yet, but the shape of the legs showed that the undue weight imposed upon them was beginning to tell. It had a long nose, and floppy ears that hung down, and a resigned expression of countenance. I did not like to ask what kind of a dog it was, or how it came to be deformed, for it was plain that the gentleman was very fond of it, and naturally he could be sensitive about it. From delicacy I thought it best not to seem to notice it too much. No doubt a man with a dog like that feels just as a person does who has a child that is out of true. The gentleman was not merely fond of the dog, he was also proud of it—just the same, again, as a mother feels about her child when it is an idiot. I could see that he was proud of it, notwithstanding it was such a long dog and looked so resigned and pious. It had been all over the world with him, and had been pilgriming like that for years and years. It had traveled fifty thousand miles by sea and rail, and had ridden in front of him on his horse eight thousand. It had a silver medal from the Geographical Society of Great Britain for its travels, and I saw it. It had won prizes in dog-shows, both in India and in England—I saw them.

He said its pedigree was on record in the Kennel Club,

and that it was a well-known dog. He said a great many people in London could recognize it the moment they saw it. I did not say anything, but I did not think it anything strange; I should know that dog again, myself, yet I am not careful about noticing dogs. He said that when he walked along in London, people often stopped and looked at the dog. Of course I did not say anything, for I did not want to hurt his feelings, but I could have explained to him that if you take a great long low dog like that and waddle it along the street anywhere in the world and not charge anything, people will stop and look. He was gratified because the dog took prizes. But that was nothing; if I were built like that I could take prizes myself. I wished I knew what kind of a dog it was, and what it was for, but I could not very well ask, for that would show that I did not know. Not that I want a dog like that, but only to know the secret of its birth.

I think he was going to hunt elephants with it, because I know, from remarks dropped by him, that he has hunted large game in India and Africa, and likes it. But I think that if he tries to hunt elephants with it, he is going to be disappointed. I do not believe that it is suited for elephants. It lacks energy, it lacks force of character, it lacks bitterness. These things all show in the meekness and resignation of its expression. It would not attack an elephant, I am sure of it. It might not run if it saw one coming, but it looked to me like a dog that would sit down and pray.

I wish he had told me what breed it was, if there are others; but I shall know the dog next time, and then if I can bring myself to it I will put delicacy aside and ask. If I seem strangely interested in dogs, I have a reason for it; for a dog saved me from an embarrassing position once, and that has made me grateful to these animals; and if by study I could learn to tell some of the kinds from the others, I should be greatly pleased. I only know one kind apart, yet, and that is

the kind that saved me that time. I always know that kind
when I meet it, and if it is hungry or lost I take care of it.
The matter happened in this way:

It was years and years ago. I had received a note from
Mr. Augustin Daly of the Fifth Avenue Theater, asking me
to call the next time I should be in New York. I was writing
plays, in those days, and he was admiring them and trying
to get me a chance to get them played in Siberia. I took the
first train—the early one—the one that leaves Hartford at
eight-twenty-nine in the morning. At New Haven I bought
a paper, and found it filled with glaring display-lines about a
"bench-show" there. I had often heard of bench-shows, but
had never felt any interest in them, because I supposed they
were lectures that were not well attended. It turned out, now,
that it was not that, but a dog-show. There was a double-
leaded column about the king-feature of this one, which was
called a Saint Bernard, and was worth ten thousand dollars,
and was known to be the largest and finest of his species in
the world. I read all this with interest, because out of my
school-boy readings I dimly remembered how the priests and
pilgrims of St. Bernard used to go out in the storms and dig
these dogs out of the snowdrifts when lost and exhausted,
and give them brandy and save their lives, and drag them to
the monastery and restore them with gruel.

Also, there was a picture of this prize-dog in the paper,
a noble great creature with a benignant countenance, standing
by a table. He was placed in that way so that one could get
a right idea of his great dimensions. You could see that he
was just a shade higher than the table—indeed, a huge fellow
for a dog. Then there was a description which went into the
details. It gave his enormous weight—150½ pounds, and his
length—4 feet 2 inches, from stem to stern-post; and his
height—3 feet 1 inch, to the top of his back. The pictures
and the figures so impressed me, that I could see the beautiful

colossus before me, and I kept on thinking about him, for the next two hours; then I reached New York, and he dropped out of my mind.

In the swirl and tumult of the hotel lobby I ran across Mr. Daly's comedian, the late James Lewis, of beloved memory, and I casually mentioned that I was going to call upon Mr. Daly in the evening at eight. He looked surprised, and said he reckoned not. For answer I handed him Mr. Daly's note. Its substance was: "Come to my private den, over the theater, where we cannot be interrupted. And come by the back way, not the front. No. 642 Sixth Avenue is a cigar shop; pass through it and you are in a paved court, with high buildings all around; enter the second door on the left, and come up-stairs."

"Is that all?"

"Yes," I said.

"Well, you'll never get in."

"Why?"

"Because you won't. Or if you do you can draw on me for a hundred dollars; for you will be the first man that has accomplished it in twenty-five years. I can't think what Mr. Daly can have been absorbed in. He has forgotten a most important detail, and he will feel humiliated in the morning when he finds that you tried to get in and couldn't."

"Why, what is the trouble?"

"I'll tell you. You see—"

At that point we were swept apart by the crowd, somebody detained me with a moment's talk, and we did not get together again. But it did not matter; I believed he was joking, anyway.

At eight in the evening I passed through the cigar shop and into the court and knocked at the second door.

"Come in!"

I entered. It was a small room, carpetless, dusty, with a

naked deal table, and two cheap wooden chairs for furniture. A giant Irishman was standing there, with shirt-collar and vest unbuttoned, and no coat on. I put my hat on the table, and was about to say something, when the Irishman took the innings himself. And not with marked courtesy of tone:

"Well, sor, what will *you* have?"

I was a little disconcerted, and my easy confidence suffered a shrinkage. The man stood as motionless as Gibraltar, and kept his unblinking eye upon me. It was very embarrassing, very humiliating, very humiliating. I stammered at a false start or two; then:

"I have just run down from—"

"Av ye plaze, ye'll not smoke here, ye understand."

I laid my cigar on the window-ledge; chased my flighty thoughts a moment, then said in a placating manner:

"I—I have come to see Mr. Daly."

"Oh, ye *have*, have ye?"

"Yes."

"Well, ye'll not see him."

"But he *asked* me to come."

"Oh, he *did*, did he?"

"Yes, he sent me this note, and—"

"Lemme see it."

For a moment I fancied there would be a change in the atmosphere, now; but this idea was premature. The big man was examining the note searchingly under the gas-jet. A glance showed me that he had it upside down—disheartening evidence that he could not read.

"Is ut his own hand-write?"

"Yes—he wrote it himself."

"He did, did he?"

"Yes."

"H'm. Well, then, why'u'd he write it like that?"

"How do you mean?"

"I mane, why w'u'dn't he put his name to ut?"

"His name *is* to it. *That's* not it—you are looking at *my* name."

I thought that that was a home shot, but he did not betray that he had been hit. He said:

"It's not an aisy one to spell; how do you pronounce ut?"

"Mark Twain."

"H'm. H'm. Mike Train. H'm. I don't remember ut. What is it ye want to see him about?"

"It isn't I that want to see *him*, he wants to see *me*."

"Oh, he does, does he?"

"Yes."

"What does he want to see ye about?"

"I don't know."

"Ye don't *know!* And ye confess it, becod! Well, I can tell ye wan thing—ye'll not see him. Are ye in the business?"

"What business?"

"The show business."

A fatal question. I recognized that I was defeated. If I answered no, he would cut the matter short and wave me to the door without the grace of a word—I saw it in his uncompromising eye; if I said I was a lecturer, he would despise me, and dismiss me with opprobrious words; if I said I was a dramatist, he would throw me out of the window. I saw that my case was hopeless, so I chose the course which seemed least humiliating: I would pocket my shame and glide out without answering. The silence was growing lengthy.

"I'll ask ye again. Are ye in the show business yerself?"

"Yes!"

I said it with splendid confidence; for in that moment the very twin of that grand New Haven dog loafed into the room, and I saw that Irishman's eye light eloquently with pride and affection.

"Ye are? Are what is it?"

"I've got a bench-show in New Haven."

The weather *did* change then.

"You don't *say,* sir! And that's *your* show, sir! Oh, it's a grand show, it's a wonderful show, sir, and a proud man I am to see your honor this day. And ye'll be an expert, sir, and ye'll know all about dogs—more than ever they know theirselves, I'll take me oath to ut."

I said, with modesty:

"I believe I have some reputation that way. In fact, my business requires it."

"Ye have *some* reputation, your honor! Bedad I believe you! There's not a jintleman in the worrld that can lay over ye in the judgmint of a dog, sir. Now I'll vinture that your honor'll know that dog's dimensions there better than he knows them his own self, and just by the casting of your educated eye upon him. Would you mind giving a guess, if ye'll be so good?"

I knew that upon my answer would depend my fate. If I made this dog bigger than the prize-dog, it would be bad diplomacy, and suspicious; if I fell too far short of the prize-dog, that would be equally damaging. The dog was standing by the table, and I believed I knew the difference between him and the one whose picture I had seen in the newspaper to a shade. I spoke promptly up and said:

"It's no trouble to guess this noble creature's figures: height, three feet; length, four feet and three-quarters of an inch; weight, a hundred and forty-eight and a quarter."

The man snatched his hat from its peg and danced on it with joy, shouting:

"Ye've hardly missed it the hair's-breadth, hardly the shade of a shade, your honor! Oh, it's the miraculous eye ye've got, for the judgmint of a dog!"

And still pouring out his admiration of my capacities, he

"YOUR HONOR'LL KNOW THAT DOG'S DIMENSIONS"

snatched off his vest and scoured off one of the wooden chairs with it, and scrubbed it and polished it, and said:

"There, sit down, your honor, I'm ashamed of meself that I forgot ye were standing all this time; and do put on your hat, ye mustn't take cold, it's a draughty place; and here is your cigar, sir, a-getting cold, I'll give ye a light. There. The place is all yours, sir, and if ye'll just put your feet on the table and make yourself at home, I'll stir around and get a candle and light ye up the ould crazy stairs and see that ye don't come to anny harm, for be this time Mr. Daly'll be that impatient to see your honor that he'll be taking the roof off."

He conducted me cautiously and tenderly up the stairs, lighting the way and protecting me with friendly warnings, then pushed the door open and bowed me in and went his way, mumbling hearty things about my wonderful eye for points of a dog. Mr. Daly was writing and had his back to me. He glanced over his shoulder presently, then jumped up and said:

"Oh, dear me, I forgot all about giving instructions. I was just writing you to beg a thousand pardons. But how is it you are here? How did you get by that Irishman? You are the first man that's done it in five and twenty years. You didn't bribe him, I know that; there's not money enough in New York to do it. And you didn't persuade him; he is all ice and iron: there isn't a soft place nor a warm one in him anywhere. What is your secret? Look here; you owe me a hundred dollars for unintentionally giving you a chance to perform a miracle—for it *is* a miracle that you've done."

"That is all right," I said, "collect it of Jimmy Lewis."

That good dog not only did me that good turn in the time of my need, but he won for me the envious reputation among all the theatrical people from the Atlantic to the Pacific of being the only man in history who had ever run the blockade of Augustin Daly's back door.

Chapter X

If the desire to kill and the opportunity to kill came always together, who would escape hanging?
            —Pudd'nhead Wilson's New Calendar.

ON the Train. Fifty years ago, when I was a boy in the then remote and sparsely peopled Mississippi valley, vague tales and rumors of a mysterious body of professional murderers came wandering in from a country which was constructively as far from us as the constellations blinking in space—India; vague tales and rumors of a sect called Thugs, who waylaid travelers in lonely places and killed them for the contentment of a god whom they worshiped; tales which everybody liked to listen to and nobody believed—except with reservations. It was considered that the stories had gathered bulk on their travels. The matter died down and a lull followed. Then Eugène Sue's *Wandering Jew* appeared, and made great talk for a while. One character in it was a chief of Thugs—Feringhea—a mysterious and terrible Indian who was as slippery and sly as a serpent, and as deadly; and he stirred up the Thug interest once more. But it did not last. It presently died again—this time to stay dead.

At first glance it seems strange that this should have happened; but really it was not strange—on the contrary, it was natural; I mean on our side of the water. For the source whence the Thug tales mainly came was a Government Report, and without doubt was not republished in America; it was probably never even seen there. Government Reports have no general circulation. They are distributed to the few, and are not always read by those few. I heard of this Report for the first time a day or two ago, and borrowed it. It is full of fascinations; and it turns those dim, dark fairy tales of my boyhood days into realities.

The Report was made in 1839 by Major Sleeman, of the Indian Service, and was printed in Calcutta in 1840. It is a clumsy, great, fat, poor sample of the printer's art, but good enough for a government printing-office in that old day and in that remote region, perhaps. To Major Sleeman was given the general superintendence of the giant task of ridding India of Thuggee, and he and his seventeen assistants accomplished it. It was the Augean Stables over again. Captain Vallancey, writing in a Madras journal in those old times, makes this remark:

> The day that sees this far-spread evil eradicated from India and known only in name, will greatly tend to immortalize British rule in the East.

He did not overestimate the magnitude and difficulty of the work, nor the immensity of the credit which would justly be due to British rule in case it was accomplished.

Thuggee became known to the British authorities in India about 1810, but its wide prevalence was not suspected; it was not regarded as a serious matter, and no systematic measures were taken for its suppression until about 1830. About that time Major Sleeman captured Eugène Sue's Thug-chief,

Feringhea, and got him to turn King's evidence. The revelations were so stupefying that Sleeman was not able to believe them. Sleeman thought he knew every criminal within his jurisdiction, and that the worst of them were merely thieves; but Feringhea told him that he was in reality living in the midst of a swarm of professional murderers; that they had been all about him for many years, and that they buried their dead close by. These seemed insane tales; but Feringhea said come and see—and he took him to a grave and dug up a hundred bodies, and told him all the circumstances of the killings, and named the Thugs who had done the work. It was a staggering business. Sleeman captured some of these Thugs and proceeded to examine them separately, and with proper precautions against collusion; for he would not believe any Indian's unsupported word. The evidence gathered proved the truth of what Feringhea had said, and also revealed the fact that gangs of Thugs were plying their trade all over India. The astonished government now took hold of Thuggee, and for ten years made systematic and relentless war upon it, and finally destroyed it. Gang after gang was captured, tried, and punished. The Thugs were harried and hunted from one end of India to the other. The government got all their secrets out of them; and also got the names of the members of the bands, and recorded them in a book, together with their birthplaces and places of residence.

The Thugs were worshipers of Bhowanee; and to this god they sacrificed anybody that came handy; but they kept the dead man's things themselves, for the god cared for nothing but the corpse. Men were initiated into the sect with solemn ceremonies. Then they were taught how to strangle a person with the sacred choke-cloth, but were not allowed to perform officially with it until after long practice. No half-educated strangler could choke a man to death quickly enough to keep him from uttering a sound—a muffled scream, gurgle, gasp, moan, or something of the sort; but the expert's work was instantaneous: the cloth was whipped around the victim's neck, there was a sudden twist, and the head fell silently forward, the eyes starting from the sockets; and all was over. The Thug carefully guarded against resistance. It was usual to get the victims to sit down, for that was the handiest position for business.

If the Thug had planned India itself it could not have been more conveniently arranged for the needs of his occupation. There were no public conveyances. There were no conveyances for hire. The traveler went on foot or in a bullock-cart or on a horse which he bought for the purpose. As soon as he was out of his own little state or principality he was among strangers; nobody knew him, nobody took note of him, and from that time his movements could no longer be traced. He did not stop in towns or villages, but camped outside of them and sent his servants in to buy provisions. There were no habitations between villages. Whenever he was between villages he was an easy prey, particularly as he usually traveled by night, to avoid the heat. He was always being overtaken by strangers who offered him the protection of their company, or asked for the protection of his—and these strangers were often Thugs, as he presently found out to his cost. The landholders, the native police, the petty princes, the village officials, the customs officers were in many cases protectors and harborers of the Thugs, and betrayed travelers to them for a share of the spoil. At first this condition of things made it next to impossible for the government to catch the marauders; they were spirited away by these watchful friends. All through a vast continent, thus infested, helpless people of every caste and kind moved along the paths and trails in couples and groups silently by night, carrying the commerce of the country—treasure, jewels, money, and petty batches of silks, spices, and all manner of wares. It was a paradise for the Thug.

When the autumn opened, the Thugs began to gather together by pre-concert. Other people had to have interpreters at every turn, but not the Thugs; *they* could talk together, no matter how far apart they were born, for they had a language of their own, and they had secret signs by which they knew each other for Thugs; and they were always friends. Even their diversities of religion and caste were sunk in devotion to their calling, and the Moslem and the high-caste and low-caste Hindu were stanch and affectionate brothers in Thuggery.

When a gang had been assembled, they had religious worship, and waited for an omen. They had definite notions about the omens. The cries of certain animals were good omens, the cries of certain other creatures were bad omens. A bad omen would stop proceedings and send the men home.

The sword and the strangling-cloth were sacred emblems. The Thugs worshiped the sword at home before going out to the assembling-place; the strangling-cloth was worshiped at the place of assembly. The chiefs of most of the bands performed the religious ceremonies themselves; but the *Kaets* delegated them to certain official stranglers (Chaurs). The rites of the Kaets were so holy that no one but the Chaur was allowed to touch the vessels and other things used in them.

Thug methods exhibited a curious mixture of caution and the absence of it; cold business calculation and sudden, unreflecting impulse; but there were two details which were constant, and not subject to caprice: patient persistence in following up the prey, and pitilessness when the time came to act.

Caution was exhibited in the strength of the bands. They

never felt comfortable and confident unless their strength exceeded that of any party of travelers they were likely to meet by four or five fold. Yet it was never their purpose to attack openly, but only when the victims were off their guard. When they got hold of a party of travelers they often moved along in their company several days, using all manner of arts to win their friendship and get their confidence. At last, when this was accomplished to their satisfaction, the real business began. A few Thugs were privately detached and sent forward in the dark to select a good killing-place and *dig the graves*. When the rest reached the spot a halt was called, for a rest or a smoke. The travelers were invited to sit. By signs, the chief appointed certain Thugs to sit down in front of the travelers as if to wait upon them, others to sit down beside them and engage them in conversation, and certain expert stranglers to stand behind the travelers and be ready when the signal was given. The signal was usually some commonplace remark, like "Bring the tobacco." Sometimes a considerable wait ensued after all the actors were in their places—the chief was biding his time, in order to make everything sure. Meantime, the talk droned on, dim figures moved about in the dull light, peace and tranquillity reigned, the travelers resigned themselves to the pleasant reposefulness and comfort of the situation, unconscious of the death-angels standing motionless at their backs. The time was ripe, now, and the signal came: "Bring the tobacco." There was a mute swift movement, all in the same instant the men at each victim's sides seized his hands, the man in front seized his feet, and pulled, the man at his back whipped the cloth around his neck and gave it a twist—the head sunk forward, the tragedy was over. The bodies were stripped and covered up in the graves, the spoil packed for transportation, then the Thugs gave pious thanks to Bhowanee, and departed on further holy service.

The Report shows that the travelers moved in exceedingly small groups—twos, threes, fours, as a rule; a party with a dozen in it was rare. The Thugs themselves seem to have been the only people who moved in force. They went about in gangs of 10, 15, 25, 40, 60, 100, 150, 200, 250, and one gang of 310 is mentioned. Considering their numbers, their catch was not extraordinary—particularly when you consider that they were not in the least fastidious, but took anybody they could get, whether rich or poor, and sometimes even killed children. Now and then they killed women, but it was considered sinful to do it, and unlucky. The "season" was six or eight months long. One season the half-dozen Bundelkand and Gwalior gangs aggregated 712 men, and they murdered 210 people. One season the Malwa and Kandeish gangs aggregated 702 men, and they murdered 232. One season the Kandeish and Berar gangs aggregated 963 men, and they murdered 385 people.

Here is the tally-sheet of a gang of *sixty* Thugs for a whole season—gang under two noted chiefs, "Chotee and Sheik Nungoo from Gwalior":

Left Poora, in Jhansee, and on arrival at Sarora murdered a traveler.

On nearly reaching Bhopal, met 3 Brahmans, and murdered them.

Cross the Nerbudda; at a village called Hutteea, murdered a Hindu.

Went through Aurungabad to Walagow; there met a Havildar of the barber caste and 5 sepoys (native soldiers); in the evening came to Jokur, and in the morning killed them near the place where the treasure-bearers were killed the year before.

Between Jokur and Dholeea met a sepoy of the shepherd caste; killed him in the jungle.

Passed through Dholeea and lodged in a village; two

miles beyond, on the road to Indore, met a Byragee (beggar—holy mendicant); murdered him at the Thapa.

In the morning, beyond the Thapa, fell in with 3 Marwarie travelers; murdered them.

Near a village on the banks of the Taptee met 4 travelers and killed them.

Between Choupra and Dhoreea met a Marwarie; murdered him.

At Dhoreea met 3 Marwaries; took them two miles and murdered them.

Two miles further on, overtaken by 3 treasure-bearers; took them two miles and murdered them in the jungle.

Came on to Khurgore Bateesa in Indore, divided spoil, and dispersed.

A total of 27 men murdered on one expedition.

Chotee (to save his neck) was informer, and furnished these facts. Several things are noticeable about his résumé. 1, Business brevity; 2, absence of emotion; 3, smallness of the parties encountered by the sixty; 4, variety in character and quality of the game captured; 5, Hindu and Mohammedan chiefs in business together for Bhowanee; 6, the sacred caste of the Brahmans not respected by either; 7, nor yet the character of that mendicant, that Byragee.

A beggar is a holy creature, and some of the gangs spared him on that account, no matter how slack business might be; but other gangs slaughtered not only him, but even that sacredest of sacred creatures, the *fakir*—that repulsive skin-and-bone thing that goes around naked and mats his bushy hair with dust and dirt, and so beflours his lean body with ashes that he looks like a specter. Sometimes a fakir trusted a shade too far in the protection of his sacredness. In the middle of a tally-sheet of Feringhea's, who had been out with forty Thugs, I find a case of the kind. After the killing of thirty-nine men and one woman, the fakir appears on the scene:

> Approaching Doregow, met 3 pundits; also a fakir, mounted on a pony; he was plastered over with sugar to collect flies, and was covered with them. Drove off the fakir, and killed the other three.
>
> Leaving Doregow, the fakir joined again, and went on in company to Raojana; met 6 Khutries on their way from Bombay to Nagpore. Drove off the fakir with stones, and killed the 6 men in camp, and buried them in the grove.
>
> Next day the fakir joined again; made him leave at Mana. Beyond there fell in with 2 Kahars and a sepoy, and came on toward the place selected for the murder. When near it, the fakir came again. Losing all patience with him, gave Mithoo, one of the gang, 5 rupees ($2.50) to murder him, and take the sin upon himself. All four were strangled, including the fakir. Surprised to find among the fakir's effects 30 pounds of coral, 350 strings of small pearls, 15 strings of large pearls, and a gilt necklace.

It is curious, the little effect that time has upon a really interesting circumstance. This one, so old, so long ago gone down into oblivion, reads with the same freshness and charm that attach to the news in the morning paper; one's spirits go up, then down, then up again, following the chances which the fakir is running; now you hope, now you despair, now you hope again; and at last everything comes out right, and you feel a great wave of personal satisfaction go weltering through you, and, without thinking, you put out your hand to pat Mithoo on the back, when—puff! the whole thing has vanished away, there is nothing there; Mithoo and all the crowd have been dust and ashes and forgotten, oh, so many, many, *many* lagging years! And then comes a sense of injury:

you don't know whether Mithoo got the swag, along with the sin, or had to divide up the swag and keep all the sin himself. There is no literary art about a government report. It stops a story right in the most interesting place.

These reports of Thug expeditions run along interminably in one monotonous tune: "Met a sepoy—killed him; met five pundits—killed them; met four Rajputs and a woman—killed them"—and so on, till the statistics get to be pretty dry. But this small trip of Feringhea's Forty had some little variety about it. Once they came across a man hiding in a *grave*—a thief; he had stolen eleven hundred rupees from Dhunroj Seith of Parowtee. They strangled him and took the money. They had no patience with thieves. They killed two treasure-bearers, and got four thousand rupees. They came across two bullocks "laden with copper pice," and killed the four drivers and took the money. There must have been half a ton of it. I think it takes a double handful of pice to make an anna, and sixteen annas to make a rupee; and even in those days the rupee was worth only half a dollar. Coming back over their tracks from Baroda, they had another picturesque stroke of luck: "The Lohars of Oodeypore" put a traveler in their charge "for safety." Dear, dear, across this abysmal gulf of time we still see Feringhea's lips uncover his teeth, and through the dim haze we catch the incandescent glimmer of his smile. He accepted that trust, good man; and so we know what went with the traveler.

Even Rajas had no terrors for Feringhea; he came across an elephant-driver belonging to the Raja of Oodeypore and promptly strangled him.

"A total of one hundred men and five women murdered on this expedition."

Among the reports of expeditions we find mention of victims of almost every quality and estate:

Native soldiers	Chuprassies	Women servants
Fakirs	Treasure-bearers	seeking work
Mendicants	Children	Shepherds
Holy-water carriers	Cowherds	Archers
Carpenters	Gardeners	Table-waiters
Peddlers	Shopkeepers	Weavers
Tailors	Palanquin-bearers	Priests
Blacksmiths	Farmers	Bankers
Policemen (native)	Bullock-drivers	Boatmen
Pastry cooks	Male servants	Merchants
Grooms	seeking work	Grass-cutters
Mecca pilgrims		

Also a prince's cook; and even the water-carrier of that sublime lord of lords and king of kings, the Governor-General of India! How broad they were in their tastes! They also murdered actors—poor wandering barn-stormers. There are two instances recorded; the first one by a gang of Thugs under a chief who soils a great name borne by a better man—Kipling's deathless Gungadin:

> After murdering four sepoys, going on toward Indore, met four strolling players, and persuaded them to come with us, on the pretense that we would see their performance at the next stage. Murdered them at a temple near Bhopal.

Second instance:

> At Deohuttee, joined by comedians. Murdered them eastward of that place.

But this gang was a particularly bad crew. On that expedition they murdered a fakir and twelve beggars. And yet Bhowanee protected them; for once when they were strangling a man in a wood when a crowd was going by close at hand and the noose slipped and the man screamed, Bhowanee made a camel burst out at the same moment with a roar that drowned the scream; and before the man could repeat it the breath was choked out of his body.

The cow is so sacred in India that to kill her keeper is an awful sacrilege, and even the Thugs recognized this; yet now and then the lust for blood was too strong, and so they did kill a few cow-keepers. In one of these instances the witness who killed the cowherd said, "In Thuggee this is strictly forbidden, and is an act from which no good can come. I was ill of a fever for ten days afterward. I do believe that evil will follow the murder of a man with a cow. If there be no cow it does not signify." Another Thug said he held the cowherd's feet while this witness did the strangling. He felt no concern, "because the bad fortune of such a deed is upon the strangler and not upon the assistants; even if there should be a hundred of them."

There were thousands of Thugs roving over India constantly, during many generations. They made Thuggee a hereditary vocation and taught it to their sons and to their sons' sons. Boys were in full membership as early as sixteen years of age; veterans were still at work at seventy. What was the fascination, what was the impulse? Apparently, it was partly piety, largely gain, and there is reason to suspect that the *sport* afforded was the chiefest fascination of all. Meadows Taylor makes a Thug in one of his books claim that the pleasure of killing men was the white man's beast-hunting instinct enlarged, refined, ennobled. I will quote the passage:

Chapter XI

Simple rules for saving money: To save half, when you are fired by an eager impulse to contribute to a charity, wait, and count forty. To save three quarters, count sixty. To save it all, count sixty-five.
—Pudd'nhead Wilson's New Calendar.

THE Thug said:

How many of you English are passionately devoted to sporting! Your days and months are passed in its excitement. A tiger, a panther, a buffalo, or a hog rouses your utmost energies for its destruction—you even risk your lives in its pursuit. How much higher game is a Thug's!

That must really be the secret of the rise and development of Thuggee. The joy of killing! the joy of seeing killing done—these are traits of the human race at large. We white people are merely modified Thugs; Thugs fretting under the restraints of a not very thick skin of civilization; Thugs who long ago enjoyed the slaughter of the Roman arena, and later the burning of doubtful Christians by authentic Christians in the public squares, and who now, with the Thugs of Spain and Nîmes, flock to enjoy the blood and misery of the bull-ring. We have no tourists of either sex or any religion who are able to resist the delights of the bull-ring when opportunity offers, and we are gentle Thugs in the hunting season, and love to chase a tame rabbit and kill it. Still, we have made some progress—microscopic, and in truth scarcely worth mentioning, and certainly nothing to be proud of—still, it is progress: we no longer take pleasure in slaughtering or burning helpless men. We have reached a little altitude where we may look down upon the Indian Thugs with a complacent shudder; and we may even hope for a day, many centuries hence, when our posterity will look down upon us in the same way.

There are many indications that the Thug often hunted men for the mere sport of it; that the fright and pain of the quarry were no more to him than are the fright and pain of the rabbit or the stag to us; and that he was no more ashamed of beguiling his game with deceits and abusing its trust than are we when we have imitated a wild animal's call and shot it when it honored us with its confidence and came to see what we wanted:

Madara, son of Nihal, and I, Ramzam, set out from Kotdee in the cold weather, and followed the high road for about twenty days in search of travelers until we came to Selempore, where we met a very old man going to the east. We won his confidence in this manner: He carried a load which was too heavy for his old age; I said to him: "You are an old man, I will aid you in carrying your load, as you are from my part of the country." He said: "Very well, take me with you." So we took him with us to Selempore, where we slept that night. We woke him next morning before dawn and set out, and at the distance of three miles we seated him to rest while it was still very dark. Madara was ready behind him, and strangled him. He never spoke a word. He was about sixty or seventy years of age.

Another gang fell in with a couple of barbers and persuaded them to come along in their company by promising them the job of shaving the whole crew—thirty Thugs. At the place appointed for the murder fifteen got shaved, and actually paid the barbers for their work. Then killed them and took back the money.

A gang of forty-two Thugs came across two Brahmans and a shopkeeper on the road, beguiled them into a grove and got up a *concert* for their entertainment. While these poor fellows were listening to the music the stranglers were standing behind them; and at the proper moment for dramatic effect they applied the noose.

The most devoted fisherman must have a bite at least as often as once a week or his passion will cool and he will put up his tackle. The tiger-sportsman must find a tiger at least once a fortnight or he will get tired and quit. The elephant-hunter's enthusiasm will waste away little by little, and his zeal will perish at last if he plod around a month without finding a member of that noble family to assassinate.

But when the lust in the hunter's heart is for the noblest of all quarries, man, how different is the case! and how watery and poor is the zeal and how childish the endurance of those other hunters by comparison. Then, neither hunger, nor thirst, nor fatigue, nor deferred hope, nor monotonous disappointment, nor leaden-footed lapse of time can conquer the hunter's patience or weaken the joy of his quest or cool the splendid rage of his desire. Of all the hunting-passions that burn in the breast of man, there is none that can lift him superior to discouragements like these but the one—the royal sport, the supreme sport, whose quarry is his brother. By comparison, tiger-hunting is a colorless poor thing, for all it has been so bragged about.

Why, the Thug was content to tramp patiently along, afoot, in the wasting heat of India, week after week, at an average of nine or ten miles a day, if he might but hope to find game some time or other and refresh his longing soul with blood. Here is an instance:

> I (Ramzam) and Hyder set out, for the purpose of strangling travelers, from Guddapore, and proceeded *via* the Fort of Julalabad, Newulgunge, Bangermow, on the banks of the Ganges (upward of one hundred miles), from whence we returned by another route. Still no travelers! till we reached Bowaneegunge, where we fell in with a traveler, a boatman; we inveigled him, and about two miles east of there Hyder strangled him as he stood—for he was troubled and afraid and would not sit. We then made a long journey (about one hundred and thirty miles) and reached Hussunpore Bundwa, where at the tank we fell in with a traveler—he slept there that night; next morning we followed him and tried to win his confidence; at the distance of two miles we endeavored to induce him to sit down—but he would not, having become aware of us. I attempted to strangle him as he walked along, but did not succeed; both of us then fell upon him. He made a great outcry, "They are murdering me!" At length we strangled him and flung his body into a well. After this we returned to our homes, having been out a month and traveled about two hundred and sixty miles. A total of two men murdered on the expedition.

And here is another case—related by the terrible Futty Khan, a man with a tremendous record, to be rementioned by and by:

> I, with three others, traveled for about forty-five days a distance of about two hundred miles in search of victims along the highway to Bundwa and returned by Davodpore (another two hundred miles), during which journey we had only one murder, which happened in this manner. Four miles to the

east of Noubustaghat we fell in with a traveler, an old man. I, with Koshal and Hyder, inveigled him and accompanied him that day within three miles of Rampoor, where, after dark, in a lonely place, we got him to sit down and rest; and while I kept him in talk, seated before him, Hyder behind strangled him: he made no resistance. Koshal stabbed him under the arms and in the throat, and we flung the body into a running stream. We got about four or five rupees each ($2 or $2.50). We then proceeded homeward. A total of one man murdered on this expedition.

There. They tramped four hundred miles, were gone about three months, and harvested two dollars and a half apiece. But the mere pleasure of the hunt was sufficient. That was pay enough. They did no grumbling.

Every now and then in this big book one comes across that pathetic remark: "We tried to get him to sit down but he would not." It tells the whole story. Some accident had awakened the suspicion in him that these smooth friends who had been petting and coddling him and making him feel so safe and so fortunate after his forlorn and lonely wanderings were the dreaded Thugs; and now their ghastly invitation to "sit and rest" had confirmed its truth. He knew there was no help for him, and that he was looking his last upon earthly things, but "he would not sit." No, not that—it was too awful to think of!

There are a number of instances which indicate that when a man had once tasted the regal joys of man-hunting he could not be content with the dull monotony of a crimeless life afterward. Example, from a Thug's testimony:

We passed through to Kurnaul, where we found a former Thug named Junooa, an old comrade of ours, who had turned religious mendicant and become a disciple and holy. He came to us in the serai and weeping with joy returned to his old trade.

Neither wealth nor honors nor dignities could satisfy a reformed Thug for long. He would throw them all away, some day, and go back to the lurid pleasures of hunting men, and being hunted himself by the British.

Ramzam was taken into a great native grandee's service and given authority over five villages. "My authority extended over these people to summons them to my presence, to make them stand or sit. I dressed well, rode my pony, and had two sepoys, a scribe and a village guard to attend me. During three years I used to pay each village a monthly visit, and no one suspected that I was a Thug! The chief man used to wait on me to transact business, and, as I passed along, old and young made their salaam to me."

And yet during that very three years he got leave of absence "to attend a wedding," and instead went off on a Thugging lark with six other Thugs and hunted the highway for fifteen days!—with satisfactory results.

Afterward he held a great office under a Raja. There he had ten miles of country under his command and a military guard of fifteen men, with authority to call out two thousand more upon occasion. But the British got on his track, and they crowded him so that he had to give himself up. See what a figure he was when he was gotten up for style and had all his things on: "I was fully armed—a sword, shield, pistols, a matchlock musket and a flint gun, for I was fond of being thus arrayed, and when so armed feared not though forty men stood before me."

He gave himself up and proudly proclaimed himself a Thug. Then by request he agreed to betray his friend and pal, Buhram, a Thug with the most tremendous record in India. "I went to the house where Buhram slept (often has he led our gangs!). I woke him, he knew me well, and came outside to me. It was a cold night, so, under pretense of warming myself, but in reality to have light for his seizure by the guards, I lighted some straw and made a blaze. We were warming our hands. The guards drew around us. I said to them, 'This is Buhram,' and he was seized just as a cat seizes a mouse. Then Buhram said, 'I am a Thug! my father was a Thug, my grandfather was a Thug, and I have thugged with many!' "

So spoke the mighty hunter, the mightiest of the mighty, the Gordon Cumming of his day. Not much regret noticeable in it.[1]

So many, many times this Official Report leaves one's curiosity unsatisfied. For instance, here is a little paragraph out of the record of a certain band of one hundred and ninety-three Thugs, which has that defect:

> Fell in with Lall Sing Subahdar and his family, consisting of nine persons. Traveled with them two days, and the third put them all to death except the two children, little boys of one and a half years old.

There it stops. What did they do with those poor little fellows? What was their subsequent history? Did they purpose training them up as Thugs? How could they take care of

[1]"Having planted a bullet in the shoulder-bone of an elephant, and caused the agonized creature to lean for support against a tree, I proceeded to brew some coffee. Having refreshed myself, taking observations of the elephant's spasms and writhings between the sips, I resolved to make experiments on vulnerable points, and, approaching very near, I fired several bullets at different parts of his enormous skull. He only acknowledged the shots by a salaam-like movement of his trunk, with the point of which he gently touched the wounds with a striking and peculiar action. Surprised and shocked to find that I was only prolonging the suffering of the noble beast, which bore its trials with such dignified composure, I resolved to finish the proceeding with all possible despatch, and accordingly opened fire upon him from the left side. Aiming at the shoulder, I fired six shots with the two-grooved rifle, which must have eventually proved mortal, after which I fired six shots at the same part with the Dutch six-pounder. Large tears now trickled down from his eyes, which he slowly shut and opened, his colossal frame shivered convulsively, and falling on his side he expired."—*Gordon Cumming*.

such little creatures on a march which stretched over several months? No one seems to have cared to ask any questions about the babies. But I do wish I knew.

One would be apt to imagine that the Thugs were utterly callous, utterly destitute of human feelings, heartless toward their own families as well as toward other people's; but this was not so. Like all other Indians, they had a passionate love for their kin. A shrewd British officer who knew the Indian character, took that characteristic into account in laying his plans for the capture of Eugène Sue's famous Feringhea. He found out Feringhea's hiding-place, and sent a guard by night to seize him, but the squad was awkward and he got away. However, they got the rest of the family—the mother, wife, child, and brother—and brought them to the officer, at Jubbulpore; the officer did not fret, but bided his time: "I knew Feringhea would not go far while links so dear to him were in my hands." He was right. Feringhea knew all the danger he was running by staying in the neighborhood, still he could not tear himself away. The officer found that he divided his time between five villages where he had relatives and friends who could get news for him from his family in Jubbulpore jail; and that he never slept two consecutive nights in the same village. The officer traced out his several haunts, then pounced upon all the five villages on the one night and at the same hour, and got his man.

Another example of family affection. A little while previously to the capture of Feringhea's family, the British officer had captured Feringhea's foster-brother, leader of a gang of ten, and had tried the eleven and condemned them to be hanged. Feringhea's captured family arrived at the jail the day before the execution was to take place. The foster-brother, Jhurhoo, entreated to be allowed to see the aged mother and the others. The prayer was granted, and this is what took place—it is the British officer who speaks:

In the morning, just before going to the scaffold, the interview took place before me. He fell at the old woman's feet and begged that she would relieve him from the obligations of the milk with which she had nourished him from infancy, as he was about to die before he could fulfil any of them. She placed her hands on his head, and he knelt, and she said she forgave him all, and bid him die like a man.

If a capable artist should make a picture of it, it would be full of dignity and solemnity and pathos; and it could touch you. You would imagine it to be anything but what it was. There is reverence there, and tenderness, and gratefulness, and compassion, and resignation, and fortitude, and self-respect—and no sense of disgrace, no thought of dishonor. Everything is there that goes to make a noble parting, and give it a moving grace and beauty and dignity. And yet one of these people is a Thug and the other a mother of Thugs! The incongruities of our human nature seem to reach their limit here.

I wish to make note of one curious thing while I think of it. One of the very commonest remarks to be found in this bewildering array of Thug confessions is this:

"Strangled him and *threw him in a well!*" In one case they threw sixteen into a well—and they had thrown others in the same well before. It makes a body thirsty to read about it.

And there is another very curious thing. The bands of Thugs had *private graveyards.* They did not like to kill and bury at random, here and there and everywhere. They preferred to wait, and toll the victims along, and get to one of their regular burying-places (bheels) if they could. In the little kingdom of Oude, which was about half as big as Ireland and about as big as the state of Maine, they had *two hundred and seventy-four bheels.* They were scattered along *fourteen hundred miles of road,* at an average of only *five miles apart,* and the British

Government traced out and located each and every one of them and set them down on the map.

The Oude bands seldom went out of their own country, but they did a thriving business within its borders. So did outside bands who came in and helped. Some of the Thug leaders of Oude were noted for their successful careers. Each of four of them confessed to above 300 murders; another to nearly 400; our friend Ramzam to 604—he is the one who got leave of absence to attend a wedding and went thugging instead; and he is also the one who betrayed Buhram to the British.

But the biggest records of all were the murder-lists of Futty Khan and Buhram. Futty Khan's number is smaller than Ramzam's, but he is placed at the head because his *average* is the best in Oude-Thug history per year of service. His slaughter was five hundred and eight men in twenty years, and he was still a young man when the British stopped his industry. Buhram's list was nine hundred and thirty-one murders, but it took him forty years. His average was one man and nearly all of another man per month for forty years, but Futty Khan's average was *two* men and a little of another man per month during his twenty years of usefulness.

There is one very striking thing which I wish to call attention to. You have surmised from the listed callings followed by the victims of the Thugs that nobody could travel the Indian roads unprotected and live to get through; that the Thugs respected no quality, no vocation, no religion, nobody; that they killed every unarmed man that came in their way. That is wholly true—with one reservation. In all the long file of Thug confessions *an English traveler is mentioned but once*—and this is what the Thug says of the circumstance:

> He was on his way from Mhow to Bombay. *We studiously avoided him.* He proceeded next morning with a number of

travelers *who had sought his protection,* and they took the road to Baroda.

We do not know who he was; he flits across the page of this rusty old book and disappears in the obscurity beyond; but he is an impressive figure, moving through that valley of death serene and unafraid, clothed in the might of the English name.

We have now followed the big official book through, and we understand what Thuggee was, what a bloody terror it was, what a desolating scourge it was. In 1830 the English found this cancerous organization embedded in the vitals of the empire, doing its devastating work in secrecy, and assisted, protected, sheltered, and hidden by innumerable confederates—big and little native chiefs, customs officers, village officials, and native police, all ready to lie for it, and the mass of the people, through fear, persistently pretending to know nothing about its doings; and this condition of things had existed for generations, and was formidable with the sanctions of age and old custom. If ever there was an unpromising task, if ever there was a hopeless task in the world, surely it was offered here—the task of conquering Thuggee. But that little handful of English officials in India set their sturdy and confident grip upon it, and ripped it out, root and branch! How modest do Captain Vallancey's words sound now, when we read them again, knowing what we know:

> The day that sees this far-spread evil completely eradicated from India, and known only in name, will greatly tend to immortalize British rule in the East.

It would be hard to word a claim more modestly than that for this most noble work.

Chapter XII

Grief can take care of itself; but to get the full value of a joy you must have somebody to divide it with.
       —Pudd'nhead Wilson's New Calender.

WE left Bombay for Allahabad by a night train. It is the custom of the country to avoid day travel when it can conveniently be done. But there is no trouble: while you can seemingly "secure" the two lower berths by making early application, there is no ticket as witness of it, and no other producible evidence in case your proprietorship shall chance to be challenged. The word "engaged" appears on the window, but it doesn't state who the compartment is engaged *for*. If your Satan and your Barney arrive before somebody else's servants, and spread the bedding on the two sofas and then stand guard till you come, all will be well; but if they step aside on an errand, they may find the beds promoted to the two shelves, and somebody else's demons standing guard over their master's beds, which in the mean time have been spread upon your sofas.

You do not pay anything extra for your sleeping-place; that is where the trouble lies. If you buy a fare-ticket and fail to use it, there is room thus made available for some one else; but if the place were secured to you it would remain vacant, and yet your ticket would secure you *another* place when you were presently ready for travel.

However, no explanation of such a system can make it seem quite rational to a person who has been used to a more rational system. If our people had the arranging of it, we should charge extra for securing the place, and then the road would suffer no loss if the purchaser did not occupy it.

The present system encourages good manners—and also discourages them. If a young girl has a lower berth and an elderly lady comes in, it is usual for the girl to offer her place to this late comer; and it is usual for the late comer to thank her courteously and take it. But the thing happens differently sometimes. When we were ready to leave Bombay my daughter's satchels were holding possession of her berth—a lower one. At the last moment, a middle-aged American lady swarmed into the compartment, followed by native porters laden with her baggage. She was growling and snarling and scolding, and trying to make herself phenomenally disagreeable; and succeeding. Without a word, she hoisted the satchels into the hanging shelf, and took possession of that lower berth.

On one of our trips Mr. Smythe and I got out at a station to walk up and down, and when we came back Smythe's bed was in the hanging shelf and an English cavalry officer was in bed on the sofa which he had lately been occupying. It was mean to be glad about it, but it is the way we are made; I could not have been gladder if it had been my enemy that had suffered this misfortune. We all like to see people in trouble, if it doesn't cost us anything. I was so happy over Mr. Smythe's chagrin that I couldn't go to sleep for thinking of it and enjoying it. I knew he supposed the officer had committed the robbery himself, whereas without a doubt the officer's servant had done it without his knowledge. Mr. Smythe kept this incident warm in his heart, and longed for a chance to get even with somebody for it. Sometime afterward the opportunity came, in Calcutta. We were leaving on a twenty-four-hour journey to Darjeeling. Mr. Barclay, the general superintendent, had made special provision for our accommodation, Mr. Smythe said; so there was no need to hurry about getting to the train; consequently, we were a little late. When we arrived, the usual immense turmoil and confusion of a great Indian station were in full blast. It was an immoderately long train, for all the natives of India were going by it somewhither, and the native officials were being pestered to frenzy by belated and anxious people. They didn't know where our car was, and couldn't remember having received any orders about it. It was a deep disappointment; moreover, it looked as if our half of our party would be left behind altogether. Then Satan came running and said he had found a compartment with one shelf and one sofa unoccupied, and had made our beds and had stowed our baggage. We rushed to the place, and just as the train was ready to pull out and the porters were slamming the doors to, all down the line, an officer of the Indian Civil Service, a good friend of ours, put his head in and said:

"I have been hunting for you everywhere. What are you doing here? Don't you know—"

The train started before he could finish. Mr. Smythe's opportunity was come. His bedding, on the shelf, at once changed places with the bedding—a stranger's—that was occupying the sofa that was opposite to mine. About ten o'clock we stopped somewhere, and a large Englishman of official military bearing stepped in. We pretended to be asleep. The lamps were covered, but there was light enough for us to note his look of surprise. He stood there, grand and fine, peering down at Smythe, and wondering in silence at the situation. After a bit he said:

"Well!" And that was all.

But that was enough. It was easy to understand. It meant: "This is extraordinary. This is high-handed. I haven't had an experience like this before."

He sat down on his baggage, and for twenty minutes we watched him through our eyelashes, rocking and swaying there to the motion of the train. Then we came to a station, and he got up and went out, muttering: "I *must* find a lower berth, or wait over." His servant came presently and carried away his things.

Mr. Smythe's sore place was healed, his hunger for revenge was satisfied. But he couldn't sleep, and neither could I; for this was a venerable old car, and nothing about it was taut. The closet door slammed all night, and defied every fastening we could invent. We got up very much jaded, at dawn, and stepped out at a way-station; and, while we were taking a cup of coffee, that Englishman ranged up alongside, and somebody said to him:

"So you didn't stop off, after all?"

"No. The guard found a place for me that had been engaged and not occupied. I had a whole saloon car all to myself—oh, quite palatial! I never had such luck in my life."

That was our car, you see. We moved into it, straight off, the family and all. But I asked the English gentleman to remain, and he did. A pleasant man, an infantry colonel; and doesn't know, yet, that Smythe robbed him of his berth, but thinks it was done by Smythe's servant without Smythe's knowledge. He was assisted in gathering this impression.

The Indian trains are manned by natives exclusively. The Indian stations—except very large and important ones—are manned entirely by natives, and so are the posts and telegraphs. The rank and file of the police are natives. All these people are pleasant and accommodating. One day I left an express-train to lounge about in that perennially ravishing show, the ebb and flow and whirl of gaudy natives, that is always surging up and down the spacious platform of a great Indian station; and I lost myself in the ecstasy of it, and when I turned, the train was moving swiftly away. I was going to sit down and wait for another train, as I would have done at home; I had no thought of any other course. But a native official, who had a green flag in his hand, saw me, and said politely:

"Don't you belong in the train, sir?"

"Yes," I said.

He waved his flag, and the train came back! And he put me aboard with as much ceremony as if I had been the General Superintendent. They are kindly people, the natives. The face and the bearing that indicate a surly spirit and a bad heart seemed to me to be so rare among Indians—so nearly non-existent, in fact—that I sometimes wondered if Thuggee wasn't a dream, and not a reality. The bad hearts *are* there, but I believe that they are in a small, poor minority. One thing is sure: They are much the most *interesting* people in the world—and the nearest to being incomprehensible. At any rate, the hardest to account for. Their character and their history, their customs and their religion, confront you with riddles at every turn—riddles which are a trifle more perplexing after they are explained than they were before. You can get the *facts* of a custom—like caste, and Suttee, and Thuggee, and so on—and with the facts a theory which tries to explain, but never quite understand *how* so strange a thing could have been born, nor *why*.

For instance—the *Suttee*. This is the explanation of it: A woman who throws away her life when her husband dies is instantly joined to him again, and is forever afterward happy with him in heaven; her family will build a little monument to her, or a temple, and will hold her in honor, and, indeed, worship her memory always; they will themselves be held in honor by the public; the woman's self-sacrifice has conferred a noble and lasting distinction upon her posterity. And, besides, see what she has escaped: If she had elected to live, she would be a disgraced person; she could not remarry; her family would despise her and disown her; she would be a friendless outcast, and miserable all her days.

Very well, you say, but the explanation is not complete yet. *How* did people come to drift into such a strange custom? What was the origin of the idea? "Well, nobody knows; it was probably a revelation sent down by the gods." One more thing: Why was such a cruel death chosen—why wouldn't a gentle one have answered? "Nobody knows; maybe that was a revelation, too."

No—you can never understand it. It all seems impossible. You resolve to believe that a widow never burnt herself willingly, but went to her death because she was afraid to defy public opinion. But you are not able to keep that position. History drives you from it. Major Sleeman has a convincing case in one of his books. In his government on the Nerbudda he made a brave attempt on the 28th of March, 1828, to put down Suttee on his own hook and without warrant from the Supreme Government of India. He could not foresee that the government would put it down itself eight months later. The only backing he had was a bold nature and a compassionate heart. He issued his proclamation abolishing the Suttee in his district. On the morning of Tuesday—note the day of the week—the 24th of the following November, Ummed Singh Upadhya, head of the most respectable and most extensive Brahman family in the district, died, and presently came a deputation of his sons and grandsons to beg that his old widow might be allowed to burn herself upon his pyre. Sleeman threatened to enforce his order, and punish severely any man who assisted; and he placed a police guard to see that no one did so. From the early morning the old widow of sixty-five had been sitting on the bank of the sacred river by her dead, waiting through the long hours for the permission; and at last the refusal came instead. In one little sentence Sleeman gives you a pathetic picture of this lonely old gray figure: all day and all night "she remained sitting by the edge of the water without eating or drinking." The next morning the body of the husband was burned to ashes in a pit eight feet square and three or four feet deep, in the view of several thousand spectators. Then the widow waded out to a bare rock in the river, and everybody went away but her sons and other relations. All day she sat there on her rock in the blazing sun without food or drink, and with no clothing but a sheet over her shoulders.

The relatives remained with her, and all tried to persuade her to desist from her purpose, for they deeply loved her. She steadily refused. Then a part of the family went to Sleeman's house, ten miles away, and tried again to get him to let her burn herself. He refused, hoping to save her yet.

All that day she scorched in her sheet on the rock, and all that night she kept her vigil there in the bitter cold. Thursday morning, in the sight of her relatives, she went through a ceremonial which said more to them than any words could have done; she put on the *dhaja* (a coarse red turban) and broke her bracelets in pieces. By these acts she became a dead person in the eye of the law, and excluded from her caste forever. By the iron rule of ancient custom, if she should now choose to live she could never return to her family. Sleeman was in deep trouble. If she starved herself to death her family would be disgraced; and, moreover, starving would be a more lingering misery than the death by fire. He went back in the evening thoroughly worried. The old woman remained on her rock, and there in the morning he found her with her *dhaja* still on her head. "She talked very collectedly, telling me that she had determined to mix her ashes with those of her departed husband, and should patiently wait my permission to do so, assured that God would enable her to sustain life till that was given, though she dared not eat or drink. Looking at the sun, then rising before her over a long and beautiful reach of the river, she said calmly, 'My soul has been for five days with my husband's near that sun; nothing but my earthly frame is left; and this, I know, you will in time suffer to be mixed with his ashes in yonder pit, because it is not in your nature or usage wantonly to prolong the miseries of a poor old woman.' "

He assured her that it was his desire and duty to save her, and to urge her to live, and to keep her family from the disgrace of being thought her murderers. But she said she was not afraid of their being thought so; that they had all, like good children, done everything in their power to induce her to live, and to abide with them; "and if I should consent I know they would love and honor me, but my duties to them have now ended. I commit them all to your care, and I go to attend my husband, Ummed Singh Upadhya, with whose ashes on the funeral pile mine have been already three times mixed."

She believed that she and he had been upon the earth three several times as wife and husband, and that she had burned herself to death three times upon his pyre. That is why she said that strange thing. Since she had broken her bracelets and put on the red turban she regarded herself as a corpse; otherwise she would not have allowed herself to do her husband the irreverence of pronouncing his name. "This was the first time in her long life that she had ever uttered her husband's name, for in India no woman, high or low, ever pronounces the name of her husband."

Major Sleeman still tried to shake her purpose. He promised to build her a fine house among the temples of her ancestors upon the bank of the river and make handsome provision for her out of rent-free lands if she would consent to live; and if she wouldn't he would allow no stone or brick to ever mark the place where she died. But she only smiled and said, "My pulse has long ceased to beat, my spirit has departed; I shall suffer nothing in the burning; and if you wish proof, order some fire and you shall see this arm consumed without giving me any pain."

Sleeman was now satisfied that he could not alter her purpose. He sent for all the chief members of the family and said he would suffer her to burn herself if they would enter into a written engagement to abandon the Suttee in their family thenceforth. They agreed; the papers were drawn out and signed, and at noon, Saturday, word was sent to the poor old woman. She seemed greatly pleased. The ceremonies of bathing were gone through with, and by three o'clock she was ready and the fire was briskly burning in the pit. She had now gone without food or drink during more than four days and a half. She came ashore from her rock, first wetting her sheet in the waters of the sacred river, for without that safeguard any shadow which might fall upon her would convey impurity to her; then she walked to the pit, leaning upon one of her sons and a nephew—the distance was a hundred and fifty yards.

I had sentries placed all around, and no other person was allowed to approach within five paces. She came on with a calm and cheerful countenance, stopped once, and, casting her eyes upward, said: "Why have they kept me five days from thee, my husband?" On coming to the sentries her supporters stopped and remained standing; she moved on, and walked once around the pit, paused a moment, and, while muttering a prayer, threw some flowers into the fire. She then walked up deliberately and steadily to the brink, stepped into the center of the flame, sat down, and, leaning back in the midst as if reposing upon a couch, was consumed without uttering a shriek or betraying one sign of agony.

It is fine and beautiful. It compels one's reverence and respect—no, has it freely, and without compulsion. We see how the custom, once started, could continue, for the soul of it is that stupendous power, Faith; faith brought to the pitch of effectiveness by the cumulative force of example and long use and custom; but we cannot understand how the first widows came to take to it. That is a perplexing detail.

Sleeman says that it was usual to play music at the Suttee, but that the white man's notion that this was to drown the screams of the martyr is not correct; that it had a quite different purpose. It was believed that the martyr died prophesying; that the prophecies sometimes foretold disaster, and it was considered a kindness to those upon whom it was to fall to drown the voice and keep them in ignorance of the misfortune that was to come.

Chapter XIII

He had had much experience of physicians, and said "the only way to keep your health is to eat what you don't want, drink what you don't like, and do what you'd druther not."
—Pudd'nhead Wilson's New Calendar.

IT was a long journey—two nights, one day, and part of another day, from Bombay eastward to Allahabad; but it was always interesting, and it was not fatiguing. At first the night travel promised to be fatiguing, but that was on account of *pajamas*. This foolish nightdress consists of jacket and drawers. Sometimes they are made of silk, sometimes of a raspy, scratchy, slazy woolen material with a sand-paper surface. The drawers are loose elephant-legged and elephant-waisted things, and instead of buttoning around the body there is a draw-string to produce the required shrinkage. The jacket is roomy, and one buttons it in front. Pajamas are hot on a hot night and cold on a cold night—defects which a nightshirt is free from. I tried the pajamas in order to be in the fashion; but I was obliged to give them up, I couldn't stand them. There was no sufficient change from day gear to night gear. I missed the refreshing and luxurious sense, induced by the nightgown, of being undressed, emancipated, set free from restraints and trammels. In place of that, I had the worried, confined, oppressed, suffocated sense of being abed with my clothes on. All through the warm half of the night the coarse surfaces irritated my skin and made it feel baked and feverish, and the dreams which came in the fitful flurries of slumber were such as distress the sleep of the damned, or ought to; and all through the cold other half of the night I could get no time for sleep because I had to employ it all in stealing blankets. But blankets are of no value at such a time; the higher they are piled the more effectively they cork the cold in and keep it from getting out. The result is that your legs are ice, and you know how you will feel by and by when you are buried. In a sane interval I discarded the pajamas, and led a rational and comfortable life thenceforth.

Out in the country in India, the day begins early. One sees a plain, perfectly flat, dust-colored and brick-yardy, stretching limitlessly away on every side in the dim gray light, striped everywhere with hard-beaten narrow paths, the vast flatness broken at wide intervals by bunches of spectral trees that mark where villages are; and along all the paths are slender women and the black forms of lanky naked men moving to their work, the women with brass water-jars on their heads, the men carrying hoes. The man is not entirely naked; always there is a bit of white rag, a loin-cloth; it amounts to a bandage, and is a white accent on his black person, like the silver band around the middle of a pipe-stem. Sometimes he also wears a fluffy and voluminous white turban, and this adds a second accent. He then answers prop-erly to Miss Gordon Cumming's flashlight picture of him— as a person who is dressed in "a turban and a pocket handker-chief."

All day long one has this monotony of dust-colored dead levels and scattering bunches of trees and mud villages. You soon realize that India is not beautiful; still there is an enchantment about it that is beguiling, and which does not pall. You cannot tell just what it is that makes the spell, perhaps, but you feel it and confess it, nevertheless. Of course, at bottom, you know in a vague way that it is *history*; it is that that affects you, a haunting sense of the myriads of human lives that have blossomed, and withered, and perished here, repeating and repeating and repeating, century after century, and age after age, the barren and meaningless process; it is this sense that gives to this forlorn, uncomely land power to speak to the spirit and make friends with it; to speak to it with a voice bitter with satire, but eloquent with melancholy. The deserts of Australia and the ice-barrens of Greenland have no speech, for they have no venerable history; with nothing to tell of man and his vanities, his fleeting glories and his miseries, they have nothing wherewith to spiritualize their ugliness and veil it with a charm.

There is nothing pretty about an Indian village—a mud one—and I do not remember that we saw any but mud ones on that long flight to Allahabad. It is a little bunch of dirt-colored mud hovels jammed together within a mud wall. As a rule, the rains had beaten down parts of some of the houses, and this gave the village the aspect of a moldering and hoary ruin. I believe the cattle and the vermin live inside the wall; for I saw cattle coming out and cattle going in; and whenever I saw a villager he was scratching. This last is only circumstantial evidence, but I think it has value. The village has a battered little temple or two, big enough to hold an idol, and with custom enough to fat up a priest and keep him comfortable. Where there are Mohammedans there are generally a few sorry tombs outside the village that have a decayed and neglected look. The villages interested me because of things which Major Sleeman says about them in his books—particularly what he says about the division of labor in them. He says that the whole face of India is parceled out into estates of villages; that nine-tenths of the vast population of the land consist of cultivators of the soil; that it is these cultivators who inhabit the villages; that there are certain "established" village servants—mechanics and others who are apparently paid a wage by the village at large, and whose callings remain in certain families and are handed down from father to son, like an estate. He gives a list of these established servants: Priest, blacksmith, carpenter, accountant, washer-man, basket-maker, potter, watchman, barber, shoe-maker, brazier, confectioner, weaver, dyer, etc. In his day witches abounded, and it was not thought good business wisdom for a man to marry his daughter into a family that hadn't a witch in it, for she would need a witch on the premises to protect her children from the evil spells which would certainly be cast upon them by the witches connected with the neighboring families.

The office of midwife was hereditary in the family of the basket-maker. It belonged to his wife. She might not be competent, but the office was hers, anyway. Her pay was not high—twenty-five cents for a boy, and half as much for a girl. The girl was not desired, because she would be a disastrous expense by and by. As soon as she should be old enough to begin to wear clothes for propriety's sake, it would be a disgrace to the family if she were not married; and to marry her meant financial ruin; for by custom the father must spend upon feasting and wedding-display everything he had and all he could borrow—in fact, reduce himself to a condition of poverty which he might nevermore recover from.

It was the dread of this prospective ruin which made the killing of girl babies so prevalent in India in the old days before England laid the iron hand of her prohibitions upon the piteous slaughter. One may judge of how prevalent the custom was, by one of Sleeman's casual electrical remarks, when he speaks of children at play in villages—*where girl voices were never heard!*

The wedding-display folly is still in full force in India, and by consequence the destruction of girl babies is still furtively practised; but not largely, because of the vigilance of the government and the sternness of the penalties it levies.

In some parts of India the village keeps in its pay three other servants: an astrologer to tell the villager when he may plant his crop, or make a journey, or marry a wife, or strangle a child, or borrow a dog, or climb a tree, or catch a rat, or swindle a neighbor, without offending the alert and solicitous heavens; and what his dream means, if he has had one and was not bright enough to interpret it himself by the details of his dinner; the two other established servants were the tiger-persuader and the hail-storm-discourager. The one kept away the tigers if he could, and collected the wages anyway, and the other kept off the hail-storms, or explained why he failed. He charged the same for explaining a failure that he did for scoring a success. A man is an idiot who can't earn a living in India.

Major Sleeman reveals the fact that the trade-union and the boycott are antiquities in India. India seems to have originated everything. The "sweeper" belongs to the bottom caste; he is the lowest of the low—all other castes despise him and scorn his office. But that does not trouble him. His caste is a caste, and that is sufficient for him, and so he is proud of it, not ashamed. Sleeman says:

> It is perhaps not known to many of my countrymen, even in India, that in every town and city in the country the right of sweeping the houses and streets is a monopoly, and is supported entirely by the pride of caste among the scavengers, who are all of the lowest class. The right of sweeping within a certain range is recognized by the caste to belong to a certain member; and if any other member presumes to sweep within that range, he is excommunicated—no other member

will smoke out of his pipe or drink out of his jug; and he can get restored to caste only by a feast to the whole body of sweepers. If any house-keeper within a particular circle happens to offend the sweeper of that range, none of his filth will be removed until he pacifies him, because no other sweeper will dare to touch it; and the people of a town are often more tyrannized over by these people than by any other.

A footnote by Major Sleeman's editor, Mr. Vincent Arthur Smith, says that in our day this tyranny of the sweepers' guild is one of the many difficulties which bar the progress of Indian sanitary reform. Think of this:

> The sweepers cannot be readily coerced, because no Hindu or Mussulman would do their work to save his life, nor will he pollute himself by beating the refractory scavenger.

They certainly do seem to have the whip-hand; it would be difficult to imagine a more impregnable position. "The vested rights described in the text are so fully recognized in practice that *they are frequently the subject of sale or mortgage.*" Just like a milk-route; or like a London crossing-sweepership. It is said that the London crossing-sweeper's right to his crossing is recognized by the rest of the guild; that they protect him in its possession; that certain choice crossings are valuable property, and are salable at high figures. I have noticed that the man who sweeps in front of the Army and Navy Stores has a wealthy South African aristocratic style about him; and when he is off his guard, he has exactly that look on his face which you always see in the face of a man who is saving up his daughter to marry her to a duke.

It appears from Sleeman that in India the occupation of elephant-driver is confined to Mohammedans. I wonder why that is. The water-carrier (*bheestie*) is a Mohammedan, but it is said that the reason of that is, that the Hindu's religion does not allow him to touch the skin of dead kine, and that is what the water-sack is made of; it would defile him. And it doesn't allow him to eat meat; the animal that furnished the meat was murdered, and to take any creature's life is a sin. It is a good and gentle religion, but inconvenient.

A great Indian river, at low water, suggests the familiar anatomical picture of a skinned human body, the intricate mesh of interwoven muscles and tendons to stand for water-channels, and the archipelagoes of fat and flesh inclosed by them to stand for the sandbars. Somewhere on this journey we passed such a river, and on a later journey we saw in the Sutlej the duplicate of that river. Curious rivers they are; low shores a dizzy distance apart, with nothing between but an enormous acreage of sand-flats with sluggish little veins of water dribbling around among them; Saharas of sand, smallpox-pitted with footprints punctured in belts as straight as the equator clear from the one shore to the other (barring the channel interruptions)—a dry-shod ferry, you see. Long railway bridges are required for this sort of rivers and India has them. You approach Allahabad by a very long one. It was now carrying us across the bed of the Jumna, a bed which did not seem to have been slept in for one while or more. It wasn't all river-bed—most of it was overflow ground.

Allahabad means "City of God." I get this from the books. From a printed curiosity—a letter written by one of those brave and confident Hindu strugglers with the English tongue, called a "babu"—I got a more compressed translation: "Godville." It is perfectly correct, but that is the most that can be said for it.

We arrived in the forenoon, and short-handed; for Satan got left behind somewhere that morning, and did not overtake us until after nightfall. It seemed very peaceful without him. The world seemed asleep and dreaming.

I did not see the native town, I think. I do not remember why; for an incident connects it with the Great Mutiny, and that is enough to make any place interesting. But I saw the English part of the city. It is a town of wide avenues and noble distances, and is comely and alluring, and full of suggestions of comfort and leisure, and of the serenity which a good conscience buttressed by a sufficient bank-account gives. The bungalows (dwellings) stand well back in the seclusion and privacy of large inclosed compounds (private grounds, as we should say) and in the shade and shelter of trees. Even the photographer and the prosperous merchant ply their industries in the elegant reserve of big compounds, and the citizens drive in there upon their business occasions. And not in cabs—no; in the Indian cities cabs are for the drifting stranger; all the white citizens have private carriages; and each carriage has a flock of white-turbaned black footmen and drivers all over it. The vicinity of a lecture-hall looks like a snow-storm, and makes the lecturer feel like an opera. India has many names, and they are correctly descriptive. It is the Land of Contradictions, the Land of Subtlety and Superstition, the Land of Wealth and Poverty, the Land of Splendor and Desolation, the Land of Plague and Famine, the Land of the Thug and the Poisoner, and of the Meek and the Patient, the Land of the Suttee, the Land of the Unreinstatable Widow, the Land where All Life is Holy, the Land of Cremation, the Land where the Vulture is a Grave and a Monument, the Land of the Multitudinous Gods; and if signs go for anything, it is the Land of the Private Carriage.

In Bombay the forewoman of a millinery shop came to the hotel in her private carriage to take the measure for a gown—not for me, but for another. She had come out to India to make a temporary stay, but was extending it indefinitely; indeed, she was purposing to end her days there. In London, she said, her work had been hard, her hours long;

for economy's sake she had had to live in shabby rooms and far away from the shop, watch the pennies, deny herself many of the common comforts of life, restrict herself in effect to its bare necessities, eschew cabs, travel third-class by underground train to and from her work, swallowing coal-smoke and cinders all the way, and sometimes troubled with the society of men and women who were less desirable than the smoke and the cinders. But in Bombay, on almost any kind of wages, she could live in comfort, and keep her carriage, and have six servants in place of the woman-of-all-work she had had in her English home. Later, in Calcutta, I found that the Standard Oil clerks had small one-horse vehicles, and did no walking; and I was told that the clerks of the other large concerns there had the like equipment. But to return to Allahabad.

I was up at dawn, the next morning. In India the tourist's servant does not sleep in a room in the hotel, but rolls himself up head and ears in his blanket and stretches himself on the veranda, across the front of his master's door, and spends the night there. I don't believe anybody's servant occupies a room. Apparently, the bungalow servants sleep on the veranda; it is roomy, and goes all around the house. I speak of men-servants; I saw none of the other sex. I think there are none, except child-nurses. I was up at dawn, and walked around the veranda, past the rows of sleepers. In front of one door a Hindu servant was squatting, waiting for his master to call him. He had polished the yellow shoes and placed them by the door, and now he had nothing to do but wait. It was freezing cold, but there he was, as motionless as a sculptured image, and as patient. It troubled me. I wanted to say to him, "Don't crouch there like that and freeze; nobody requires it of you; stir around and get warm." But I hadn't the words. I thought of saying *jeldy jow,* but I couldn't remember what it meant, so I didn't say it. I knew another

phrase, but it wouldn't come to my mind. I moved on, purposing to dismiss him from my thoughts, but his bare legs
and bare feet kept him there. They kept drawing me back
from the sunny side to a point whence I could see him. At
the end of an hour he had not changed his attitude in the
least degree. It was a curious and impressive exhibition of
meekness and patience, or fortitude, or indifference, I did not
know which. But it worried me, and it was spoiling my
morning. In fact, it spoiled two hours of it quite thoroughly.
I quitted this vicinity, then, and left him to punish himself as
much as he might want to. But up to that time the man had
not changed his attitude a hair. He will always remain with
me, I suppose; his figure never grows vague in my memory.
Whenever I read of Indian resignation, Indian patience under
wrongs, hardships, and misfortunes, he comes before me.
He becomes a personification, and stands for India in trouble.
And for untold ages India in trouble has been pursued with
the very remark which I was going to utter but didn't, because
its meaning had slipped me: *Jeldy jow!* ("Come, shove
along!") Why, it was the very thing.

In the early brightness we made a long drive out to the
Fort. Part of the way was beautiful. It led under stately trees
and through groups of native houses and by the usual village
well, where the picturesque gangs are always flocking to and
fro and laughing and chattering; and this time brawny men
were deluging their bronze bodies with the limpid water, and
making a refreshing and enticing show of it; enticing, for the
sun was already transacting business, firing India up for the
day. There was plenty of this early bathing going on, for it
was getting toward breakfast-time, and with an unpurified
body the Hindu must not eat.

Then we struck into the hot plain, and found the roads
crowded with pilgrims of both sexes, for one of the great
religious fairs of India was being held, just beyond the Fort,

at the junction of the sacred rivers, the Ganges and the Jumna. Three sacred rivers, I should have said, for there is a subterranean one. Nobody has seen it, but that doesn't signify. The fact that it is there is enough. These pilgrims had come from all over India; some of them had been months on the way, plodding patiently along in the heat and dust, worn, poor, hungry, but supported and sustained by an unwavering faith and belief; they were supremely happy and content, now; their full and sufficient reward was at hand; they were going to be cleansed from every vestige of sin and corruption by these holy waters which make utterly pure whatsoever thing they touch, even the dead and rotten. It is wonderful, the power of a faith like that, that can make multitudes upon multitudes of the old and weak and the young and frail enter without hesitation or complaint upon such incredible journeys and endure the resultant miseries without repining. It is done in love, or it is done in fear; I do not know which it is. No matter what the impulse is, the act born of it is beyond imagination marvelous to our kind of people, the cold whites. There are choice great natures among us that could exhibit the equivalent of this prodigious self-sacrifice, but the rest of us know that we should not be equal to anything approaching it. Still, we all talk self-sacrifice, and this makes me hope that we are large enough to honor it in the Hindu.

Two millions of natives arrive at this fair every year. How many start, and die on the road, from age and fatigue and disease and scanty nourishment, and how many die on the return, from the same causes, no one knows; but the tale is great, one may say enormous. Every twelfth year is held to be a year of peculiar grace; a greatly augmented volume of pilgrims results then. The twelfth year has held this distinction since the remotest times, it is said. It is said also that there is to be but one more twelfth year—for the Ganges. After that, that holiest of all scared rivers will cease to be holy, and will be abandoned by the pilgrims for many centuries; how many, the wise men have not stated. At the end of that interval it will become holy again. Meantime, the data will be arranged by those people who have charge of all such matters, the great chief Brahmans. It will be like shutting down a mint. At first glance it looks most unbrahmanically uncommercial, but I am not disturbed, being soothed and tranquilized by their reputation. "Brer fox he lay low," as Uncle Remus says; and at the judicious time he will spring something on the Indian public which will show that he was not financially asleep when he took the Ganges out of the market.

Great numbers of the natives along the roads were bringing away holy water from the rivers. They would carry it far and wide in India and sell it. Tavernier, the French traveler (seventeenth century), notes that Ganges water is often given at weddings, "each guest receiving a cup or two, according to the liberality of the host; sometimes two or three thousand rupees' worth of it is consumed at a wedding."

The Fort is a huge old structure, and has had a large experience in religions. In its great court stands a monolith which was placed there more than two thousand years ago to preach Buddhism by its pious inscription; the Fort was built three centuries ago by a Mohammedan Emperor—a resanctification of the place in the interest of *that* religion. There is a Hindu temple, too, with subterranean ramifications stocked with shrines and idols; and now the Fort belongs to the English, it contains a Christian Church. Insured in all the companies.

From the lofty ramparts one has a fine view of the sacred rivers. They join at that point—the pale-blue Jumna, apparently clean and clear, and the muddy Ganges, dull yellow and not clean. On a long curved spit between the rivers, towns of tents were visible, with a multitude of fluttering pennons, and a mighty swarm of pilgrims. It was a troublesome place to get down to, and not a quiet place when you arrived; but it was interesting. There was a world of activity and turmoil and noise, partly religious, partly commercial; for the Mohammedans were there to curse and sell, and the Hindus to buy and pray. It is a fair as well as a religious festival. Crowds were bathing, praying, and drinking the purifying waters, and many sick pilgrims had come long journeys in palanquins to be healed of their maladies by a bath; or if that might not be, then to die on the blessed banks and so make sure of heaven. There were fakirs in plenty, with their bodies dusted over with ashes and their long hair caked together with cow-dung; for the cow is holy and so is the rest of it; so holy that the good Hindu peasant frescoes the walls of his hut with this refuse, and also constructs ornamental figures out of it for the gracing of his dirt floor. There were seated families, fearfully and wonderfully painted, who by attitude and grouping represented the families of certain great gods. There was a holy man who sat naked by the day and by the week on a cluster of iron spikes, and did not seem to mind it; and another holy man, who stood all day holding his withered arms motionless aloft, and was said to have been doing it for years. All of these performers have a cloth on the ground beside them for the reception of contributions, and even the poorest of the people give a trifle and hope that the sacrifice will be blessed to him. At last came a procession of naked holy people marching by and chanting, and I wrenched myself away.

Chapter XIV

The man who is ostentatious of his modesty is twin to the statue that wears a fig-leaf.
                    —Pudd'nhead Wilson's New Calendar.

THE journey to Benares was all in daylight, and occupied but a few hours. It was admirably dusty. The dust settled upon you in a thick ashy layer and turned you into a fakir, with nothing lacking to the rôle but the cow-manure and the sense of holiness. There was a change of cars about midafternoon at Moghul-serai—if that was the name—and a wait of two hours there for the Benares train. We could have found a carriage and driven to the sacred city, but we should have lost the wait. In other countries a long wait at a station is a dull thing and tedious, but one has no right to have that feeling in India. You have the monster crowd of bejeweled natives, the stir, the bustle, the confusion, the shifting splendors of the costumes—dear me, the delight of it, the charm of it are beyond speech. The two-hour wait was over too soon. Among other satisfying things to look at was a minor native prince from the backwoods somewhere, with his guard of honor, a ragged but wonderfully gaudy gang of fifty dark barbarians armed with rusty flintlock muskets. The general show came so near to exhausting variety that one would have said that no addition to it could be conspicuous, but when this Falstaff and his motleys marched through it one saw that that seeming impossibility had happened.

We got away by and by, and soon reached the outer edge of Benares; then there was another wait; but, as usual, with something to look at. This was a cluster of little canvas-boxes—palanquins. A canvas-box is not much of a sight—when empty; but when there is a lady in it, it is an object of interest. These boxes were grouped apart, in the full blaze of the terrible sun, during the three-quarters of an hour that we tarried there. They contained zenana ladies. They had to sit up; there was not room enough to stretch out. They probably did not mind it. They are used to the close captivity of their dwellings all their lives; when they go a journey they are carried to the train in these boxes; in the train they have to be secluded from inspection. Many people pity them, and I always did it myself and never charged anything; but it is doubtful if this compassion is valued. While we were in India some good-hearted Europeans in one of the cities proposed to restrict a large park to the use of zenana ladies, so that they could go there and in assured privacy go about unveiled and enjoy the sunshine and air as they had never enjoyed them before. The good intentions back of the proposition were recognized, and sincere thanks returned for it, but the proposition itself met with a prompt declination at the hands of those who were authorized to speak for the zenana ladies. Apparently, the idea was shocking to the ladies—indeed, it was quite manifestly shocking. Was that proposition the equivalent of inviting European ladies to assemble scantily and scandalously clothed in the seclusion of a private park? It seemed to be about that.

Without doubt modesty is nothing less than a holy feeling; and without doubt the person whose rule of modesty has been transgressed feels the same sort of wound that he would feel if something made holy to him by his religion had suffered a desecration. I say "rule of modesty" because there are about a million rules in the world, and this makes a million standards to be looked out for. Major Sleeman mentions the case of some high-caste veiled ladies who were profoundly scandalized when some English young ladies passed by with faces bare to the world; so scandalized that they spoke out with strong indignation and wondered that people could be so shameless as to expose their persons like that. And yet "the legs of the objectors were naked to mid-thigh." Both parties were clean-minded and irreproachably modest, while abiding by their separate rules, but they couldn't have traded rules for a change without suffering considerable discomfort. All human rules are more or less idiotic, I suppose. It is best so, no doubt. The way it is now, the asylums can hold the sane people, but if we tried to shut up the insane we should run out of building materials.

You have a long drive through the outskirts of Benares before you get to the hotel. And all the aspects are melancholy. It is a vision of dusty sterility, decaying temples, crumbling tombs, broken mud walls, shabby huts. The whole region seems to ache with age and penury. It must take ten thousand years of want to produce such an aspect. We were still outside of the great native city when we reached the hotel. It was a quiet and homelike house, inviting, and manifestly comfortable. But we liked its annex better, and went thither. It was a mile away, perhaps, and stood in the midst of a large compound, and was built bungalow fashion, everything on the ground floor, and a veranda all around. They have doors in India, but I don't know why. They don't fasten, and they stand open, as a rule, with a curtain hanging in the doorspace to keep out the glare of the sun. Still, there is plenty of privacy, for no white person will come in without notice, of course. The native men-servants will, but they don't seem to count. They glide in, barefoot and noiseless, and are in the midst before one knows it. At first this is a shock, and sometimes it is an embarrassment; but one has to get used to it, and does.

There was one tree in the compound, and a monkey lived in it. At first I was strongly interested in the tree, for I was told that it was the renowned *peepul*—the tree in whose shadow you cannot tell a lie. This one failed to stand the test, and I went away from it disappointed. There was a softly creaking well close by, and a couple of oxen drew water from it by the hour, superintended by two natives dressed in the usual "turban and pocket handkerchief." The tree and the well were the only scenery, and so the compound was a soothing and lonesome and satisfying place; and very restful after so many activities. There was nobody in our bungalow but ourselves; the other guests were in the next one, where the table d'hôte was furnished. A body could not be more pleasantly situated. Each room had the customary bath attached—a room ten or twelve feet square, with a roomy stone-paved pit in it and abundance of water. One could not easily improve upon this arrangement, except by furnishing it with cold water and excluding the hot, in deference to the fervency of the climate; but that is forbidden. It would damage the bather's health. The stranger is warned against taking cold baths in India, but even the most intelligent strangers are fools, and they do not obey, and so they presently get laid up. I was the most intelligent fool that passed through, that year. But I am still more intelligent now. Now that it is too late.

I wonder if the *dorian*, if that is the name of it, is another superstition, like the peepul tree. There was a great abundance and variety of tropical fruits, but the dorian was never in evidence. It was never the season for the dorian. It was always going to arrive from Burma some time or other, but it never did. By all accounts, it was a most strange fruit, and incomparably delicious to the taste, but not to the smell. Its rind was said to exude a stench of so atrocious a nature that when a dorian was in the room even the presence of a polecat was a refreshment. We found many who had eaten the dorian, and they all spoke of it with a sort of rapture. They said that if you could hold your nose until the fruit was in your mouth a sacred joy would suffuse you from head to foot that would make you oblivious to the smell of the rind, but that if your grip slipped and you caught the smell of the rind before the fruit was in your mouth, you would faint. There is a fortune in that rind. Some day somebody will import it into Europe and sell it for cheese.

Benares was not a disappointment. It justified its reputation as a curiosity. It is on high ground, and overhangs a grand curve of the Ganges. It is a vast mass of building, compactly crusting a hill, and is cloven in all directions by an intricate confusion of cracks which stand for streets. Tall, slim minarets and beflagged temple-spires rise out of it and give it picturesqueness, viewed from the river. The city is as busy as an anthill, and the hurly-burly of human life swarming along the web of narrow streets reminds one of the ants. The sacred cow swarms along, too, and goes whither she pleases, and takes toll of the grain-shops, and is very much in the way, and is a good deal of a nuisance, since she must not be molested.

Benares is older than history, older than tradition, older even than legend, and looks twice as old as all of them put together. From a Hindu statement quoted in Rev. Mr. Parker's compact and lucid *Guide to Benares*, I find that the site of the town was the beginning-place of the Creation. It was merely an upright "lingam," at first, no larger than a stovepipe, and stood in the midst of a shoreless ocean. This was the work of the God Vishnu. Later he spread the lingam out till its surface was ten miles across. Still it was not large enough for the business; therefore he presently built the globe around it. Benares is thus the center of the earth. This is considered an advantage.

It has had a tumultuous history, both materially and spiritually. It started Brahmanically, many ages ago; then by and by Buddha came in recent times twenty-five hundred years ago, and after that it was Buddhist during many centuries—twelve, perhaps—but the Brahmans got the upper hand again, then, and have held it ever since. It is unspeakably sacred in Hindu eyes, and is as unsanitary as it is sacred, and smells like the rind of the dorian. It is the headquarters of the Brahman faith, and one-eighth of the population are priests of that church. But it is not an overstock, for they have all India as a prey. All India flocks thither on pilgrimage, and pours its savings into the pockets of the priests in a generous stream, which never fails. A priest with a good stand on the shore of the Ganges is much better off than the sweeper of the best crossing in London. A good stand is worth a world of money. The holy proprietor of it sits under his grand spectacular umbrella and blesses people all his life, and collects his commission, and grows fat and rich; and the stand passes from father to son, down and down and down through the ages, and remains a permanent and lucrative estate in the family. As Mr. Parker suggests, it can become a subject of dispute, at one time or another, and then the matter will be settled, not by prayer and fasting and consultations with Vishnu, but by the intervention of a much more puissant power—an English court. In Bombay I was told by an American missionary that in India there are 640 Protestant missionaries at work. At first it seemed an immense force, but of course that was a thoughtless idea. One missionary to 500,000 natives—no, that is not a force; it is the reverse of it; 640 marching against an intrenched camp of 300,000,000—the odds are too great. A force of 640 in Benares alone would have its hands overfull with 8,000 Brahman priests for adversary. Missionaries need to be well equipped with hope and confidence, and this equipment they seem to have always had in all parts of the world. Mr. Parker has it. It enables him to get a favorable outlook out of statistics which might add up differently with other mathematicians. For instance:

"During the past few years competent observers declare that the number of pilgrims to Benares has increased."

And then he adds up this fact and gets this conclusion:

"But the revival, if so it may be called, has in it the marks of death. It is a spasmodic struggle before dissolution."

In this world we have seen the Roman Catholic power dying, upon these same terms, for many centuries. Many a time we have gotten all ready for the funeral and found it postponed again, on account of the weather or something. Taught by experience, we ought not to put on our things for this Brahmanical one till we see the procession move. Apparently one of the most uncertain things in the world is the funeral of a religion.

I should have been glad to acquire some sort of idea of Hindu theology, but the difficulties were too great, the matter was too intricate. Even the mere A B C of it is baffling. There is a trinity—Brahma, Shiva, and Vishnu—independent powers, apparently, though one cannot feel quite sure of that, because in one of the temples there is an image where an attempt has been made to concentrate the three in one person. The three have other names and plenty of them, and this makes confusion in one's mind. The three have wives and the wives have several names, and this increases the confusion. There are children, the children have many names, and thus the confusion goes on and on. It is not worth while to try to get any grip upon the cloud of minor gods, there are too many of them.

It is even a justifiable economy to leave Brahma, the chiefest god of all, out of your studies, for he seems to cut no great figure in India. The vast bulk of the national worship is lavished upon Shiva and Vishnu and their families. Shiva's symbol—the "lingam" with which Vishnu began the Creation—is worshiped by everybody, apparently. It is the commonest object in Benares. It is on view everywhere, it is garlanded with flowers, offerings are made to it, it suffers no neglect. Commonly it is an upright stone, shaped like a thimble—sometimes like an elongated thimble. This priapus-worship, then, is older than history. Mr. Parker says that the lingams in Benares "*outnumber the inhabitants.*"

In Benares there are many Mohammedan mosques. There are Hindu temples without number—these quaintly shaped and elaborately sculptured little stone jugs crowd all the lanes. The Ganges itself and every individual drop of water in it are temples. Religion, then, is the *business* of Benares, just as gold-production is the business of Johannesburg. Other industries count for nothing as compared with the vast and all-absorbing rush and drive and boom of the town's specialty. Benares is the sacredest of sacred cities. The moment you step across the sharply defined line which separates it from the rest of the globe, you stand upon ineffably and unspeakably holy ground. Mr. Parker says: "It is impossible to convey any adequate idea of the intense feelings of veneration and affection with which the pious Hindu regards 'Holy Kashi' (Benares)." And then he gives you this vivid and moving picture:

> Let a Hindu regiment be marched through the district, and as soon as they cross the line and enter the limits of the holy place they rend the air with cries of "Kashi ji ki jai—jai!"

(Holy Kashi! Hail to thee! Hail! Hail! Hail!) The weary pilgrim, scarcely able to stand with age and weakness, blinded by the dust and heat, and almost dead with fatigue, crawls out of the ovenlike railway-carriage, and as soon as his feet touch the ground he lifts up his withered hands and utters the same pious exclamation. Let a European in some distant city in casual talk in the bazar mention the fact that he has lived at Benares, and at once voices will be raised to call down blessings on his head, for a dweller in Benares is of all men most blessed.

It makes our own religious enthusiasm seem pale and cold. Inasmuch as the life of religion is in the heart, not the head, Mr. Parker's touching picture seems to promise a sort of indefinite postponement of that funeral.

Chapter XV

Let me make the superstitions of a nation and I care not who makes its laws or its songs either.
—Pudd'nhead Wilson's New Calendar.

YES, the city of Benares is in effect just a big church, a religious hive, whose every cell is a temple, a shrine, or a mosque, and whose every conceivable earthly and heavenly good is procurable under one roof, so to speak—a sort of Army and Navy Stores, theologically stocked.

I will make out a little itinerary for the pilgrim; then you will see how handy the system is, how convenient, how comprehensive. If you go to Benares with a serious desire to spiritually benefit yourself, you will find it valuable. I got some of the facts from conversations with the Rev. Mr. Parker and the others from his *Guide to Benares*; they are therefore trustworthy.

1. *Purification.* At sunrise you must go down to the Ganges and bathe, pray, and drink some of the water. This is for your general purification.

2. *Protection against Hunger.* Next, you must fortify yourself against the sorrowful earthly ill just named. This you will

do by worshiping for a moment in the Cow Temple. By the door of it you will find an image of Ganesh, son of Shiva; it has the head of an elephant on a human body; its face and hands are of silver. You will worship it a little, and pass on, into a covered veranda, where you will find devotees reciting from the sacred books, with the help of instructors. In this place are groups of rude and dismal idols. You may contribute something for their support; then pass into the temple, a grim and stenchy place, for it is populous with sacred cows and with beggars. You will give something to the beggars, and "reverently kiss the tails" of such cows as pass along, for these cows are peculiarly holy, and this act of worship will secure you from hunger for the day.

3. *"The Poor Man's Friend."* You will next worship this god. He is at the bottom of a stone cistern in the temple of Dalbhyeswar, under the shade of a noble peepul tree on the bluff overlooking the Ganges, so you must go back to the river. The Poor Man's Friend is the god of *material prosperity* in general, and the god of the *rain* in particular. You will secure material prosperity, or both, by worshiping him. He is Shiva, under a new alias, and he abides in the bottom of that cistern in the form of a stone lingam. You pour Ganges water over him and in return for this homage you get the promised benefits. If there is any delay about the rain you must pour water in until the cistern is full; the rain will then be sure to come.

4. *Fever.* At the Kedar Ghat you will find a long flight of stone steps leading down to the river. Half-way down is a tank filled with sewage. Drink as much of it as you want. It is for fever.

5. *Smallpox.* Go straight from there to the central Ghat. At its up-stream end you will find a small whitewashed building, which is a temple sacred to Sitala, goddess of smallpox. Her understudy is there—a rude human figure behind a brass

screen. You will worship this for reasons to be furnished presently.

6. *The Well of Fate.* For certain reasons you will next go and do homage at this well. You will find it in the Dandpan Temple, in the city. The sunlight falls into it from a square hole in the masonry above. You will approach it with awe, for your life is now at stake. You will bend over and look. If the fates are propitious, you will see your face pictured in the water far down in the well. If matters have been otherwise ordered, a sudden cloud will mask the sun and you will see nothing. This means that you have not six months to live. If you are already at the point of death, your circumstances are now serious. There is no time to lose. Let this world go, arrange for the next one. Handily situated, at your very elbow, is opportunity for this. You turn and worship the image of Maha Kal, the Great Fate, and happiness in the life to come is secured. If there is breath in your body yet, you should now make an effort to get a further lease of the present life. You have a chance. There is a chance for everything in this admirably stocked and wonderfully systemized Spiritual and Temporal Army and Navy Store. You must get yourself carried to the

7. *Well of Long Life.* This is within the precincts of the moldering and venerable Briddhkal Temple, which is one of the oldest in Benares. You pass in by a stone image of the monkey god, Hanuman, and there, among the ruined courtyards, you will find a shallow pool of stagnant sewage. It smells like the best limburger cheese, and is filthy with the washings of rotting lepers, but that is nothing, bathe in it; bathe in it gratefully and worshipfully, for this is the Fountain of Youth; these are the Waters of Long Life. Your gray hairs will disappear, and with them your wrinkles and your rheumatism, the burdens of care and the weariness of age, and you will come out young, fresh, elastic, and full of eager-

ness for the new race of life. Now will come flooding upon you the manifold desires that haunt the dear dreams of the morning of life. You will go whither you will find

8. *Fulfilment of Desire.* To wit, to the Kameshwar Temple, sacred to Shiva as the Lord of Desires. Arrange for yours there. And if you like to look at idols among the pack and jam of temples, there you will find enough to stock a museum. You will begin to commit sins now with a fresh, new vivacity; therefore, it will be well to go frequently to a place where you can get

9. *Temporary Cleansing from Sin.* To wit, to the Well of the Earring. You must approach this with the profoundest reverence, for it is unutterably sacred. It is, indeed, the most sacred place in Benares, the very Holy of Holies, in the estimation of the people. It is a railed tank, with stone stairways leading down to the water. The water is not clean. Of course it could not be, for people are always bathing in it. As long as you choose to stand and look, you will see the files of sinners descending and ascending—descending soiled with sin, ascending purged from it. "The liar, the thief, the murderer, and the adulterer may here wash and be clean," says the Rev. Mr. Parker, in his book. Very well. I know Mr. Parker, and I believe it; but if anybody else had said it, I should consider him a person who had better go down in the tank and take another wash. The god Vishnu dug this tank. He had nothing to dig with but his "discus." I do not know what a discus is, but I know it is a poor thing to dig tanks with, because, by the time this one was finished, it was full of sweat—Vishnu's sweat. He constructed the site that Benares stands on, and afterward built the globe around it, and thought nothing of it, yet sweated like that over a little thing like this tank. One of these statements is doubtful. I do not know which one it is, but I think it difficult not to believe that a god who could build a world around Benares would

not be intelligent enough to build it around the tank too, and not have to dig it. Youth, long life, temporary purification from sin, salvation through propitiation of the Great Fate— these are all good. But you must do something more. You must

10. *Make Salvation Sure.* There are several ways. To get drowned in the Ganges is one, but that is not pleasant. To die within the limits of Benares is another; but that is a risky one, because you might be out of town when your time came. The best one of all is the Pilgrimage Around the City. You must walk; also, you must go barefoot. The tramp is forty-four miles, for the road winds out into the country a piece, and you will be marching five or six days. But you will have plenty of company. You will move with throngs and hosts of happy pilgrims whose radiant costumes will make the spectacle beautiful and whose glad songs and holy pæans of triumph will banish your fatigues and cheer your spirit; and at intervals there will be temples where you may sleep and be refreshed with food. The pilgrimage completed, you have purchased salvation, and paid for it. But you may not get it unless you

11. *Get Your Redemption Recorded.* You can get this done at the Sakhi Binayak Temple, and it is best to do it, for otherwise you might not be able to prove that you had made the pilgrimage in case the matter should some day come to be disputed. That temple is in a lane back of the Cow Temple. Over the door is a red image of Ganesh of the elephant head, son and heir of Shiva, and Prince of Wales to the Theological Monarchy, so to speak. Within is a god whose office it is to record your pilgrimage and be responsible for you. You will not see him, but you will see a Brahman who will attend to the matter and take the money. If he should forget to collect the money, you can remind him. *He* knows that your salvation is now secure, but of course you would like to know it

yourself. You have nothing to do but go and pray, and pay at the

12. *Well of the Knowledge of Salvation.* It is close to the Golden Temple. There you will see, sculptured out of a single piece of black marble, a bull which is much larger than any living bull you have ever seen, and yet is not a good likeness after all. And there also you will see a very uncommon thing—an image of Shiva. You have seen his lingam fifty thousand times already, but this is Shiva himself, and said to be a good likeness. It has three eyes. He is the only god in the firm that has three. "The well is covered by a fine canopy of stone supported by forty pillars," and around it you will find what you have already seen at almost every shrine you have visited in Benares, a mob of devout and eager pilgrims. The sacred water is being ladled out to them; with it comes to them the knowledge, clear, thrilling, absolute, that they are saved; and you can see by their faces that there is one happiness in this world which is supreme, and to which no other joy is comparable. You receive your water, you make your deposit, and now what more would you have? Gold, diamonds, power, fame? All in a single moment these things have withered to dirt, dust, ashes. The world has nothing to give you now. For you it is bankrupt.

I do not claim that the pilgrims do their acts of worship in the order and sequence above charted out in this Itinerary of mine, but I think logic suggests that they ought to do so. Instead of a helter-skelter worship, we then have a definite starting-place, and a march which carries the pilgrim steadily forward by reasoned and logical progression to a definite goal. Thus, his Ganges bath in the early morning gives him an appetite; he kisses the cow-tails, and that removes it. It is now business hours, and longings for material prosperity rise in his mind, and he goes and pours water over Shiva's symbol;

this insures the prosperity, but also brings on a rain, which gives him a fever. Then he drinks the sewage at the Kedar Ghat to cure the fever; it cures the fever but gives him the smallpox. He wishes to know how it is going to turn out; he goes to the Dandpan Temple and looks down the well. A clouded sun shows him that death is near. Logically, his best course for the present, since he cannot tell at what moment he may die, is to secure a happy hereafter; this he does, through the agency of the Great Fate. He is safe, now, for heaven; his next move will naturally be to keep out of it as long as he can. Therefore he goes to the Briddhkal Temple and secures Youth and long life by bathing in a puddle of leper-pus which would kill a microbe. Logically, Youth has re-equipped him for sin and with a disposition to commit it; he will naturally go to the fane which is consecrated to the Fulfilment of Desires, and make arrangements. Logically, he will now go to the Well of the Earring from time to time to unload and freshen up for further banned enjoyments. But first and last and all the time he is human, and therefore in his reflective intervals he will always be speculating in "futures." He will make the Great Pilgrimage around the city and so make his salvation absolutely sure; he will also have record made of it, so that it may remain absolutely sure and not be forgotten or repudiated in the confusion of the Final Settlement. Logically, also, he will wish to have satisfying and tranquilizing *personal* knowledge that that salvation is secure; therefore he goes to the Well of the Knowledge of Salvation, adds that completing detail, and then goes about his affairs serene and content; serene and content, for he is now royally endowed with an advantage which no religion in this world could give him but his own; for henceforth he may commit as many million sins as he wants to and nothing can come of it.

Thus the system, properly and logically ordered, is neat, compact, clearly defined, and covers the whole ground. I desire to recommend it to such as find the other systems too difficult, exacting, and irksome for the uses of this fretful brief life of ours.

However, let me not deceive any one. My Itinerary lacks a detail. I must put it in. The truth is, that after the pilgrim has faithfully followed the requirements of the Itinerary through to the end and has secured his salvation and also the personal knowledge of that fact, there is still an accident possible to him which can annul the whole thing. If he should ever cross to the other side of the Ganges and get caught out and die there he would at once come to life again in the form of an ass. Think of that, after all this trouble and expense. You see how capricious and uncertain salvation is there. The Hindu has a childish and unreasoning aversion to being turned into an ass. It is hard to tell why. One could properly expect an ass to have an aversion to being turned into a Hindu. One could understand that he could lose dignity by it; also self-respect, and nine-tenths of his intelligence. But the Hindu changed into an ass wouldn't lose anything, unless you count his religion. And he would gain much—release from his slavery to two million gods and twenty million priests, fakirs, holy mendicants, and other sacred bacilli; he would escape the Hindu hell; he would also escape the Hindu heaven. These are advantages which the Hindu ought to consider; then he would go over and die on the other side.

Benares is a religious Vesuvius. In its bowels the theological forces have been heaving and tossing, rumbling, thundering, and quaking, boiling, and weltering and flaming and smoking for ages. But a little group of missionaries have taken post at its base, and they have hopes. There are the Baptist Missionary Society, the Church Missionary Society, the London Missionary Society, the Wesleyan Missionary

Society, and the Zenana Bible and Medical Mission. They have schools, and the principal work seems to be among the children. And no doubt that part of the work prospers best, for grown people everywhere are always likely to cling to the religion they were brought up in.

Chapter XVI

IN one of those Benares temples we saw a devotee working for salvation in a curious way. He had a huge wad of clay beside him and was making it up into little wee gods no bigger than carpet-tacks. He stuck a grain of rice into each—to represent the lingam, I think. He turned them out nimbly, for he had had long practice and had acquired great facility. Every day he made two thousand gods, then threw them into the holy Ganges. This act of homage brought him the profound homage of the pious—also their coppers. He had a sure living here, and was earning a high place in the hereafter.

The Ganges front is the supreme show-place of Benares. Its tall bluffs are solidly caked from water to summit, along a stretch of three miles, with a splendid jumble of massive and picturesque masonry, a bewildering and beautiful confusion of stone platforms, temples, stair-flights, rich and stately palaces—nowhere a break, nowhere a glimpse of the bluff itself; the long face of it is compactly walled from sight by this crammed perspective of platforms, soaring stairways, sculptured temples, majestic palaces, softening away into the distances; and there is movement, motion, human life everywhere, and brilliantly costumed—streaming in rainbows up and down the lofty stairways, and massed in metaphorical flower-gardens on the miles of great platforms at the river's edge.

All this masonry, all this architecture represents piety. The palaces were built by native princes whose homes, as a rule, are far from Benares, but who go there from time to time to refresh their souls with the sight and touch of the Ganges, the river of their idolatry. The stairways are records of acts of piety; the crowd of costly little temples are tokens of money spent by rich men for present credit and hope of future reward. Apparently, the rich Christian who spends large sums upon his religion is conspicuous with us, by his rarity, but the rich Hindu who doesn't spend large sums upon his religion is seemingly non-existent. With us the poor spend money on their religion, but they keep back some to live on. Apparently, in India, the poor bankrupt themselves daily for their religion. The rich Hindu can afford his pious outlays; he gets much glory for his spendings, yet keeps back a sufficiency of his income for temporal purposes; but the poor Hindu is entitled to compassion, for his spendings keep him poor, yet get him no glory.

We made the usual trip up and down the river, seated in chairs under an awning on the deck of the usual commodious hand-propelled ark; made it two or three times, and could have made it with increasing interest and enjoyment many times more; for, of course, the palaces and temples would grow more and more beautiful every time one saw them, for that happens with all such things; also, I think one would not get tired of the bathers, nor their costumes, nor of their ingenuities in getting out of them and into them again with-

out exposing too much bronze, nor of their devotional gestic-
ulations and absorbed bead-tellings.

But I should get tired of seeing them wash their mouths
with that dreadful water and drink it. In fact, I did get tired
of it, and very early, too. At one place where we halted for
a while, the foul gush from a sewer was making the water
turbid and murky all around, and there was a random corpse
slopping around in it that had floated down from up country.
Ten steps below that place stood a crowd of men, women,
and comely young maidens waist-deep in the water—and
they were scooping it up in their hands and drinking it. Faith
can certainly do wonders, and this is an instance of it. Those
people were not drinking that fearful stuff to assuage thirst,
but in order to purify their souls and the interior of their
bodies. According to their creed, the Ganges water makes
everything pure that it touches—instantly and utterly pure.
The sewer-water was not an offense to them, the corpse did
not revolt them; the sacred water had touched both, and both
were now snow-pure, and could defile no one. The memory
of that sight will always stay by me; but not by request.

A word further concerning the nasty but all-purifying
Ganges water. When we went to Agra, by and by, we happened there just in time to be in at the birth of a marvel—a
memorable scientific discovery—the discovery that in certain
ways the foul and derided Ganges water *is* the most puissant
purifier in the world! This curious fact as I have said, had just
been added to the treasury of modern science. It had long
been noted as a strange thing that while Benares is often
afflicted with the cholera she does not spread it beyond her
borders. This could not be accounted for. Mr. Henkin, the
scientist in the employ of the government of Agra, concluded
to examine the water. He went to Benares and made his tests.
He got water at the mouths of the sewers where they empty
into the river at the bathing-ghats; a cubic centimeter of it

contained millions of germs; at the end of six hours they were *all dead*. He caught a floating corpse, towed it to the shore, and from beside it he dipped up water that was swarming with cholera germs; at the end of six hours they were *all dead*. He added swarm after swarm of cholera germs to this water; within the six hours *they always died*, to the last sample. Repeatedly, he took pure well-water which was barren of animal life, and put into it a few cholera germs; they always began to propagate at once, and always within six hours they swarmed—and were *numerable by millions upon millions*.

For ages and ages the Hindus have had absolute faith that the water of the Ganges was absolutely pure, could not be defiled by any contact whatsoever, and infallibly made pure and clean whatsoever thing touched it. They still believe it, and that is why they bathe in it and drink it, caring nothing for its *seeming* filthiness and the floating corpses. The Hindus have been laughed at, these many generations, but the laughter will need to modify itself a little from now on. How did they find out the water's secret in those ancient ages? Had they germ-scientists then? We do not know. We only know that they had a civilization long before we emerged from savagery. But to return to where I was before; I was about to speak of the burning ghat.

They do not burn fakirs—those revered mendicants. They are so holy that they can get to their place without that sacrament, provided they be consigned to the consecrating river. We saw one carried to mid-stream and thrown overboard. He was sandwiched between two great slabs of stone.

We lay off the cremation-ghat half an hour and saw nine corpses burned. I should not wish to see any more of it, unless I might select the parties. The mourners follow the bier through the town and down to the ghat; then the bier-bearers deliver the body to some low-caste natives—Doms—and the mourners turn about and go back home. I heard no crying and saw no tears, there was no ceremony of parting. Apparently, these expressions of grief and affection are reserved for the privacy of the home. The dead women came draped in red, the men in white. They are laid in the water at the river's edge while the pyre is being prepared.

The first subject was a man. When the Doms unswathed him to wash him, he proved to be a sturdily built, well-nourished, and handsome old gentleman, with not a sign about him to suggest that he had ever been ill. Dry wood was brought and built up into a loose pile; the corpse was laid upon it and covered over with fuel. Then a naked holy man who was sitting on high ground a little distance away began to talk and shout with great energy, and he kept up this noise right along. It may have been the funeral sermon, and probably was. I forgot to say that one of the mourners remained behind when the others went away. This was the dead man's son, a boy of ten or twelve, brown and handsome, grave and self-possessed, and clothed in flowing white. He was there to burn his father. He was given a torch, and while he slowly walked seven times around the pyre the naked black man on the high ground poured out his sermon more clamorously than ever. The seventh circuit completed, the boy applied the torch at his father's head, then at his feet; the flames sprang briskly up with a sharp crackling noise, and the lad went away. Hindus do not want daughters, because their weddings make such a ruinous expense; but they want sons, so that at death they may have honorable exit from the world; and there is no honor equal to the honor of having one's pyre lighted by one's son. The father who dies sonless is in a grievous situation indeed, and is pitied. Life being uncertain, the Hindu marries while he is still a boy, in the hope that he will have a son ready when the day of his need shall come. But if he have no son, he will adopt one. This answers every purpose.

Meantime, the corpse is burning, also several others. It is a dismal business. The stokers did not sit down in idleness, but moved briskly about, punching up the fires with long poles, and now and then adding fuel. Sometimes they hoisted the half of a skeleton into the air, then slammed it down and beat it with the pole, breaking it up so that it would burn better. They hoisted skulls up in the same way and banged and battered them. The sight was hard to bear; it would have been harder if the mourners had stayed to witness it. I had but a moderate desire to see a cremation, so it was soon satisfied. For sanitary reasons it would be well if cremation were universal; but this form is revolting, and not to be recommended.

The fire used is sacred, of course—for there is money in it. Ordinary fire is forbidden; there is no money in it. It was told that this sacred fire is all furnished by one person, and that he has a monopoly of it and charges a good price for it. Sometimes a rich mourner pays a thousand rupees for it. To get to paradise from India is an expensive thing. Every detail connected with the matter costs something, and helps to fatten a priest. I suppose it is quite safe to conclude that that fire-bug is in holy orders.

Close to the cremation-ground stand a few time-worn stones which are remembrances of the Suttee. Each has a rough carving upon it, representing a man and a woman standing or walking hand in hand, and marks the spot where a widow went to her death by fire in the days when the suttee flourished. Mr. Parker said that widows would burn themselves now if the government would allow it. The family that can point to one of these little memorials and say, "She who burned herself there was an ancestress of ours," is envied.

It is a curious people. With them, all life seems to be sacred, except human life. Even the life of vermin is sacred, and must not be taken. The good Jain wipes off a seat before using it, lest he cause the death of some valueless insect by sitting down on it. It grieves him to have to drink water, because the provisions in his stomach may not agree with the microbes. Yet India invented Thuggery and the Suttee. India is a hard country to understand.

We went to the temple of the Thug goddess, Bhowanee, or Kali, or Durga. She has these names and others. She is the only god to whom living sacrifices are made. Goats are sacrificed to her. Monkeys would be cheaper. There are plenty of them about the place. Being scared, they make themselves very free, and scramble around wherever they please. The temple and its porch are beautifully carved, but this is not the case with the idol. Bhowanee is not pleasant to look at. She has a silver face, and tongue painted a deep red. She wears a necklace of skulls.

In fact, none of the idols in Benares are handsome or attractive. And what a swarm of them there is! The town is a vast museum of idols—and all of them crude, misshapen, and ugly. They flock through one's dreams at night, a wild mob of nightmares. When you get tired of them in the temples and take a trip on the river, you find idol giants, flashily painted, stretched out side by side on the shore. And apparently wherever there is room for one more lingam, a lingam is there. If Vishnu had foreseen what his town was going to be, he would have called it Idolville or Lingamburg.

The most conspicuous feature of Benares is the pair of slender white minarets which tower like masts from the great Mosque of Aurangzeb. They seem to be always in sight, from everywhere, those airy, graceful, inspiring things. But masts is not the right word, for masts have a perceptible taper, while these minarets have not. They are 142 feet high, and only 8½ feet in diameter at the base, and 7½ at the summit—scarcely any taper at all. These are the proportions of a candle;

and fair and fairylike candles these are. Will be, anyway, some day, when the Christians inherit them and top them with the electric light. These is a great view from up there—a wonderful view. A large gray monkey was part of it, and damaged it. A monkey has no judgment. This one was skipping about the upper great heights of the mosque—skipping across empty yawning intervals which were almost too wide for him, and which he only just barely cleared, each time, by the skin of his teeth. He got me so nervous that I couldn't look at the view. I couldn't look at anything but him. Every time he went sailing over one of those abysses my breath stood still, and when he grabbed for the perch he was going for, I grabbed too, in sympathy. And he was perfectly indifferent, perfectly unconcerned, and I did all the panting myself. He came within an ace of losing his life a dozen times, and I was so troubled about him that I would have shot him if I had had anything to do it with. But I strongly recommend the view. There is more monkey than view, and there is always going to be more monkey while that idiot survives, but what view you get is superb. All Benares, the river, and the region round about are spread before you. Take a gun, and look at the view.

The next thing I saw was more reposeful. It was a new kind of art. It was a picture painted on water. It was done by a native. He sprinkled fine dust of various colors on the still surface of a basin of water, and out of these sprinklings a dainty and pretty picture gradually grew, a picture which a breath could destroy. Somehow it was impressive, after so much browsing among massive and battered and decaying fanes that rest upon ruins, and those ruins upon still other ruins, and those upon still others again. It was a sermon, an allegory, a symbol of Instability. Those creations in stone were only a kind of water pictures, after all.

A prominent episode in the Indian career of Warren

Hastings had Benares for its theater. Wherever that extraordinary man set his foot, he left his mark. He came to Benares in 1781 to collect a fine of five hundred thousand pounds which he had levied upon its Raja, Cheit Singh, on behalf of the East India Company. Hastings was a long way from home and help. There were, probably, not a dozen Englishmen within reach; the Raja was in his fort with his myriads around him. But no matter. From his little camp in a neighboring garden, Hastings sent a party to arrest the sovereign. He sent on this daring mission a couple of hundred native soldiers—sepoys—under command of three young English lieutenants. The Raja submitted without a word. The incident lights up the Indian situation electrically, and gives one a vivid sense of the strides which the English had made and the mastership they had acquired in the land since the date of Clive's great victory. In a quarter of a century, from being nobodies, and feared by none, they were become confessed lords and masters, feared by all, sovereigns included, and served by all, sovereigns included. It makes the fairy tales sound true. The English had not been afraid to enlist native soldiers to fight against their own people and keep them obedient. And now Hastings was not afraid to come away out to this remote place with a handful of such soldiers and send them to arrest a native sovereign.

The lieutenants imprisoned the Raja in his own fort. It was beautiful, the pluckiness of it, the impudence of it. The arrest enraged the Raja's people, and all Benares came storming about the place and threatening vengeance. And yet, but for an accident, nothing important would have resulted, perhaps. The mob found out a most strange thing, an almost incredible thing—that this handful of soldiers had come on this hardy errand with empty guns and no ammunition. This has been attributed to thoughtlessness, but it could hardly have been that, for in such large emergencies as this, intelligent people *do* think. It must have been indifference, an over-confidence born of the proved submissiveness of the native character, when confronted by even one or two stern Britons in their war-paint. But, however that may be, it was a fatal discovery that the mob had made. They were full of courage now, and they broke into the fort and massacred the helpless soldiers and their officers. Hastings escaped from Benares by night and got safely away, leaving the principality in a state of wild insurrection: but he was back again within the month, and quieted it down in his prompt and virile way, and took the Raja's throne away from him and gave it to another man. He was a capable kind of person was Warren Hastings. This was the only time he was ever out of ammunition. Some of his acts have left stains upon his name which can never be washed away, but he saved to England the Indian Empire, and that was the best service that was ever done to the Indians themselves, those wretched heirs of a hundred centuries of pitiless oppression and abuse.

Chapter XVII

True irreverence is disrespect for another man's god.
                              —Pudd'nhead Wilson's New Calendar.

I T was in Benares that I saw another living god. That makes two. I believe I have seen most of the greater and lesser wonders of the world, but I do not remember that any of them interested me so overwhelmingly as did that pair of gods.

When I try to account for this effect I find no difficulty about it. I find that, as a rule, when a thing is a wonder to us it is not because of what *we* see in it, but because of what *others* have seen in it. We get almost all our wonders at second hand. We are eager to see any celebrated thing—and we never fail of our reward; just the deep privilege of gazing upon an object which has stirred the enthusiasm or evoked the reverence or affection or admiration of multitudes of our race is a thing which we value; we are profoundly glad that we have seen it, we are permanently enriched from having seen it, we would not part with the memory of that experience for a great price. And yet that very spectacle may be the *Taj*. You cannot keep your enthusiasms down, you cannot keep your emotions within bounds when that soaring bubble of marble breaks upon your view. But these are not *your* enthusiasms and emotions—they are the accumulated emotions and enthusiasms of a thousand fervid writers, who have been slowly and steadily storing them up in your heart day by day and year by year all your life; and now they burst out in a flood and overwhelm you; and you could not be a whit happier if they were your very own. By and by you sober down, and then you perceive that you have been drunk on the smell of somebody else's cork. For ever and ever the memory of my distant first glimpse of the Taj will compensate me for creeping around the globe to have that great privilege.

But the Taj—with all your inflation of delusive emotions, acquired at second hand from people to whom in the majority of cases they were also delusions acquired at second hand—a thing which you fortunately did not think of or it might have made you doubtful of what you imagined were your own—what is the Taj as a marvel, a spectacle, and an uplifting and overpowering wonder, compared with a living, breathing, speaking personage whom several millions of human beings devoutly and sincerely and unquestioningly believe to be a god, and humbly and gratefully worship as a god?

He was sixty years old when I saw him. He is called Sri 108 Swami Bhaskarananda Saraswati. That is one form of it. I think that that is what you would call him in speaking to him—because it is short. But you would use more of his name in addressing a letter to him; courtesy would require this. Even then you would not have to use all of it, but only this much:

Sri 108 Matparamahansaparivrajakacharyaswamibhaskaranandasaraswati.

You do not put "Esq." after it, for that is not necessary. The word which opens the volley is itself a title of honor— "Sri." The "108" stands for the rest of his names, I believe. Vishnu has 108 names which he does not use in business, and no doubt it is a custom of gods and a privilege sacred to their order to keep 108 extra ones in stock. Just the restricted name set down above is a handsome property, without the 108. By my count it has fifty-eight letters in it. This removes the long German words from competition; they are permanently out of the race.

Sri 108 S. B. Saraswati has attained to what among the Hindus is called the "state of perfection." It is a state which other Hindus reach by being born again and again, and over and over again into this world, through one reincarnation after another—a tiresome long job covering centuries and decades of centuries, and one that is full of risks, too, like the accident of dying on the wrong side of the Ganges some time or other and waking up in the form of an ass, with a fresh start necessary and the numerous trips to be made all over again. But in reaching perfection, Sri 108 S. B. S. has escaped all that. He is no longer a part or a feature of this world; his substance has changed, all earthiness has departed out of it; he is utterly holy, utterly pure; nothing can desecrate this holiness or stain this purity; he is no longer of the earth, its concerns are matters foreign to him, its pains and griefs and troubles cannot reach him. When he dies, Nirvana is his; he will be absorbed into the substance of the Supreme Deity and be at peace forever.

The Hindu Scriptures point out how this state is to be reached, but it is only once in a thousand years, perhaps, that a candidate accomplishes it. This one has traversed the course required, stage by stage, from the beginning to the end, and now has nothing left to do but wait for the call which shall release him from a world in which he has now no part nor lot. First, he passed through the student stage, and became learned in the holy books. Next he became citizen, householder, husband, and father. That was the required second stage. Then—like John Bunyan's Christian—he bade perpetual good-by to his family, as required, and went wandering away. He went far into the desert and served a term as hermit. Next, he became a beggar, "in accordance with the rites laid down in the Scriptures," and wandered about India eating the bread of mendicancy. A quarter of a century ago he reached the stage of purity. This needs no garment; its symbol is nudity; he discarded the waist-cloth which he had previously worn. He could resume it now if he chose, for neither that nor any other contact can defile him; but he does not choose.

There are several other stages, I believe, but I do not remember what they are. But he has been through them. Throughout the long course he was perfecting himself in holy learning, and writing commentaries upon the sacred books. He was also meditating upon Brahma, and he does that now.

White marble relief-portraits of him are sold all about India. He lives in a good house in a noble great garden in Benares, all meet and proper to his stupendous rank. Necessarily, he does not go abroad in the streets. Deities would never be able to move about handily in any country. If one whom we recognized and adored as a god should go abroad in our streets, and the day it was to happen were known, all traffic would be blocked and business would come to a standstill.

This god is comfortably housed, and yet modestly, all things considered, for if he wanted to live in a palace he would only need to speak and his worshipers would gladly build it. Sometimes he sees devotees for a moment, and comforts them and blesses them, and they kiss his feet and go away happy. Rank is nothing to him, he being a god. To him all men are alike. He sees whom he pleases and denies himself to whom he pleases. Sometimes he sees a prince and denies himself to a pauper; at other times he receives the pauper and turns the prince away. However, he does not receive many of either class. He has to husband his time for his meditations. I think he would receive Rev. Mr. Parker at any time. I think he is sorry for Mr. Parker, and I think Mr. Parker is sorry for him; and no doubt this compassion is good for both of them.

When we arrived we had to stand around in the garden a little while and wait, and the outlook was not good, for he had been turning away Maharajas that day and receiving only the riffraff, and we belonged in between, somewhere. But presently, a servant came out saying it was all right, he was coming.

And sure enough, he came, and I saw him—that object of the worship of millions. It was a strange sensation, and thrilling. I wish I could feel it stream through my veins again. And yet, to me he was not a god, he was only a Taj. The thrill was not my thrill, but had come to me second hand from those invisible millions of believers. By a handshake with their god I had ground-circuited their wire and got their monster battery's whole charge.

He was tall and slender, indeed emaciated. He had a clean-cut and conspicuously intellectual face, and a deep and kindly eye. He looked many years older than he really was, but much study and meditation and fasting and prayer, with the arid life he had led as hermit and beggar, could account for that. He is wholly nude when he receives natives, of whatever rank they may be, but he had white cloth around his loins now, a concession to Mr. Parker's European prejudices, no doubt.

As soon as I had sobered down a little we got along very well together, and I found him a most pleasant and friendly deity. He had heard a deal about Chicago, and showed a quite remarkable interest in it, for a god. It all came of the World's Fair and the Congress of Religions. If India knows about nothing else American, she knows about those, and will keep them in mind one while.

He proposed an exchange of autographs, a delicate attention which made me believe in him, but I had been having my doubts before. He wrote his in his book, and I have a reverent regard for that book, though the words run from right to left, and so I can't read it. It was a mistake to print in that way. It contains his voluminous comments on the Hindu holy writings, and if I could make them out I would try for perfection myself. I gave him a copy of *Huckleberry Finn*. I thought it might rest him up a little to mix it in along with his meditations on Brahma, for he looked tired, and I knew that if it didn't do him any good it wouldn't do him any harm.

He has a scholar meditating under him—Mina Bahadur Rana—but we did not see him. He wears clothes and is very imperfect. He has written a little pamphlet about his master, and I have that. It contains a wood-cut of the master and himself seated on a rug in the garden. The portrait of the master is very good, indeed. The posture is exactly that which Brahma himself affects, and it requires long arms and limber legs, and can be accumulated only by gods and the india-rubber man. There is a life-size marble relief of Sri 108 S. B. S. in the garden. It represents him in this same posture.

Dear me! It is a strange world. Particularly the Indian division of it. This pupil, Mina Bahadur Rana, is not a commonplace person, but a man of distinguished capacities and attainments, and, apparently, he had a fine worldly career in front of him. He was serving the Nepal Government in a high capacity at the Court of the Viceroy of India, twenty years ago. He was an able man, educated, a thinker, a man of property. But the longing to devote himself to a religious life came upon him, and he resigned his place, turned his back upon the vanities and comforts of the world, and went away into the solitudes to live in a hut and study the sacred writings and meditate upon virtue and holiness and seek to attain them. This sort of religion resembles ours. Christ recommended the rich to give away all their property and follow Him in poverty, not in worldly comfort. American and English millionaires do it every day, and thus verify and confirm to the world the tremendous forces that lie in religion. Yet many people scoff at them for this loyalty to duty, and many will scoff at Mina Bahadur Rana and call him a crank. Like many Christians of great character and intellect, he has made the study of his Scriptures and the writing of books of commentaries upon them the loving labor of his life. Like them, he has believed that this was not an idle and foolish waste of his life, but a most worthy and honorable employment of it. Yet, there are many people who will see in those others, men worthy of homage and deep reverence, but in him merely a crank. But I shall not. He has my reverence. And I don't offer it as a common thing and poor, but as an unusual thing and of value. The ordinary reverence, the reverence defined and explained by the dictionary, costs nothing. Reverence for one's own sacred things—parents, religion, flag, laws, and respect for one's own beliefs—these are feelings which we cannot even help. They come natural to us; they are involuntary, like breathing. There is no personal merit in breathing. But the reverence which is difficult, and which has personal merit in it, is the respect which you pay, without compulsion, to the political or religious attitude of a man whose beliefs are not yours. You can't revere his gods or his politics, and no one expects you to do that, but you could respect his belief in them if you tried hard enough; and you could respect *him*, too, if you tried hard enough. But it is very, very difficult; it is next to impossible, and so we hardly ever try. If the man doesn't believe as we do, we say he is a crank, and that settles it. I mean it does nowadays because now we can't burn him.

We are always canting about people's "irreverence," always charging this offense upon somebody or other, and thereby intimating that we are better than that person and do not commit that offense ourselves. Whenever we do this we are in a lying attitude, and our speech is cant; for none of us are reverent—in a meritorious way; deep down in our hearts we are all irreverent. There is probably not a single exception to this rule in the earth. There is probably not one person whose reverence rises higher than respect for his *own* sacred things; and therefore, it is not a thing to boast about and be proud of, since the most degraded savage has that—and, like the best of us, has nothing higher. To speak plainly, we despise all reverences and all objects of reverence which are outside the pale of our own list of sacred things. And yet, with strange inconsistency, we are shocked when other people despise and defile the things which are holy to us. Suppose we should meet with a paragraph like the following, in the newspapers:

"Yesterday a visiting party of the British nobility had a picnic at Mount Vernon, and in the tomb of Washington they ate their luncheon, sang popular songs, played games, and danced waltzes and polkas."

Should we be shocked? Should we feel outraged? Should we be amazed? Should we call the performance a desecration? Yes, that would all happen. We should denounce those people in round terms, and call them hard names.

And suppose we found this paragraph in the newspapers:

"Yesterday a visiting party of American pork-millionaires had a picnic in Westminster Abbey, and in that sacred place they ate their luncheon, sang popular songs, played games, and danced waltzes and polkas."

Would the English be shocked? Would they feel out-raged? Would they be amazed? Would they call the perfor-mance a desecration? That would all happen. The pork-millionaires would be denounced in round terms; they would be called hard names.

In the tomb at Mount Vernon lie the ashes of America's most honored son; in the Abbey, the ashes of England's great-est dead; the tomb of tombs, the costliest in the earth, the wonder of the world, the Taj, was built by a great Emperor to honor the memory of a perfect wife and perfect mother, one in whom there was no spot or blemish, whose love was his stay and support, whose life was the light of the world to him; in it her ashes lie, and to the Mohammedan millions of India it is a holy place; to them it is what Mount Vernon is to Americans, it is what the Abbey is to the English.

Major Sleeman wrote forty or fifty years ago (the italics are mine):

> I would here enter my humble protest against the *quadrille and lunch parties* which are sometimes given to European ladies and gentlemen of the station at this imperial tomb; drinking and dancing are no doubt very good things in their season, but they are sadly out of place *in a sepulcher*.

Were there any Americans among those lunch-parties? If they were invited, there were.

If my imagined lunch-parties in Westminster and the tomb of Washington should take place, the incident would cause a vast outbreak of bitter eloquence about Barbarism and Irreverence; and it would come from two sets of people who would go next day and dance in the Taj if they had a chance.

As we took our leave of the Benares god and started away we noticed a group of natives waiting respectfully just within the gate—a Raja from somewhere in India, and some people of lesser consequence. The god beckoned them to come, and as we passed out the Raja was kneeling and reverently kissing his sacred feet.

If Barnum—but Barnum's ambitions are at rest. This god will remain in the holy peace and seclusion of his garden, undisturbed. Barnum could not have gotten him, anyway. Still, he would have found a substitute that would answer.

Chapter XVIII

Do not undervalue the headache. While it is at its sharpest it seems a bad investment; but when relief begins, the unexpired remainder is worth four dollars a minute.
—Pudd'nhead Wilson's New Calendar.

A COMFORTABLE railway journey of seventeen and a half hours brought us to the capital of India, which is likewise the capital of Bengal—Calcutta. Like Bombay, it has a population of nearly a million natives and a small gathering of white people. It is a huge city and fine, and is called the City of Palaces. It is rich in historical memories; rich in British achievement—military, political, commercial; rich in the results of the miracles done by that brace of mighty magicians, Clive and Hastings. And has a cloud-kissing monument to one Ochterlony.

It is a fluted candlestick two hundred and fifty feet high. This lingam is the only large monument in Calcutta, I believe. It is a fine ornament, and will keep Ochterlony in mind.

Wherever you are, in Calcutta, and for miles around, you can see it; and always when you see it you think of Ochterlony. And so there is not an hour in the day that you do not think of Ochterlony and wonder who he was. It is good that Clive cannot come back, for he would think it was for Plassey; and then that great spirit would be wounded when the revelation came that it was not. Clive would find out that it was for Ochterlony; and he would think Ochterlony was a battle. And he would think it was a great one, too, and he would say, "With three thousand I whipped sixty thousand and founded the Empire—and there is no monument; this other soldier must have whipped a billion with a dozen and saved the world."

But he would be mistaken. Ochterlony was a man, not a battle. And he did good and honorable service, too; as good and honorable service as has been done in India by seventy-five or a hundred other Englishmen of courage, rectitude, and distinguished capacity. For India has been a fertile breeding-ground of such men, and remains so; great men, both in war and in the civil service, and as modest as great. But they have no monuments, and were not expecting any. Ochterlony could not have been expecting one, and it is not at all likely that he desired one—certainly not until Clive and Hastings should be supplied. Every day Clive and Hastings lean on the battlements of heaven and look down and wonder which of the two the monument is for; and they fret and worry because they cannot find out, and so the peace of heaven is spoiled for them and lost. But not for Ochterlony. Ochterlony is not troubled. He doesn't suspect that it is his monument. Heaven is sweet and peaceful to him. There is a sort of unfairness about it all.

Indeed, if monuments were always given in India for high achievements, duty straightly performed, and smirchless records, the landscape would be monotonous with them. The handful of English in India govern the Indian myriads with apparent ease, and without noticeable friction, through tact, training, and distinguished administrative ability, reinforced by just and liberal laws—and by keeping their word to the native whenever they give it.

England is far from India and knows little about the eminent services performed by her servants there, for it is the newspaper correspondent who makes fame, and he is not sent to India but to the continent, to report the doings of the princelets and the dukelets, and where they are visiting and whom they are marrying. Often a British official spends thirty or forty years in India, climbing from grade to grade by services which would make him celebrated anywhere else, and finishes as a vice-sovereign, governing a great realm and millions of subjects; then he goes home to England substantially unknown and unheard of, and settles down in some modest corner, and is as one extinguished. Ten years later there is a twenty-line obituary in the London papers, and the reader is paralyzed by the splendors of a career which he is not sure that he had ever heard of before. But meanwhile he has learned all about the continental princelets and dukelets.

The average man is profoundly ignorant of countries that lie remote from his own. When they are mentioned in his presence one or two facts and maybe a couple of names rise like torches in his mind, lighting up an inch or two of it and leaving the rest all dark. The mention of Egypt suggests some Biblical facts and the Pyramids—nothing more. The mention of South Africa suggests Kimberley and the diamonds and there an end. Formerly the mention, to a Hindu, of America suggested a name—George Washington—with that his familiarity with our country was exhausted. Latterly his familiarity with it has doubled in bulk; so that when America is mentioned now, two torches flare up in the dark caverns of his mind and he says, "Ah, the country of the great man—Washington; and of the Holy City—Chicago."

For he knows about the Congress of Religions, and this has enabled him to get an erroneous impression of Chicago.

When India is mentioned to the citizen of a far country it suggests Clive, Hastings, the Mutiny, Kipling, and a number of other great events; and the mention of Calcutta infallibly brings up the Black Hole. And so, when that citizen finds himself in the capital of India he goes first of all to see the Black Hole of Calcutta—and is disappointed.

The Black Hole was not preserved; it is gone, long, long ago. It is strange. Just as it stood, it was itself a monument; a ready-made one. It was finished, it was complete, its materials were strong and lasting, it needed no furbishing up, no repairs; it merely needed to be let alone. It was the first brick, the Foundation Stone, upon which was reared a mighty Empire—the Indian Empire of Great Britain. It was the ghastly episode of the Black Hole that maddened the British and brought Clive, that young military marvel, raging up from Madras; it was the seed from which sprung Plassey; and it was that extraordinary battle, whose like had not been seen in the earth since Agincourt, that laid deep and strong the foundations of England's colossal Indian sovereignty.

And yet within the time of men who still live, the Black Hole was torn down and thrown away as carelessly as if its bricks were common clay, not ingots of historic gold. There is no accounting for human beings.

The supposed site of the Black Hole is marked by an engraved plate. I saw that; and better that than nothing. The Black Hole was a prison—a *cell* is nearer the right word—eighteen feet square, the dimensions of an ordinary bedchamber; and into this place the victorious Nabob of Bengal packed one hundred and forty-six of his English prisoners. There was hardly standing-room for them; scarcely a breath of air was to be got; the time was night, the weather sweltering hot. Before the dawn came, the captives were all dead but twenty-three. Mr. Holwell's long account of the awful episode was familiar to the world a hundred years ago, but one seldom sees in print even an extract from it in our day. Among the striking things in it is this. Mr. Holwell, perishing with thirst, kept himself alive by sucking the perspiration from his sleeves. It gives one a vivid idea of the situation. He presently found that while he was busy drawing life from one of his sleeves a young English gentleman was stealing supplies from the other one. Holwell was an unselfish man, a man of the most generous impulses; he lived and died famous for these fine and rare qualities; yet when he found out what was happening to that unwatched sleeve, he took the precaution to suck that one dry first. The miseries of the Black Hole were able to change even a nature like his. But that young gentleman was one of the twenty-three survivors, and he said it was the stolen perspiration that saved his life. From the middle of Mr. Holwell's narrative I will make a brief extract:

> Then a general prayer to Heaven, to hasten the approach of the flames to the right hand and left of us, and put a period to our misery. But these failing, they whose strength and spirits were quite exhausted laid themselves down and expired quietly upon their fellows; others who had yet some strength and vigor left made a last effort at the windows, and several succeeded by leaping and scrambling over the backs and heads of those in the first rank, and got hold of the bars, from which there was no removing them. Many to the right and left sunk with the violent pressure, and were soon suffocated; for now a steam arose from the living and the dead, which affected us in all its circumstances as if we were forcibly held with our heads over a bowl full of strong volatile spirit of hartshorn, until suffocated; nor could the effluvia of the one be distinguished from the other, and frequently, when I was forced by

the load upon my head and shoulders to hold my face down, I was obliged, near as I was to the window, instantly to raise it again to avoid suffocation. I need not, my dear friend, ask your commiseration, when I tell you, that in this plight, from half an hour past eleven till near two in the morning, I sustained the weight of a heavy man, with his knees in my back, and the pressure of his whole body on my head, a Dutch surgeon who had taken his seat upon my left shoulder, and a Topaz (a black Christian soldier) bearing on my right; all which nothing could have enabled me to support but the props and pressure equally sustaining me all around. The two latter I frequently dislodged by shifting my hold on the bars and driving my knuckles into their ribs; but my friend above stuck fast, held immovable by two bars.

I exerted anew my strength and fortitude; but the repeated trials and efforts I made to dislodge the insufferable incumbrances upon me at last quite exhausted me; and toward two o'clock, finding I must quit the window or sink where I was, I resolved on the former, having borne, truly for the sake of others, infinitely more for life than the best of it is worth. In the rank close behind me was an officer of one of the ships, whose name was Cary, and who had behaved with much bravery during the siege (his wife, a fine woman, though country-born, would not quit him, but accompanied him into the prison, and was one who survived). This poor wretch had been long raving for water and air; I told him I was determined to give up life, and recommended his gaining my station. On my quitting it he made a fruitless attempt to get my place; but the Dutch surgeon who sat on my shoulder supplanted him. Poor Cary expressed his thankfulness, and said he would give up life too; but it was with the utmost labor we forced our way from the window (several in the inner ranks appearing to me dead standing, unable to fall by the throng and equal pressure around). He laid himself down to die; and his death, I believe, was very sudden; for he was a short, full, sanguine man. His strength was great; and, I imagine, had he not retired with me, I should never have been able to force my way. I was at this time sensible of no pain, and little uneasiness; I can give you no better idea of my situation than by repeating my simile of the bowl of spirit of hartshorn. I found a stupor coming on apace, and laid myself down by that gallant old man, the Rev. Mr. Jervas Bellamy, who lay dead with his son, the lieutenant, hand in hand, near the southernmost wall of the prison. When I had lain there some little time, I still had reflection enough to suffer some uneasiness in the thought that I should be trampled upon, when dead, as I myself had done to others. With some difficulty I raised myself, and gained the platform a second time, where I presently lost all sensation; the last trace of sensibility that I have been able to recollect after my lying down, was my sash being uneasy about my waist, which I untied and threw from me. Of what passed in this interval, to the time of my resurrection from this hole of horrors, I can give you no account.

There was plenty to see in Calcutta, but there was not plenty of time for it. I saw the fort that Clive built; and the place where Warren Hastings and the author of the Junius Letters fought their duel; and the great botanical gardens; and the fashionable afternoon turnout in the Maidan; and a grand review of the garrison in a great plain at sunrise; and a military tournament in which great bodies of native soldiery exhibited the perfection of their drill at all arms, a spectacular and beautiful show occupying several nights and closing with the mimic storming of a native fort which was as good as the reality for thrilling and accurate detail, and better than the reality for security and comfort; we had a pleasure excursion on the *Hoogly* by courtesy of friends, and devoted the rest of the time to social life and the Indian museum. One should spend a month in the museum, an enchanted palace of Indian antiquities. Indeed, a person might spend half a year among the beautiful and wonderful things without exhausting their interest.

It was winter. We were of Kipling's "hosts of tourists who travel up and down India in the cold weather showing how things ought to be managed." It is a common expression there, "the cold weather," and the people think there is such a thing. It is because they have lived there half a lifetime, and their perceptions have become blunted. When a person is accustomed to one hundred and thirty-eight in the shade, his ideas about cold weather are not valuable. I had read, in the histories, that the June marches made between Lucknow and Cawnpore by the British forces in the time of the Mutiny were made in that kind of weather—one hundred and thirty-eight in the shade—and had taken it for historical embroidery. I had read it again in Sergeant-Major Forbes-Mitchell's account of his military experiences in the Mutiny—at least I thought I had—and in Calcutta I asked him if it was true, and he said it was. An officer of high rank who had been in the thick of the Mutiny said the same. As long as those men were talking about what they knew, they were trustworthy, and I believed them; but when they said it was now "cold weather," I saw that they had traveled outside of their sphere of knowledge and were floundering. I believe that in India "cold weather" is merely a conventional phrase and has come into use through the necessity of having some way to distinguish between weather which will melt a brass door-knob and weather which will only make it mushy. It was observable that brass ones were in use while I was in Calcutta, showing that it was not yet time to change to porcelain; I was told the change to porcelain was not usually made until May. But this cold weather was too warm for us; so we started to Darjeeling, in the Himalayas—a twenty-four-hour journey.

Chapter XIX

There are eight hundred and sixty-nine different forms of lying, but only one of them has been squarely forbidden. Thou shalt not bear false witness against thy neighbor.

—Pudd'nhead Wilson's New Calender.

FROM DIARY:

February 14. We left at 4.30 P.M. Until dark we moved through rich vegetation, then changed to a boat and crossed the Ganges.

February 15. Up with the sun. A brilliant morning, and frosty. A double suit of flannels is found necessary. The plain is perfectly level, and seems to stretch away and away and away, dimming and softening, to the uttermost bounds of nowhere. What a soaring, strenuous, gushing fountain-spray of delicate greenery a bunch of bamboo is! As far as the eye can reach, these grand vegetable geysers grace the view, their spoutings refined to steam by distance. And there are fields of bananas, with the sunshine glancing from the varnished surface of their drooping vast leaves. And there are frequent groves of palm; and an effective accent is given to the landscape by isolated individuals of this picturesque family, towering, clean-stemmed, their plumes broken and hanging

ragged, Nature's imitation of an umbrella that has been out
to see what a cyclone is like and is trying not to look disappointed. And everywhere through the soft morning vistas
we glimpse the villages, the countless villages, the myriad
villages, thatched, built of clean new matting, snuggling
among grouped palms and sheaves of bamboo; villages, villages, no end of villages, not three hundred yards apart, and
dozens and dozens of them in sight all the time; a mighty
City, hundreds of miles long, hundreds of miles broad,
made of all villages, the biggest city in the earth, and as
populous as a European kingdom. I have seen no such city
as this before. And there is a continuously repeated and re-
plenished multitude of naked men in view on both sides and
ahead. We fly through it mile after mile, but still it is always
there, on both sides and ahead—brown-bodied, naked men
and boys, plowing in the fields. But *not a woman*. In these
two hours I have not seen a woman or a girl working in the
fields.

> From Greenland's icy mountains,
>   From India's coral strand,
> Where Afric's sunny fountains
>   Roll down their golden sand;
> From many an ancient river,
>   From many a palmy plain,
> They call us to deliver
>   Their land from error's chain.

Those are beautiful verses, and they have remained in
my memory all my life. But if the closing lines are true, let
us hope that when we come to answer the call and deliver
the land from its errors, we shall secrete from it some of our
high-civilization ways, and at the same time borrow some of
its pagan ways to enrich our high system with. We have a

right to do this. If we lift those people up, we have a right to lift ourselves up nine or ten grades or so, at their expense. A few years ago I spent several weeks at Tölz, in Bavaria. It is a Roman Catholic region, and not even Benares is more deeply or pervasively or intelligently devout. In my diary of those days I find this:

> We took a long drive yesterday around about the lovely country roads. But it was a drive whose pleasure was damaged in a couple of ways: by the dreadful shrines and by the shameful spectacle of gray and venerable old grandmothers toiling in the fields. The shrines were frequent along the roads— figures of the Saviour nailed to the cross and streaming with blood from the wounds of the nails and thorns.
>
> When missionaries go from here do they find fault with the pagan idols? I saw many women, seventy and even eighty years old, mowing and binding in the fields, and pitchforking the loads into the wagons.

I was in Austria later, and in Munich. In Munich I saw gray old women pushing trucks uphill and down, long distances, trucks laden with barrels of beer, incredible loads. In my Austrian diary I find this:

> In the fields I often see a woman and a cow harnessed to the plow, and a man driving.
>
> In the public street of Marienbad to-day, I saw an old, bent, gray-headed woman *in harness with a dog*, drawing a laden sled over bare dirt roads and bare pavements; and at his ease walked the driver, smoking his pipe, a hale fellow not thirty years old.

Five or six years ago I bought an open boat, made a kind of a canvas wagon-roof over the stern of it to shelter me from sun and rain; hired a courier and a boatman, and made a twelve-day floating voyage down the Rhone from Lake Bourget to Marseilles. In my diary of that trip I find this entry. I was far down the Rhone then:

Passing St. Étienne, 2.15 P.M. On a distant ridge inland, a tall open-work structure commandingly situated, with a statue of the Virgin standing on it. A devout country. All down this river, wherever there is a crag there is a statue of the Virgin on it. I believe I have seen a hundred of them. And yet, in many respects, the peasantry seem to be mere pagans, and destitute of any considerable degree of civilization.

. . . We reached a not very promising-looking village about four o'clock, and I concluded to tie up for the day; munching fruit and fogging the hood with pipe-smoke had grown monotonous; I could not have the hood furled, because the floods of rain fell unceasingly. The tavern was on the river-bank, as is the custom. It was dull there, and melancholy— nothing to do but look out of the window into the drenching rain and shiver; one could do that, for it was bleak and cold and windy, and country France furnishes no fire. Winter overcoats did not help me much; they had to be supplemented with rugs. The raindrops were so large and struck the river with such force that they knocked up the water like pebble-splashes.

With the exception of a very occasional wooden-shod peasant, nobody was abroad in this bitter weather—I mean nobody of our sex. But all weathers are alike to the women in these continental countries. To them and the other animals, life is serious; nothing interrupts their slavery. Three of them were washing clothes in the river under the window when I arrived, and they continued at it as long as there was light to work by. One was apparently thirty; another—the mother!— above fifty; the third—grandmother!—so old and worn and gray she could have passed for eighty; I took her to be that old. They had no waterproofs nor rubbers, of course; over their shoulders they wore gunnysacks—simply conductors for rivers of water; some of the volume reached the ground; the rest soaked in on the way.

At last, a vigorous fellow of thirty-five arrived, dry and comfortable, smoking his pipe under his big umbrella in an open donkey-cart—husband, son, and grandson of those women! He stood up in the cart, sheltering himself, and began to superintend, issuing his orders in a masterly tone of command, and showing temper when they were not obeyed swiftly enough. Without complaint or murmur the drowned women patiently carried out the orders, lifting the immense baskets of soggy, wrung-out clothing into the cart and stowing them to the man's satisfaction. There were six of the great baskets, and a man of mere ordinary strength could not have lifted any one of them. The cart being full now, the Frenchman descended, still sheltered by his umbrella, entered the tavern, and the women went drooping homeward, trudging in the wake of the cart, and soon were blended with the deluge and lost to sight.

When I went down into the public room, the Frenchman had his bottle of wine and plate of food on a bare table black with grease, and was "chomping" like a horse. He had the little religious paper which is in everybody's hands on the Rhone borders, and was enlightening himself with the histories of French saints who used to flee to the desert in the Middle Ages to escape the contamination of woman. For two hundred years France has been sending missionaries to other savage lands. To spare to the needy from poverty like hers is fine and true generosity.

But to get back to India—where, as my favorite poem says:

> Every prospect pleases,
> And only man is vile.

It is because Bavaria and Austria and France have not introduced their civilization to him yet. But Bavaria and Austria and France are on their way. They are coming. They will rescue him; they will refine the vileness out of him.

Some time during the forenoon, approaching the mountains, we changed from the regular train to one composed of little canvas-sheltered cars that skimmed along within a foot of the ground and seemed to be going fifty miles an hour when they were really making about twenty. Each car had seating capacity for half a dozen persons; and when the curtains were up one was substantially out-of-doors, and could see everywhere, and get all the breeze, and be luxuriously comfortable. It was not a pleasure excursion in name only, but in fact.

After a while we stopped at a little wooden coop of a station just within the curtain of the somber jungle, a place with a deep and dense forest of great trees and scrub and vines all about it. The royal Bengal tiger is in great force there, and is very bold and unconventional. From this lonely little station a message once went to the railway manager in Calcutta: "Tiger eating station-master on front porch; telegraph instructions."

It was there that I had my first tiger-hunt. I killed thirteen. We were presently away again, and the train began to climb the mountains. In one place seven wild elephants crossed the track, but two of them got away before I could overtake them. The railway journey up the mountain is forty miles, and it takes eight hours to make it. It is so wild and interesting and exciting and enchanting that it ought to take a week. As for the vegetation, it is a museum. The jungle seemed to contain samples of every rare and curious tree and bush that we had ever seen or heard of. It is from that museum, I think, that the globe must have been supplied with the trees and vines and shrubs that it holds precious.

The road is infinitely and charmingly crooked. It goes winding in and out under lofty cliffs that are smothered in vines and foliage, and around the edges of bottomless chasms; and all the way one glides by files of picturesque natives, some carrying burdens up, others going down from their work in the tea-gardens; and once there was a gaudy wedding procession, all bright tinsel and color, and a bride, comely and girlish, who peeped out from the curtains of her palanquin, exposing her face with that pure delight which the young and happy take in sin for sin's own sake.

By and by we were well up in the region of the clouds, and from that breezy height we looked down and afar over a wonderful picture—the Plains of India, stretching to the horizon, soft and fair, level as a floor, shimmering with heat, mottled with cloud-shadows, and cloven with shining rivers. Immediately below us, and receding down, down, down, toward the valley, was a shaven confusion of hilltops, with ribbony roads and paths squirming and snaking cream-yellow all over them and about them, every curve and twist sharply distinct.

At an elevation of 6,000 feet we entered a thick cloud, and it shut out the world and kept it shut out. We climbed 1,000 feet higher, then began to descend, and presently got down to Darjeeling, which is 6,000 feet above the level of the Plains.

We had passed many a mountain village on the way up, and seen some new kinds of natives, among them many samples of the fighting Ghurkas. They are not large men, but they are strong and resolute. There are no better soldiers among Britain's native troops. And we had passed shoals of their women climbing the forty miles of steep road from the valley to their mountain homes, with tall baskets on their backs hitched to their foreheads by a band, and containing a freightage weighing—I will not say how many hundreds of pounds, for the sum is unbelievable. These were young women, and they strode smartly along under these astonishing burdens with the air of people out for a holiday. I was told that a woman will carry a piano on her back all the way up the mountain; and that more than once a woman had done it. If these were old women I should regard the Ghurkas as no more civilized than the Europeans.

At the railway-station at Darjeeling you find plenty of cab-substitutes—open coffins, in which you sit, and are then borne on men's shoulders up the steep roads into the town.

Up there we found a fairly comfortable hotel, the property of an indiscriminate and incoherent landlord, who looks after nothing, but leaves everything to his army of Indian servants. No, he does look after the bill—to be just to him—and the tourist cannot do better than follow his example. I was told by a resident that the summit of Kinchinjunga is often hidden in the clouds, and that sometimes a tourist has waited twenty-two days, and then been obliged to go away without a sight of it. And yet went not disappointed; for when he got his hotel bill he recognized that he was now seeing the highest thing in the Himalayas. But this is probably a lie.

After lecturing I went to the Club that night, and that was a comfortable place. It is loftily situated, and looks out over a vast spread of scenery; from it you can see where the boundaries of three countries come together, some thirty miles away; Thibet is one of them, Nepaul another, and I think Herzegovina was the other. Apparently, in every town and city in India the gentlemen of the British civil and military service have a club; sometimes it is a palatial one, always it is pleasant and homelike. The hotels are not always as good as they might be, and the stranger who has access to the Club is grateful for his privilege and knows how to value it.

Next day was Sunday. Friends came in the gray dawn

with horses, and my party rode away to a distant point where Kinchinjunga and Mount Everest show up best, but I stayed at home for a private view; for it was very cold, and I was not acquainted with the horses, anyway. I got a pipe and a few blankets and sat for two hours at the window, and saw the sun drive away the veiling gray and touch up the snow-peaks one after another with pale pink splashes and delicate washes of gold, and finally flood the whole mighty convulsion of snow-mountains with a deluge of rich splendors.

Kinchinjunga's peak was but fitfully visible, but in the betweentimes it was vividly clear against the sky—away up there in the blue dome more than 28,000 feet above sea-level—the loftiest land I had ever seen, by 12,000 feet or more. It was 45 miles away. Mount Everest is a thousand feet higher, but it was not a part of that sea of mountains piled up there before me, so I did not see it; but I did not care, because I think that mountains that are as high as that are disagreeable.

I changed from the back to the front of the house and spent the rest of the morning there, watching the swarthy strange tribes flock by from their far homes in the Himalayas. All ages and both sexes were represented, and the breeds were quite new to me, though the costumes of the Thibetans made them look a good deal like Chinamen. The prayer-wheel was a frequent feature. It brought me near to these people and made them seem kinfolk of mine. Through our preacher we do much of our praying by proxy. We do not whirl him around a stick, as they do, but that is merely a detail. The swarm swung briskly by, hour after hour, a strange and striking pageant. It was wasted there, and it seemed a pity. It should have been sent streaming through the cities of Europe or America, to refresh eyes weary of the pale monotonies of the circus pageant. These people were bound for the bazar,

with things to sell. We went down there, later, and saw that
novel congress of the wild peoples, and plowed here and
there through it, and concluded that it would be worth coming from Calcutta to see, even if there were no Kinchinjunga
and Everest.

Chapter XX

There are two times in a man's life when he should not speculate: when he can't afford it, and when he can.
—Pudd'nhead Wilson's New Calendar

O N Monday and Tuesday at sunrise we again had fair-to-middling views of the stupendous mountains; then, being well cooled off and refreshed, we were ready to chance the weather of the lower world once more.

We traveled uphill by the regular train five miles to the summit, then changed to a little canvas-canopied hand-car for the thirty-five-mile descent. It was the size of a sleigh, it had six seats and was so low that it seemed to rest on the ground. It had no engine or other propelling power, and needed none to help it fly down those steep inclines. It only needed a strong brake to modify its flight, and it had that. There was a story of a disastrous trip made down the mountain once in this little car by the Lieutenant-Governor of Bengal, when the car jumped the track and threw its passengers over a precipice. It was not true, but the story had value for me, for it made me nervous, and nervousness wakes a person up and makes him alive and alert, and heightens the thrill of a new and doubtful experience. The car could really jump the track, of course; a pebble on the track, placed there by either accident or malice, at a sharp curve where one might strike it before the eye could discover it, could derail the car and fling it down into India; and the fact that the Lieutenant-Governor had escaped was no proof that I would have the same luck. And standing there, looking down upon the Indian Empire from the airy altitude of seven thousand feet, it seemed unpleasantly far, dangerously far, to be flung from a hand-car.

But after all, there was but small danger—for me. What there was, was for Mr. Pugh, inspector of a division of the Indian police, in whose company and protection we had come from Calcutta. He had seen long service as an artillery officer, was less nervous than I was, and so he was to go ahead of us in a pilot hand-car, with a Ghurka and another native; and the plan was that when we should see his car jump over a precipice we must put on our brake and send for another pilot. It was a good arrangement. Also Mr. Barnard, chief engineer of the mountain division of the road, was to take personal charge of our car, and he had been down the mountain in it many a time.

Everything looked safe. Indeed, there was but one questionable detail left: the regular train was to follow us as soon as we should start, and it might run over us. Privately, I thought it would.

The road fell sharply down in front of us and went corkscrewing in and out around the crags and precipices, down, down, forever down, suggesting nothing so exactly or so uncomfortably as a crooked toboggan-slide with no end to it. Mr. Pugh waved his flag and started, like an arrow from a bow, and before I could get out of the car we were gone too. I had previously had but one sensation like the shock of that departure, and that was the gaspy shock that took my breath away the first time that I was discharged from the summit of a toboggan-slide. But in both instances the sensation was pleasurable—intensely so; it was a sudden and immense exaltation, a mixed ecstasy of deadly fright and unimaginable joy. I believe that this combination makes the perfection of human delight.

The pilot-car's flight down the mountain suggested the swoop of a swallow that is skimming the ground, so swiftly and smoothly and gracefully it swept down the long straight reaches and soared in and out of the bends and around the corners. We raced after it, and seemed to flash by the capes and crags with the speed of light; and now and then we almost overtook it—and had hopes; but it was only playing with us; when we got near, it released its brake, made a spring around a corner, and the next time it spun into view, a few seconds later, it looked as small as a wheelbarrow, it was so far away. We played with the train in the same way. We often got out to gather flowers or sit on a precipice and look at the scenery, then presently we would hear a dull and growing roar, and the long coils of the train would come into sight behind and above us; but we did not need to start till the locomotive was close down upon us—then we soon left it far behind. It had to stop at every station, therefore it was not an embarrassment to us. Our brake was a good piece of machinery; it could bring the car to a standstill on a slope as steep as a house-roof.

The scenery was grand and varied and beautiful, and there was no hurry; we could always stop and examine it. There was abundance of time. We did not need to hamper the train; if it wanted the road, we could switch off and let it go by, then overtake it and pass it later. We stopped at one place to see the Gladstone Cliff, a great crag which the ages and the weather have sculptured into a recognizable portrait of the venerable statesman. Mr. Gladstone is a stockholder in the road, and Nature began this portrait ten thousand years ago, with the idea of having the compliment ready in time for the event.

We saw a banyan tree which sent down supporting stems from branches which were sixty feet above the ground. That is, I suppose it was a banyan; its bark resembled that of the great banyan in the botanical gardens at Calcutta, that spider-legged thing with its wilderness of vegetable columns. And there were frequent glimpses of a totally leafless tree upon whose innumerable twigs and branches a cloud of crimson butterflies had lighted—apparently. In fact these brilliant red butterflies were flowers, but the illusion was good. Afterward in South Africa, I saw another splendid effect made by red flowers. This flower was probably called the torchplant—should have been so named, anyway. It had a slender stem several feet high, and from its top stood up a single tongue of flame, an intensely red flower of the size and shape of a small corn-cob. The stems stood three or four feet apart all over a great hill-slope that was a mile long, and made one think of what the Place de la Concorde would be if its myriad lights were red instead of white and yellow.

A few miles down the mountain we stopped half an hour to see a Thibetan dramatic performance. It was in the open air on the hillside. The audience was composed of Thibetans, Ghurkas, and other unusual people. The costumes of the actors were in the last degree outlandish, and the performance was in keeping with the clothes. To an accompaniment of barbarous noises the actors stepped out one after another and began to spin around with immense swiftness and vigor and violence, chanting the while, and soon the whole troupe would be spinning and chanting and raising the dust. They were performing an ancient and celebrated historical play, and a Chinaman explained it to me in pidjin English as it went along. The play was obscure enough without the explanation;

with the explanation added, it was opaque. As a drama this ancient historical work of art was defective, I thought, but as a wild and barbarous spectacle the representation was beyond criticism.

Far down the mountain we got out to look at a piece of remarkable loop-engineering—a spiral where the road curves upon itself with such abruptness that when the regular train came down and entered the loop, we stood over it and saw the locomotive disappear under our bridge, then in a few moments appear again, chasing its own tail; and we saw it gain on it, overtake it, draw ahead past the rear cars, and run a race with that end of the train. It was like a snake swallowing itself.

Half-way down the mountain we stopped about an hour at Mr. Barnard's house for refreshments, and while we were sitting on the veranda looking at the distant panorama of hills through a gap in the forest, we came very near seeing a leopard kill a calf.[1] It is a wild place and lovely. From the woods all about came the songs of birds—among them the contributions of a couple of birds which I was not then acquainted with: the brain-fever bird and the coppersmith. The song of the brain-fever demon starts on a low but steadily rising key, and is a spiral twist which augments in intensity and severity with each added spiral, growing sharper and sharper, and more and more painful, more and more agonizing, more and more maddening, intolerable, unendurable, as it bores deeper and deeper and deeper into the listener's brain, until at last the brain-fever comes as a relief and the man dies. I am bringing some of these birds home to America. They will be a great curiosity there, and it is believed that in our climate they will multiply like rabbits.

The coppersmith bird's note at a certain distance away

[1] It killed it the day before.

has the ring of a sledge on granite; at a certain other distance the hammering has a more metallic ring, and you might think that the bird was mending a copper kettle; at another distance it has a more woodeny thump, but it is a thump that is full of energy, and sounds just like starting a bung. So he is a hard bird to name with a single name; he is a stone-breaker, coppersmith, and bung-starter, and even then he is not completely named, for when he is close by you find that there is a soft, deep, melodious quality in his thump, and for that no satisfying name occurs to you. You will not mind his other notes, but when he camps near enough for you to hear that one, you presently find that his measured and monotonous repetition of it is beginning to disturb you; next it will weary you, soon it will distress you, and before long each thump will hurt your head; if this goes on, you will lose your mind with the pain and misery of it, and go crazy. I am bringing some of these birds home to America. There is nothing like them there. They will be a great surprise, and it is said that in a climate like ours they will surpass expectation for fecundity.

I am bringing some nightingales, too, and some cue-owls. I got them in Italy. The song of the nightingale is the deadliest known to ornithology. That demoniacal shriek can kill at thirty yards. The note of the cue-owl is infinitely soft and sweet—soft and sweet as the whisper of a flute. But penetrating—oh, beyond belief; it can bore through boiler-iron. It is a lingering note, and comes in triplets, on the one unchanging key: *hoo-o-o, hoo-o-o, hoo-o-o*; then a silence of fifteen seconds, then the triplet again; and so on, all night. At first it is divine; then less so; then trying; then distressing; then excruciating; then agonizing, and at the end of two hours the listener is a maniac.

And so, presently, we took to the hand-car and went flying down the mountain again; flying and stopping, flying and stopping, till at last we were in the plain once more and stowed for Calcutta in the regular train. That was the most enjoyable day I have spent in the earth. For rousing, tingling, rapturous pleasure there is no holiday trip that approaches the bird-flight down the Himalayas in a hand-car. It has no fault, no blemish, no lack, except that there are only thirty-five miles of it instead of five hundred.

Chapter XXI

She was not quite what you would call refined. She was not quite what you would call unrefined. She was the kind of person that keeps a parrot.
—Pudd'nhead Wilson's New Calendar.

SO far as I am able to judge, nothing has been left undone, either by man or Nature, to make India the most extraordinary country that the sun visits on his round. Nothing seems to have been forgotten, nothing overlooked. Always, when you think you have come to the end of her tremendous specialties and have finished hanging tags upon her as the Land of the Thug, the Land of the Plague, the Land of Famine, the Land of Giant Illusions, the Land of Stupendous Mountains, and so forth, another specialty crops up and another tag is required. I have been overlooking the fact that India is by an unapproachable supremacy—the Land of Murderous Wild Creatures. Perhaps it will be simplest to throw away the tags and generalize her with one all-comprehensive name, as the Land of Wonders.

For many years the British Indian Government has been trying to destroy the murderous wild creatures, and has spent a great deal of money in the effort. The annual official returns show that the undertaking is a difficult one.

These returns exhibit a curious annual uniformity in results; the sort of uniformity which you find in the annual output of suicides in the world's capitals, and the proportions of deaths by this, that, and the other disease. You can always come close to foretelling how many suicides will occur in Paris, London, and New York, next year, and also how many deaths will result from cancer, consumption, dog-bite, falling out of the window, getting run over by cabs, etc., if you know the statistics of those matters for the present year. In the same way, with one year's Indian statistics before you, you can guess closely at how many people were killed in that Empire by tigers during the previous year, and the year before that, and the year before that, and at how many were killed in each of those years by bears, how many by wolves, and how many by snakes; and you can also guess closely at how many people are going to be killed each year for the coming five years by each of those agencies. You can also guess closely at how many of each agency the government is going to kill each year for the next five years.

I have before me statistics covering a period of six consecutive years. By these, I know that in India the tiger kills something over 800 persons every year, and that the government responds by killing about double as many tigers every year. In four of the six years referred to, the tiger got 800 odd; in one of the remaining two years he got only 700, but in the other remaining year he made his average good by scoring 917. He is always sure of his average. Any one who bets that the tiger will kill 2,400 people in India in any three consecutive years has invested his money in a certainty; any one who bets that he will kill 2,600 in any three consecutive years, is absolutely sure to lose.

Strikingly uniform as are the statistics of suicide, they

are not any more so than are those of the tiger's annual output of slaughtered human beings in India. The government's work is quite uniform, too; it about doubles the tiger's average. In six years the tiger killed 5,000 persons, minus 50; in the same six years 10,000 tigers were killed, minus 400.

The wolf kills nearly as many people as the tiger—700 a year to the tiger's 800 odd—but while he is doing it, more than 5,000 of his tribe fall.

The leopard kills an average of 230 people per year, but loses 3,300 of his own mess while he is doing it.

The bear kills 100 people per year at a cost of 1,250 of his own tribe.

The tiger, as the figures show, makes a very handsome fight against man. But it is nothing to the elephant's fight. The king of beasts, the lord of the jungle, loses four of his mess per year, but he kills *forty-five* persons to make up for it.

But when it comes to killing cattle, the lord of the jungle is not interested. He kills but 100 in six years—horses of hunters, no doubt—but in the same six the tiger kills more than 84,000, the leopard 100,000, the bear 4,000, the wolf 70,000, the hyena more than 13,000, other wild beasts 27,000, and the snakes 19,000, a grand total of more than 300,000; an average of 50,000 head per year.

In response, the government kills, in the six years, a total of 3,201,232 wild beasts and snakes. Ten for one.

It will be perceived that the snakes are not much interested in cattle; they kill only 3,000 odd per year. The snakes are much more interested in man. India swarms with deadly snakes. At the head of the list is the cobra, the deadliest known to the world, a snake whose bite kills where the rattlesnake's bite merely entertains.

In India, the annual man-killings by snakes are as uniform, as regular, and as forecastable as are the tiger average and the suicide average. Any one who bets that in India, in any three consecutive years, the snakes will kill 49,500 persons, will win his bet; and any one who bets that in India in any three consecutive years the snakes will kill 53,500 persons, will lose his bet. In India the snakes kill 17,000 people a year; they hardly ever fall short of it; they as seldom exceed it. An insurance actuary could take the Indian census tables and the government's snake tables and tell you within sixpence how much it would be worth to insure a man against death by snake-bite there. If I had a dollar for every person killed per year in India, I would rather have it than any other property, as it is the only property in the world not subject to shrinkage.

I should like to have a royalty on the government end of the snake business, too, and am in London now trying to get it; but when I get it it is not going to be as regular an income as the other will be if I get that; I have applied for it. The snakes transact their end of the business in a more orderly and systematic way than the government transacts its end of it, because the snakes have had a long experience and know all about the traffic. You can make sure that the government will never kill fewer than 110,000 snakes in a year, and that it will never quite reach 300,000—too much room for oscillation; good speculative stock, to bear or bull, and buy and sell long and short, and all that kind of thing, but not eligible for investment like the other. The man that speculates in the government's snake crop wants to go carefully. I would not advise a man to buy a single crop at all—I mean a crop of futures—for the possible wabble is something quite extraordinary. If he can buy *six* future crops in a bunch, seller to deliver 1,500,000 altogether, that is another matter. I do not know what snakes are worth now, but I know what they would be worth then, for the statistics show that the seller could not come within 427,000 of carrying out his contract.

However, I think that a person who speculates in snakes is a fool, anyway. He always regrets it afterward.

To finish the statistics. In six years the wild beasts kill 20,000 persons, and the snakes kill 103,000. In the same six the government kills 1,073,546 snakes. Plenty left.

There are narrow escapes in India. In the very jungle where I killed sixteen tigers and all those elephants, a cobra bit me, but it got well; every one was surprised. This could not happen twice in ten years, perhaps. Usually death would result in fifteen minutes.

We struck out westward or northwestward from Calcutta on an itinerary of a zigzag sort, which would in the course of time carry us across India to its northwestern corner and the border of Afghanistan. The first part of the trip carried us through a great region which was an endless garden— miles and miles of the beautiful flower from whose juices comes the opium, and at Muzaffurpore we were in the midst of the indigo culture; thence by a branch road to the Ganges at a point near Dinapore, and by a train which would have missed the connection by a week but for the thoughtfulness of some British officers who were along, and who knew the ways of trains that are run by natives without white supervision. This train stopped at every village; for no purpose connected with business, apparently. We put out nothing, we took nothing aboard. The train-hands stepped ashore and gossiped with friends a quarter of an hour, then pulled out and repeated this at the succeeding villages. We had thirty-five miles to go and six hours to do it in, but it was plain that we were not going to make it. It was then that the English officers said it was now necessary to turn this gravel-train into an express. So they gave the engine-driver a rupee and told him to fly. It was a simple remedy. After that we made ninety miles an hour. We crossed the Ganges just at dawn, made our connection, and went to Benares, where we stayed twenty-four hours and inspected that strange and fascinating piety-hive again; then left for Lucknow, a city which is perhaps the most conspicuous of the many monuments of British fortitude and valor that are scattered about the earth.

The heat was pitiless, the flat plains were destitute of grass, and, baked dry by the sun, they were the color of pale dust, which was flying in clouds. But it was much hotter than this when the relieving forces marched to Lucknow in the time of the Mutiny. Those were the days of one hundred and thirty-eight degrees in the shade.

Chapter XXII

Make it a point to do something every day that you don't want to do. This is the golden rule for acquiring the habit of doing your duty without pain.
—Pudd'nhead Wilson's New Calendar.

IT seems to be settled, now, that among the many causes from which the Great Mutiny sprang, the main one was the annexation of the kingdom of Oudh by the East India Company—characterized by Sir Henry Lawrence as "the most unrighteous act that was ever committed." In the spring of 1857, a mutinous spirit was observable in many of the native garrisons, and it grew day by day and spread wider and wider. The younger military men saw something very serious in it, and would have liked to take hold of it vigorously and stamp it out promptly; but they were not in authority. Old men were in the high places of the army—men who should have been retired long before, because of their great age—and they regarded the matter as a thing of no consequence. They loved their native soldiers, and would not believe that anything could move them to revolt. Everywhere these obstinate veterans listened serenely to the rumbling of the volcanoes under them, and said it was nothing.

And so the propagators of mutiny had everything their own way. They moved from camp to camp undisturbed, and painted to the native soldier the wrongs his people were suffering at the hands of the English, and made his heart burn for revenge. They were able to point to two facts of formidable value as backers of their persuasions: In Clive's day, native armies were incoherent mobs, and without effective arms; therefore, they were weak against Clive's organized handful of well-armed men, but the thing was the other way, now. The British forces were native; they had been trained by the British, organized by the British, armed by the British, all the power was in their hands—they were a club made by British hands to beat out British brains with. There was nothing to oppose their mass, nothing but a few weak battalions of British soldiers scattered about. India, a force not worth speaking of. This argument, taken alone, might not have succeeded, for the bravest and best Indian troops had a wholesome dread of the white soldier, whether he was weak or strong; but the agitators backed it with their second and best point—*prophecy*—a prophecy a hundred years old. The Indian is open to prophecy at all times; argument may fail to convince him, but not prophecy. There was a prophecy that a hundred years from the year of that battle of Clive's which founded the British Indian Empire, the British power would be overthrown and swept away by the natives.

The Mutiny broke out at Meerut on the 10th of May, 1857, and fired a train of tremendous historical explosions. Nana Sahib's massacre of the surrendered garrison of Cawnpore occured in June, and the long siege of Lucknow began. The military history of England is old and great, but I think it must be granted that the crushing of the Mutiny is the greatest chapter in it. The British were caught asleep and unprepared. They were a few thousands, swallowed up in an ocean of hostile populations. It would take months to inform

England and get help, but they did not falter or stop to count the odds, but with English resolution and English devotion they took up their task, and went stubbornly on with it, through good fortune and bad, and fought the most unpromising fight that one may read of in fiction or out of it, and won it thoroughly.

The Mutiny broke out so suddenly and spread with such rapidity that there was but little time for occupants of weak outlying stations to escape to places of safety. Attempts were made, of course, but they were attended by hardships as bitter as death in the few cases which were successful; for the heat ranged between one hundred and twenty and one hundred and thirty-eight in the shade; the way led through hostile peoples, and food and water were hardly to be had. For ladies and children accustomed to ease and comfort and plenty, such a journey must have been a cruel experience. Sir G. O. Trevelyan quotes an example:

This is what befell Mrs. M———, the wife of the surgeon at a certain station on the southern confines of the insurrection. "I heard," she says, "a number of shots fired, and, looking out, I saw my husband driving furiously from the mess-house, waving his whip. I ran to him, and, seeing a bearer with my child in his arms, I caught her up, and got into the buggy. At the mess-house we found all the officers assembled, together with sixty sepoys, who had remained faithful. We went off in one large party, amidst a general conflagration of our late homes. We reached the caravanserai at Chattapore the next morning, and thence started for Callinger. At this point our sepoy escort deserted us. We were fired upon by match-lockmen, and one officer was shot dead. We heard, likewise, that the people had risen at Callinger, so we returned and walked back ten miles that day. M——— and I carried the child alternately. Presently Mrs. Smalley died of sunstroke. We had no food among us. An officer kindly lent us a horse. We were very faint. The Major died, and was buried; also the Sergeant-Major and some women. The bandsmen left us on the nineteenth of June. We were fired at again by matchlockmen, and changed direction for Allahabad. Our party consisted of nine gentlemen, two children, the sergeant and his wife. On the morning of the twentieth, Captain Scott took Lottie on to his horse. I was riding behind my husband, and she was so crushed between us. She was two years old on the first of the month. We were both weak through want of food and the effect of the sun. Lottie and I had no head-covering. M—— had a sepoy's cap I found on the ground. Soon after sunrise we were followed by villagers armed with clubs and spears. One of them struck Captain Scott's horse on the leg. He galloped off with Lottie, and my poor husband never saw his child again. We rode on several miles, keeping away from villages, and then crossed the river. Our thirst was extreme. M—— had dreadful cramps, so that I had to hold him on the horse. I was very uneasy about him. The day before I saw the drummer's wife eating chupatties, and asked her to give a piece to the child, which she did. I now saw water in a ravine. The descent was steep, and our only drinking-vessel was M——'s cap. Our horse got water, and I bathed my neck. I had no stockings, and my feet were torn and blistered. Two peasants came in sight, and we were frightened and rode off. The sergeant held our horse, and M—— put me up and mounted. I think he must have got suddenly faint, for I fell and he over me, on the road, when the horse started off. Some time before he said, and Barber, too, that he could not live many hours. I felt he was dying before we came to the ravine. He told me his wishes about his children and myself, and took leave. My brain seemed burnt up. No tears came. As soon as we fell, the sergeant let go the horse, and it went off; so that escape was cut off. We sat down on the ground waiting for death. Poor fellow! he was very weak; his thirst was frightful, and I went to get him water. Some villagers came, and took my rupees and watch. I took off my wedding ring and twisted it in my hair, and replaced the guard. I tore off my skirt of my dress to bring water in, but it was no use, for when I returned my beloved's eyes were fixed, and though I called and tried to restore him, and poured water into his mouth, it only rattled in his throat. He never spoke to me again. I held him in my arms till he sank gradually down. I felt frantic, but could not cry. I was alone. I bound his head and face in my dress, for there was no earth to bury him. The pain in my hands and feet was dreadful. I went down to the ravine, and sat in the water on a stone, hoping to get off at night and look for Lottie. When I came back from the water, I saw they had not taken her little watch, chain, and seals, so I tied them under my petticoat. In an hour about thirty villagers came; they dragged me out of the ravine, and took off my jacket, and found the little chain. They then dragged me to a village, mocking me all the way, and disputing as to whom I was to belong to. The whole population came to look at me. I asked for a bedstead, and lay down outside the door of a hut. They had a dozen of cows, and yet refused me milk. When night came, and the village was quiet, some old woman brought me a leafful of rice. I was too parched to eat, and they gave me water. The morning after a neighboring Raja sent a palanquin and a horseman to fetch me, who told me that a little child and three Sahibs had come to his master's house." And so the poor mother found her lost one, "greatly blistered," poor little creature. It is not for Europeans in India to pray that their flight be not in the winter.

In the first days of June the aged general, Sir Hugh Wheeler, commanding the forces at Cawnpore, was deserted by his native troops; then he moved out of the fort and into an exposed patch of open flat ground and built a four-foot mud wall around it. He had with him a few hundred white soldiers and officers, and apparently more women and children than soldiers. He was short of provisions, short of arms short of ammunition, short of military wisdom, short of everything but courage and devotion to duty. The defense of that open lot through twenty-one days and nights of hunger, thirst, Indian heat, and a never-ceasing storm of bullets, bombs, and cannon-balls—a defense conducted, not by the aged and infirm general, but by a young officer named Moore—is one of the most heroic episodes in history. When at last the Nana found it impossible to conquer these starving men and women with powder and ball, he resorted to treachery, and that succeeded. He agreed to supply them with food and send them to Allahabad in boats. Their mud wall and their barracks were in ruins, their provisions were at the point of exhaustion, they had done all that the brave could do, they had conquered an honorable compromise, their forces had been fearfully reduced by casualties and by disease, they were not able to continue the contest longer. They came forth helpless but suspecting no treachery, the Nana's host closed around them, and at a signal from a trumpet the massacre began. About two hundred women and children were spared—for the present—but all the men except three or four were killed. Among the incidents of the massacre quoted by Sir G. O. Trevelyan, is this:

When, after the lapse of some twenty minutes, the dead began to outnumber the living;—when the fire slackened, as the marks grew few and far between; then the troopers who had been drawn up to the right of the temple plunged into the river, saber between teeth, and pistol in hand. Thereupon two half-caste Christian women, the wives of musicians in the band of the Fifty-sixth, witnessed a scene which should not be related at second hand. "In the boat where I was to have gone," says Mrs. Bradshaw, confirmed throughout by Mrs. Setts, "was the schoolmistress and twenty-two misses. General Wheeler came last in a palkee. They carried him into the water near the boat. I stood close by. He said, 'Carry me a little further toward the boat.' But a trooper said, 'No, get out here.' As the General got out of the palkee, head foremost, the trooper gave him a cut with his sword into the neck, and he fell into the water. My son was killed near him. I saw it; alas! alas! Some were stabbed with bayonets; others cut down. Little infants were torn in pieces. We saw it; we did; and tell you only what we saw. Other children were stabbed and thrown into the river. The school-girls were burnt to death. I saw their clothes and hair catch fire. In the water, a few paces off, by the next boat, we saw the youngest daughter of Colonel Williams. A sepoy was going to kill her with his bayonet. She said, 'My father was always kind to sepoys.' He turned away, and just then a villager struck her on the head with a club, and she fell into the water. These people likewise saw good Mr. Moncrieff, the clergyman, take a book from his pocket that he never had leisure to open, and heard him commence a prayer for mercy which he was not permitted to conclude." Another deponent observed an European making for a drain like a scared water-rat, when some boatmen, armed with cudgels, cut off his retreat, and beat him down dead into the mud.

The women and children who had been reserved from the massacre were imprisoned during a fortnight in a small building, one story high—a cramped place, a slightly modified Black Hole of Calcutta. They were waiting in suspense; there was none who could forecast their fate. Meantime the news of the massacre had traveled far, and an army of rescuers with Havelock at its head was on its way—at least an army which hoped to be rescuers. It was crossing the country by forced marches, and strewing its way with its own dead— men struck down by cholera, and by a heat which reached one hundred and thirty-five degrees. It was in a vengeful fury, and it stopped for nothing—neither heat, nor fatigue, nor disease, nor human opposition. It tore its impetuous way through hostile forces, winning victory after victory, but still striding on and on, not halting to count results. And at last, after, this extraordinary march, it arrived before the walls of Cawnpore, met the Nana's massed strength, delivered a crushing defeat, and entered.

But too late—only a few hours too late. For at the last moment the Nana had decided upon the massacre of the captive women and children, and had commissioned three Mohammedans and two Hindus to do the work. Sir G. O. Trevelyan says:

> Thereupon the five men entered. It was the short gloaming of Hindustan—the hour when ladies take their evening drive. She who had accosted the officer was standing in the doorway. With her were the native doctor and two Hindu menials. That much of the business might be seen from the veranda, but all else was concealed amidst the interior gloom. Shrieks and scuffling acquainted those without that the journeymen were earning their hire. Survur Khan soon emerged with his sword broken off at the hilt. He procured another from the Nana's house, and a few minutes after appeared again on the same errand. The third blade was of better temper; or perhaps the thick of the work was already over. By the time darkness had closed in, the men came forth and locked up the house for the night. Then the screams ceased, but the groans lasted till morning.
>
> The sun rose as usual. When he had been up nearly three hours the five repaired to the scene of their labors overnight. They were attended by a few sweepers, who proceeded to transfer the contents of the house to a dry well situated behind some trees which grew hard by. "The bodies," says one who was present throughout, "were dragged out, most of them by the hair of the head. Those who had clothing worth taking were stripped. Some of the women were alive. I cannot say how many, but *three could speak*. They prayed for the sake of God that an end might be put to their sufferings. I remarked

one very stout woman, a half-caste, who was severely wounded in both arms, who entreated to be killed. She and two or three others were placed against the bank of the cut by which bullocks go down in drawing water. The dead were first thrown in. Yes: there was a great crowd looking on; they were standing along the walls of the compound. They were principally city people and villagers. Yes: there were also sepoys. *Three boys were alive.* They were fair children. The eldest, I think, must have been six or seven, and the youngest five years. They were running around the well (where else could they go to?) and there was none to save them. No: none said a word or tried to save them."

At length the smallest of them made an infantile attempt to get away. The little thing had been frightened past bearing by the murder of one of the surviving ladies. He thus attracted the observation of a native, who flung him and his companions down the well.

The soldiers had made a march of eighteen days, almost without rest, to save the women and the children, and now they were too late—all were dead and the assassin had flown. What happened then, Trevelyan hesitated to put into words. "Of what took place, the less said is the better."

Then he continues:

But there was a spectacle to witness which might excuse much. Those, who, straight from the contested field, wandered sobbing through the rooms of the ladies' house, saw what it were well could the outraged earth have straightway hidden. The inner apartment was ankle-deep in blood. The plaster was scored with sword-cuts; not high up as where men have fought, but low down, and about the corners, as if a creature had crouched to avoid the blow. Strips of dresses, vainly tied around the handles of the doors, signified the contrivance to which feminine despair had resorted as a means of keeping out the murderers. Broken combs were there, and the frills of children's trousers, and torn cuffs and pinafores, and little round hats, and one or two shoes with burst latchets, and one or two daguerreotype cases with cracked glasses. An officer picked up a few curls, preserved in a bit of cardboard, and marked "Ned's hair, with love"; but around were strewn locks, some near a yard in length, dissevered, not as a keepsake, by quite other scissors.

The battle of Waterloo was fought on the 18th of June, 1815. I do not state this fact as a reminder to the reader, but as news to him. For a forgotten fact *is* news when it comes again. Writers of books have the fashion of whizzing by vast and renowned historical events with the remark, "The details of this tremendous episode are too familiar to the reader to need repeating here." They know that that is not true. It is a low kind of flattery. They know that the reader had forgotten every detail of it, and that nothing of the tremendous event is left in his mind but a vague and formless luminous smudge. Aside from the desire to flatter the reader, they have another reason for making the remark—two reasons, indeed. They do not remember the details themselves, and do not want the trouble of hunting them up and copying them out; also, they are afraid that if they search them out and print them they will be scoffed at by the book-reviewers for retelling those worn old things which are familiar to everybody. They should not mind the reviewer's jeer; *he* doesn't remember any of the worn old things until the book which he is reviewing has retold them to him.

I have made the quoted remark myself, at one time and another, but I was not doing it to flatter the reader; I was merely doing it to save work. If I had known the details without brushing up, I would have put them in; but I didn't, and I did not want the labor of posting myself; so I said, "The details of this tremendous episode are too familiar to the reader to need repeating here." I do not like that kind of a lie; still, it does save work.

I am not trying to get out of repeating the details of the Siege of Lucknow in fear of the reviewer; I am not leaving them out in fear that they would not interest the reader; I am leaving them out partly to save work; mainly for lack of room. It is a pity, too; for there is not a dull place anywhere in the great story.

Ten days before the outbreak (May 10th) of the Mutiny, all was serene at Lucknow, the huge capital of Oudh, the kingdom which had recently been seized by the East India Company. There was a great garrison, composed of about 7,000 native troops and between 700 and 800 whites. These white soldiers and their families were probably the only people of their race there; at their elbow was that swarming population of warlike natives, a race of born soldiers, brave, daring, and fond of fighting. On high ground just outside the city stood the palace of that great personage, the Resident, the representative of British power and authority. It stood in the midst of spacious grounds, with its due compliment of outbuildings, and the grounds were inclosed by a wall—a wall not for defense, but for privacy. The mutinous spirit was in the air, but the whites were not afraid, and did not feel much troubled.

Then came the outbreak at Meerut, then the capture of Delhi by the mutineers; in June came the three-weeks leaguer of Sir Hugh Wheeler in his open lot at Cawnpore—forty miles distant from Lucknow—then the treacherous massacre of that gallant little garrison; and now the great revolt was in full flower, and the comfortable condition of things at Lucknow was instantly changed.

There was an outbreak there, and Sir Henry Lawrence marched out of the Residency on the 30th of June to put it down, but was defeated with heavy loss, and had difficulty in getting back again. That night the memorable siege of the Residency—called the siege of Lucknow—began. Sir Henry was killed three days later, and Brigadier Inglis succeeded him in command.

Outside of the Residency fence was an immense host of hostile and confident native besiegers; inside it were 480 loyal native soldiers, 730 white ones, and 500 women and children. In those days the English garrisons always managed to hamper themselves sufficiently with women and children.

The natives established themselves in houses close at hand and began to rain bullets and cannon-balls into the Residency; and this they kept up, night and day, during four months and a half, the little garrison industriously replying all the time. The women and children soon became so used to the roar of the guns that it ceased to disturb their sleep. The children imitated siege and defense in their play. The women—with any pretext, or with none—would sally out into the storm-swept grounds.

The defense was kept up week after week, with stubborn fortitude, in the midst of death, which came in many forms— by bullet, smallpox, cholera, and by various diseases induced by unpalatable and insufficient food, by the long hours of wearying and exhausting overwork in the daily and nightly battle in the oppressive Indian heat, and by the broken rest caused by the intolerable pest of mosquitoes, flies, mice, rats, and fleas.

Six weeks after the beginning of the siege more than one-half of the original force of white soldiers was dead, and close upon three-fifths of the original native force.

But the fighting went on just the same. The enemy mined, the English counter-mined, and, turn about, they blew up each other's posts. The Residency grounds were honeycombed with the enemy's tunnels. Deadly courtesies were constantly exchanged—sorties by the English in the night; rushes by the enemy in the night—rushes whose purpose was to breach the walls or scale them; rushes which cost heavily, and always failed.

The ladies got used to all the horrors of war—the shrieks of mutilated men, the sight of blood and death. Lady Inglis makes this mention in her diary:

> Mrs. Bruere's nurse was carried past our door to-day, wounded in the eye. To extract the bullet it was found necessary to take out the eye—a fearful operation. Her mistress held her while it was performed.

The first relieving force failed to relieve. It was under Havelock and Outram, and arrived when the siege had been going on for three months. It fought its desperate way to Lucknow, then fought its way through the city against odds of a hundred to one, and entered the Residency; but there was not enough left of it, then, to do any good. It lost more men in its last fight than it found in the Residency when it got in. It became captive itself.

The fighting and starving and dying by bullets and disease went steadily on. Both sides fought with energy and industry. Captain Birch puts this striking incident in evidence. He is speaking of the third month of the siege:

> As an instance of the heavy firing brought to bear on our position this month may be mentioned the cutting down of the upper story of a brick building simply by *musketry firing*. This building was in a most exposed position. All the shots which just missed the top of the rampart cut into the dead wall pretty much in a straight line, and at length cut right through and brought the upper story tumbling down. The upper struc-

ture on the top of the brigade mess also fell in. The Residency
house was a wreck. Captain Anderson's post had long ago
been knocked down, and Innes's post also fell in. These two
were riddled with round shot. As many as two hundred were
picked up by Colonel Masters.

The exhausted garrison fought doggedly on all through
the next month—October. Then, November 2d, news
came—Sir Colin Campbell's relieving force would soon be
on its way from Cawnpore.

On the 12th the boom of his guns was heard.

On the 13th the sounds came nearer—he was slowly,
but steadily, cutting his way through, storming one strong-
hold after another.

On the 14th he captured the Martinère College, and ran
up the British flag there. It was seen from the Residency.

Next he took the Dilkoosha.

On the 17th he took the former mess-house of the
Thirty-second regiment—a fortified building, and very
strong. "A most exciting, anxious day," writes Lady Inglis
in her diary. "About 4 P.M., two strange officers walked
through our yard, leading their horses"—and by that sign
she knew that communication was established between the
forces, that the relief was real, this time, and that the long
siege of Lucknow was ended.

The last eight or ten miles of Sir Colin Campbell's march
was through seas of blood. The weapon mainly used was
the bayonet, the fighting was desperate. The way was mile-
stoned with detached strong buildings of stone, fortified, and
heavily garrisoned, and these had to be taken by assault.
Neither side asked for quarter, and neither gave it. At the
Secundrabagh, where nearly two thousand of the enemy occupied a great stone house in a garden, the work of slaughter

was continued until every man was killed. That is a sample of the character of that devastating march.

There were but few trees in the plain at that time, and from the Residency the progress of the march, step by step, victory by victory, could be noted; the ascending clouds of battle-smoke marked the way to the eye, and the thunder of the guns marked it to the ear.

Sir Colin Campbell had not come to Lucknow to hold it, but to save the occupants of the Residency, and bring them away. Four or five days after his arrival the secret evacuation by the troops took place, in the middle of a dark night, by the principal gate (the Bailie Guard). The two hundred women and two hundred and fifty children had been previously removed. Captain Birch says:

> And now commenced a movement of the most perfect arrangement and successful generalship—the withdrawal of the whole of the various forces, a combined movement requiring the greatest care and skill. First, the garrison in immediate contact with the enemy at the furthest extremity of the Residency position was marched out. Every other garrison in turn fell in behind it, and so passed out through the Bailie Guard gate, till the whole of our position was evacuated. Then Havelock's force was similarly withdrawn, post by post, marching in rear of our garrison. After them in turn came the forces of the Commander-in-Chief, which joined on in the rear of Havelock's force. Regiment by regiment was withdrawn with the utmost order and regularity. The whole operation resembled the movement of a telescope. Stern silence was kept, and the enemy took no alarm.

Lady Inglis, referring to her husband and to General Sir James Outram, sets down the closing detail of this impressive midnight retreat, in darkness and by stealth, of this shadowy

host through the gate which it had defended so long and so
well:

> At twelve precisely they marched out, John and Sir James
> Outram remaining till all had passed, and then they took off
> their hats to the Bailie Guard, the scene of as noble a defense
> as I think history will ever have to relate.

Chapter XXIII

*Don't part with your illusions. When they are gone you
may still exist but you have ceased to live.*
                    —Pudd'nhead Wilson's New Calendar.

*Often, the surest way to convey misinformation is to tell
the strict truth.*
                    —Pudd'nhead Wilson's New Calendar.

W E were driven over Sir Colin Campbell's route by a
British officer, and when I arrived at the Residency I
was so familiar with the road that I could have led a retreat
over it myself; but the compass in my head has been out of
order from my birth, and so, as soon as I was within the
battered Bailie Guard and turned about to review the march
and imagine the relieving forces storming their way along it,
everything was upside down and wrong end first in a moment, and I was never able to get straightened out again. And
now, when I look at the battle-plan, the confusion remains.
In me the east was born west, the battle-plans which have the
east on the right-hand side are of no use to me.

The Residency ruins are draped with flowering vines,
and are impressive and beautiful. They and the grounds are
sacred now, and will suffer no neglect nor be profaned by any
sordid or commercial use while the British remain masters of

India. Within the grounds are buried the dead who gave up their lives there in the long siege.

After a fashion, I was able to imagine the fiery storm that raged night and day over the place during so many months, and after a fashion I could imagine the men moving through it, but I could not satisfactorily place the two hundred women, and I could do nothing at all with the two hundred and fifty children. I knew by Lady Inglis's diary that the children carried on their small affairs very much as if blood and carnage and the crash and thunder of a siege were natural and proper features of nursery life, and I tried to realize it; but when her little Johnny came rushing, all excitement, through the din and smoke, shouting, "Oh, mama, the white hen has laid an egg!" I saw that I could not do it. Johnny's place was under the bed. I could imagine him there, because I could imagine myself there; and I think I should not have been interested in a hen that was laying an egg; my interest would have been with the parties that were laying the bomb-shells. I sat at dinner with one of those children in the Club's Indian palace, and I knew that all through the siege he was perfecting his teething and learning to talk; and while to me he was the most impressive object in Lucknow after the Residency ruins, I was not able to imagine what his life had been during that tempestuous infancy of his, nor what sort of a curious surprise it must have been to him to be marched suddenly out into a strange dumb world where there wasn't any noise, and nothing going on. He was only forty-one when I saw him, a strangely youthful link to connect the present with so ancient an episode as the Great Mutiny.

By and by we saw Cawnpore, and the open lot which was the scene of Moore's memorable defense, and the spot on the shore of the Ganges where the massacre of the betrayed garrison occurred, and the small Indian temple whence the bugle-signal notified the assassins to fall on. This latter was a lonely spot, and silent. The sluggish river drifted by, almost currentless. It was dead low water, narrow channels with vast sandbars between, all the way across the wide bed; and the only living thing in sight was that grotesque and solemn bald-headed bird, the Adjutant, standing on his six-foot stilts, solitary on a distant bar, with his head sunk between his shoulders, thinking; thinking of his prize, I suppose—the dead Hindu that lay awash at his feet, and whether to eat him alone or invite friends. He and his prey were a proper accent to that mournful place. They were in keeping with it, they emphasized its loneliness and its solemnity.

And we saw the scene of the slaughter of the helpless women and children, and also the costly memorial that is built over the well which contains their remains. The Black Hole of Calcutta is gone, but a more reverent age is come, and whatever remembrancer still exists of the moving and heroic sufferings and achievements of the garrisons of Lucknow and Cawnpore will be guarded and preserved.

In Agra and its neighborhood, and afterward at Delhi, we saw forts, mosques, and tombs, which were built in the great days of the Mohammedan emperors, and which are marvels of cost, magnitude, and richness of materials and ornamentation, creations of surpassing grandeur, wonders which do indeed make the like things in the rest of the world seem tame and inconsequential by comparison. I am not purposing to describe them. By good fortune I had not read much about them, and therefore was able to get a natural and rational focus upon them, with the result that they thrilled, blessed, and exalted me. But if I had previously overheated my imagination by drinking too much pestilential literary hot Scotch, I should have suffered disappointment and sorrow.

I mean to speak of only one of these many world-renowned buildings, the Taj Mahal, the most celebrated construction in the earth. I had read a great deal too much about it. I saw it in the daytime, I saw it in the moonlight, I saw it near at hand, I saw it from a distance; and I knew all the time, that of its kind it was *the* wonder of the world, with no competitor now and no possible future competitor; and yet, it was not *my* Taj. My Taj had been built by excitable literary people; it was solidly lodged in my head, and I could not blast it out.

I wish to place before the reader some of the usual descriptions of the Taj, and ask him to take note of the impressions left in his mind. These descriptions do really state the truth—as nearly as the limitations of language will allow. But language is a treacherous thing, a most unsure vehicle, and it can seldom arrange descriptive words in such a way that they will not inflate the facts—by help of the reader's imagination, which is always ready to take a hand, and work for nothing, and do the bulk of it at that.

I will begin with a few sentences from the excellent little local guide-book of Mr. Satya Chandra Mukerji. I take them from here and there in his description:

> The inlaid work of the Taj and the flowers and petals that are to be found on all sides on the surface of the marble evince a most delicate touch.

That is true.

> The inlaid work, the marble, the flowers, the buds, the leaves, the petals, and the lotus stems are almost without a rival in the whole of the civilized world.
> The work of inlaying with stones and gems is found in the highest perfection in the Taj.

Gems, inlaid flowers, buds, and leaves to be found on all sides. What do you see before you? Is the fairy structure growing? Is it becoming a jewel casket?

The whole of the Taj produces a wonderful effect that is equally sublime and beautiful.

Then Sir William Wilson Hunter:

The Taj Mahal with its beautiful domes, "a dream of marble," rises on the river-bank.

The materials are white marble and red sandstone.

The complexity of its design and the delicate intricacy of the workmanship baffle description.

Sir William continues. I will italicize some of his words:

The mausoleum stands on a raised marble platform, at each of whose corners rises a tall and slender minaret of graceful proportions and of exquisite beauty. Beyond the platform stretch the two wings, one of which is itself a mosque of great architectural merit. In the center of the whole design the mausoleum occupies a square of one hundred and eighty-six feet, with the angles deeply truncated so as to form an unequal octagon. The main feature in this central pile is the great dome, which swells upward to nearly two-thirds of a sphere and tapers at its extremity into a pointed spire crowned by a crescent. Beneath it an inclosure of marble trellis-work surrounds the tomb of the princess and of her husband, the Emperor. Each corner of the mausoleum is covered by a similar though much smaller dome erected on a pediment pierced with graceful Saracenic arches. Light is admitted into the interior through a double screen of pierced marble, which tempers the glare of an Indian sky, while its whiteness prevents the mellow effect from degenerating into gloom. The internal decorations consist of inlaid work in *precious stones, such as agate, jasper, etc., with which every spandrel or salient point in the architecture is richly fretted.* Brown and violet marble is also freely employed in wreaths, scrolls, and lintels to relieve the monotony of white wall. *In regard to color and design, the interior of the Taj may rank first in the world for purely decorative workmanship;* while the perfect symmetry of its exterior, once seen, can never be forgotten, nor the aerial grace of its domes, rising like marble bubbles into the clear sky. The Taj represents the most highly elaborated stage of ornamentation reached by the Indo-Mohammedan builders, the stage in which the architect ends and the *jeweler* begins. In its magnificent gateway the diagonal ornamentation at the corners, which satisfied the designers of the gateways of Itimad-ud-doulah and Sikandra mausoleums, is superseded by fine marble cables, in bold twists, strong and handsome. The triangular insertions of white marble and large flowers have in like manner given place to *fine inlaid work.* Firm perpendicular lines in black marble with well-proportioned panels of the same material are effectively used in the interior of the gateway. On its top the Hindu brackets and monolithic architraves of Sikandra are replaced by Moorish carped arches, usually single blocks of red sandstone, in the kiosks and pavilions which adorn the roof. From the pillared pavilions a magnificent view is obtained of the Taj gardens below, with the noble Jumna River at their further end, and the city and fort of Agra in the distance. From this beautiful and splendid gateway one passes up a straight alley shaded by evergreen trees cooled by a broad shallow piece of water running along the middle of the path to the Taj itself. *The Taj is entirely of marble and gems.* The red sandstone of the other Mohammedan buildings has entirely disappeared, or rather the red sandstone which used to form the thickness of the walls is in the Taj itself overlaid completely with white marble, and the white marble is itself *inlaid with precious stones arranged in lovely patterns of flowers.* A feeling of purity impresses itself on the eye and the mind from the absence of the coarser material which forms so invariable a material in Agra architecture. The lower wall and panels are covered with tulips, oleanders, and full-blown lilies, in flat carving on the white marble; and *although the inlaid work of flowers done in gems* is very *brilliant* when looked at closely, there is on the whole but little color, and the all-prevailing sentiment is one of whiteness, silence, and calm. The whiteness is broken only by the fine color of the inlaid gems, by lines in black marble, and by delicately written inscriptions, also in black, from the Koran. Under the dome of *the vast mausoleum* a high and beautiful screen of open tracery in white marble rises around the two tombs, or rather cenotaphs of the emperor and his princess; and in this *marvel of marble* the carving has advanced from the old geometrical patterns to a trellis-work of flowers and foliage, handled with great freedom and spirit. The two cenotaphs in the center of the *exquisite* inclosure have no carving except the plain *Kalamdan* or oblong pen-box on the tomb of Emperor Shah Jehan. But both cenotaphs are *inlaid with flowers made of costly gems,* and with the ever-graceful oleander scroll.

Bayard Taylor, after describing the details of the Taj, goes on to say:

> On both sides the palm, the banyan, and the feathery bamboo mingle their foliage; the song of birds meets your ears, and the odor of roses and lemon flowers sweetens the air. Down such a vista and over such a foreground rises the Taj. There is no mystery, no sense of partial failure about the Taj. *A thing of perfect beauty and of absolute finish* in every detail, it might pass for the work of genii who knew naught of the weaknesses and ills with which mankind are beset.

All of these details are true. But, taken together, they state a falsehood—to *you.* You cannot add them up correctly. Those writers know the values of their words and phrases, but to you the words and phrases convey other and uncertain values. To those writers their phrases have values which I think I am now acquainted with; and for the help of the reader I will here repeat certain of those words and phrases, and

follow them with numerals which shall represent those values—then we shall see the difference between a writer's ciphering and a mistaken reader's:

> *Precious stones, such as agate, jasper, etc.—5.*
>
> *With which every salient point is richly fretted—5.*
>
> *First in the world for purely decorative workmanship—9.*
>
> *The Taj represents the stage where the architect ends and the
> jeweler begins—5.*
>
> *The Taj is entirely of marble and gems—7.*
>
> *Inlaid with precious stones in lovely patterns of flowers—5.*
>
> *The inlaid work of flowers done in gems is very brilliant—*
> (followed by a most important modification which the
> reader is sure to read too carelessly)—2.
>
> *The vast mausoleum—5.*
>
> *This marvel of marble—5.*
>
> *The exquisite inclosure—5.*
>
> *Inlaid with flowers made of costly gems—5.*
>
> *A thing of perfect beauty and absolute finish—5.*

Those details are correct; the figures which I have placed
after them represent quite fairly their individual values. Then
why, as a whole, do they convey a false impression to the
reader? It is because the reader—beguiled by his heated imagination—masses them in the wrong way. The *writer* would
mass the first three figures in the following way, and they
would speak the truth:

$$
\begin{array}{r}
5 \\
5 \\
\underline{9} \\
\end{array}
$$

Total—19

But the reader masses them thus—and then they tell a
lie—559.

The writer would add all of his twelve numerals together, and then the sum would express the whole truth about the Taj, and the truth only—63.

But the reader—always helped by his imagination— would put the figures in a row one after the other, and get this sum, which would tell him a noble big lie:

559575255555.

You must put in the commas yourself; I have to go on with my work.

The reader will always be sure to put the figures together in that wrong way, and then as surely before him will stand, sparkling in the sun, a gem-crusted Taj tall as the Matterhorn.

I had to visit Niagara fifteen times before I succeeded in getting my imaginary Falls gaged to the actuality and could begin to sanely and wholesomely wonder at them for what they were, not what I had expected them to be. When I first approached them it was with my face lifted toward the sky, for I thought I was going to see an Atlantic Ocean pouring down thence, over cloud-vexed Himalayan heights, a sea-green wall of water sixty miles front and six miles high, and so, when the toy reality came suddenly into view—that beruffled little wet apron hanging out to dry—the shock was too much for me, and I fell with a dull thud.

Yet slowly, surely, steadily, in the course of my fifteen visits, the proportions adjusted themselves to the facts, and I came at last to realize that a waterfall a hundred and sixty-five feet high and a quarter of a mile wide was an impressive thing. It was not a dipperful to my vanished great vision, but it would answer.

I know that I ought to do with the Taj as I was obliged to do with Niagara—see it fifteen times, and let my mind gradually get rid of the Taj built in it by its describers, by help of my imagination, and substitute for it the Taj of fact.

It would be noble and fine, then, and a marvel; not the marvel which it replaced, but still a marvel, and fine enough. I am a careless reader, I suppose—an *impressionist* reader; an impressionist reader of what is *not* an impressionist picture; a reader who overlooks the informing details or masses their sum improperly, and gets only a large, splashy, general effect—an effect which is not correct, and which is not warranted by the particulars placed before me—particulars which I did not examine, and whose meanings I did not cautiously and carefully estimate. It is an effect which is some thirty-five or forty times finer than the reality, and is therefore a great deal better and more valuable than the reality; and so, I ought never to hunt up the reality, but stay miles away from it, and thus preserve undamaged my own private mighty Niagara tumbling out of the vault of heaven, and my own ineffable Taj, built of tinted mists upon jeweled arches of rainbows supported by colonnades of moonlight. It is a mistake for a person with an unregulated imagination to go and look at an illustrious world's wonder.

I suppose that many, many years ago I gathered the idea that the Taj's place in the achievements of man was exactly the place of the ice-storm in the achievements of Nature; that the Taj represented man's supremest possibility in the creation of grace and beauty and exquisiteness and splendor, just as the ice-storm represents Nature's supremest possibility in the combination of those same qualities. I do not know how long ago that idea was bred in me, but I know that I cannot remember back to a time when the thought of either of these symbols of gracious and unapproachable perfection did not at once suggest the other. If I thought of the ice-storm, the Taj rose before me divinely beautiful; if I thought of the Taj, with its encrustings and inlayings of jewels, the vision of the ice-storm rose. And so, to me, all these years, the Taj has had no rival among the temples and palaces of men, none that even remotely approached it—it was man's architectural ice-storm.

Here in London the other night I was talking with some Scotch and English friends, and I mentioned the ice-storm, using it as a figure—a figure which failed, for none of them had heard of the ice-storm. One gentleman, who was very familiar with American literature, said he had never seen it mentioned in any book. That is strange. And I, myself, was not able to say that I had seen it mentioned in a book; and yet the autumn foliage, with all other American scenery, has received full and competent attention.

The oversight is strange, for in America the ice-storm is an event. And it is not an event which one is careless about. When it comes, the news flies from room to room in the house, there are bangings on the doors, and shoutings, "The ice-storm! the ice-storm!" and even the laziest sleepers throw off the covers and join the rush for the windows. The ice-storm occurs in midwinter, and usually its enchantments are wrought in the silence and the darkness of the night. A fine drizzling rain falls hour after hour upon the naked twigs and branches of the trees, and as it falls it freezes. In time the trunk and every branch and twig are incased in hard pure ice; so that the tree looks like a skeleton tree made all of glass— glass that is crystal-clear. All along the under side of every branch and twig is a comb of little icicles—the frozen drip. Sometimes these pendants do not quite amount to icicles, but are round beads—frozen tears.

The weather clears, toward dawn, and leaves a brisk, pure atmosphere and a sky without a shred of cloud in it— and everything is still, there is not a breath of wind. The dawn breaks and spreads, the news of the storm goes about the house, and the little and the big, in wraps and blankets, flock to the window and press together there, and gaze intently out upon the great white ghost in the grounds, and nobody says a word, nobody stirs. All are waiting; they know what is coming, and they are waiting—waiting for the miracle. The minutes drift on and on and on, with not a sound but the ticking of the clock; at last the sun fires a sudden sheaf of rays into the ghostly tree and turns it into a white splendor of glittering diamonds. Everybody catches his breath, and feels a swelling in his throat and a moisture in his eyes—but waits again; for he knows what is coming; there is more yet. The sun climbs higher, and still higher, flooding the tree from its loftiest spread of branches to its lowest, turning it to a glory of white fire; then in a moment, without warning, comes the great miracle, the supreme miracle, the miracle without its fellow in the earth; a gust of wind sets every branch and twig to swaying, and in an instant turns the whole white tree into a spouting and spraying explosion of flashing gems of every conceivable color; and there it stands and sways this way and that, flash! flash! flash! a dancing and glancing world of rubies, emeralds, diamonds, sapphires, the most radiant spectacle, the most blinding spectacle, the divinest, the most exquisite, the most intoxicating vision of fire and color and intolerable and unimaginable splendor that ever any eye has rested upon in this world, or will ever rest upon outside of the gates of heaven.

By all my senses, all my faculties, I know that the ice-storm is Nature's supremest achievement in the domain of the superb and the beautiful; and by my reason, at least, I know that the Taj is man's ice-storm.

In the ice-storm every one of the myriad ice-beads pendent from twig and branch is an individual gem, and changes color with every motion caused by the wind; each tree carries a million, and a forest-front exhibits the splendors of the single tree multiplied by a thousand.

It occurs to me now that I have never seen the ice-storm put upon canvas, and have not heard that any painter has tried to do it. I wonder why that is. Is it that paint cannot counterfeit the intense blaze of a sun-flooded jewel? There should be, and must be, a reason, and a good one, why the most enchanting sight that Nature has created has been neglected by the brush.

Often, the surest way to convey misinformation is to tell the strict truth. The describers of the Taj have used the word *gem* in its strictest sense—its scientific sense. In that sense it is a mild word, and promises but little to the eye— nothing bright, nothing brilliant, nothing sparkling, nothing splendid in the way of color. It *accurately* describes the sober and unobtrusive gem-work of the Taj; that is, to the very highly educated one person in a thousand; but it most falsely describes it to the 999. But the 999 are the people who ought to be especially taken care of, and to them it does not mean quiet-colored designs wrought in carnelians, or agates, or such things; they know the word in its wide and ordinary sense only, and so to them it means diamonds and rubies and opals and their kindred, and the moment their eyes fall upon it in print they see a vision of glorious colors clothed in fire.

These describers are writing for the "general," and so, in order to make sure of being understood, they ought to use words in their ordinary sense, or else explain. The word *fountain* means one thing in Syria, where there is but a handful of people; it means quite another thing in North America, where there are seventy-five million. If I were describing some Syrian scenery, and should exclaim, "Within the nar- row space of a quarter of a mile square I saw, in the glory of the flooding moonlight, two hundred noble fountains— imagine the spectacle!" the North American would have a vision of clustering columns of water soaring aloft, bending over in graceful arches, bursting in beaded spray and raining white fire in the moonlight—and he would be deceived. But the Syrian would not be deceived; he would merely see two

hundred fresh-water springs—two hundred drowsing pud-
dles, as level and unpretentious and unexcited as so many
door-mats, and even with the help of the moonlight he would
not lose his grip in the presence of the exhibition. My word
"fountain" would be correct; it would speak the strict truth;
and it would convey the strict truth to the handful of Syrians,
and the strictest misinformation to the North American millions. With their gems—and gems—and more gems—and
gems again—and still other gems—the describers of the Taj
are within their legal but not their moral rights; they are
dealing in the strictest scientific truth; and in doing it they
succeed to admiration in telling "what ain't so."

Chapter XXIV

SATAN (impatiently) to NEW-COMER. The trouble with you Chicago people is, that you think you are the best people down here; whereas you are merely the most numerous.

—Pudd'nhead Wilson's New Calendar.

WE wandered contentedly around here and there in India; to Lahore, among other places, where the Lieutenant-Governor lent me an elephant. This hospitality stands out in my experiences in a stately isolation. It was a fine elephant, affable, gentlemanly, educated, and I was not afraid of it. I even rode it with confidence through the crowded lanes of the native city, where it scared all the horses out of their senses, and where children were always just escaping its feet. It took the middle of the road in a fine, independent way, and left it to the world to get out of the way or take the consequences. I am used to being afraid of collisions when I ride or drive, but when one is on top of an elephant that feeling is absent. I could have ridden in comfort through a regiment of runaway teams. I could easily learn to prefer an elephant to any other vehicle, partly because of that immunity from collisions, and partly because of the fine view one has from up there, and partly because of the dignity one feels in that high place, and partly because one can look in at the windows and see what is going on privately among the family. The Lahore horses were used to elephants, but they were rapturously afraid of them just the same. It seemed curious. Perhaps the better they know the elephant the more they respect him in that peculiar way. In our own case we are not afraid of dynamite till we get acquainted with it.

We drifted as far as Rawal Pindi, away up on the Afghan frontier—I think it was the Afghan frontier, but it may have been Herzegovina—it was around there somewhere—and down again to Delhi, to see the ancient architectural wonders there and in Old Delhi and not describe them, and also to see the scene of the illustrious assault, in the Mutiny days, when the British carried Delhi by storm, one of the marvels of history for impudent daring and immortal valor.

We had a refreshing rest, there in Delhi, in a great old mansion which possessed historical interest. It was built by a rich Englishman who had become orientalized—so much so that he had a zenana. But he was a broad-minded man, and remained so. To please his harem he built a mosque; to please himself he built an English church. That kind of a man will arrive, somewhere. In the Mutiny days the mansion was the British general's headquarters. It stands in a great garden—oriental fashion—and about it are many noble trees. The trees harbor monkeys; and they are monkeys of a watchful and enterprising sort, and not much troubled with fear. They invade the house whenever they get a chance, and carry off everything they don't want. One morning the master of the house was in his bath, and the window was open. Near it stood a pot of yellow paint and a brush. Some monkeys appeared in the window; to scare them away, the gentleman threw his sponge at them. They did not scare at all; they jumped into the room and threw yellow paint all over him from the brush, and drove him out; then they painted the walls and the floor and the tank and the windows and the furniture yellow, and were in the dressing-room painting that when help arrived and routed them.

Two of these creatures came into my room in the early morning, through a window whose shutters I had left open, and when I woke one of them was before the glass brushing his hair, and the other one had my note-book, and was reading a page of humorous notes and crying. I did not mind the one with the hair-brush, but the conduct of the other one hurt me; it hurts me yet. I threw something at him, and that was wrong, for my host had told me that the monkeys were best left alone. They threw everything at me that they could lift, and then went into the bathroom to get some more things, and I shut the door on them.

At Jeypore, in Rajputana, we made a considerable stay. We were not in the native city, but several miles from it, in the small European official suburb. There were but few Europeans—only fourteen—but they were all kind and hospitable, and it amounted to being at home. In Jeypore we found again what we had found all about India—that while the Indian servant is in his way a very real treasure, he will sometimes bear watching, and the Englishman watches him. If he sends him on an errand, he wants more than the man's word for it that he did the errand. When fruit and vegetables were sent to us, a "chit" came with them—a receipt for us to sign; otherwise the things might not arrive. If a gentleman sent up his carriage, the chit stated "from" such-and-such an hour "to" such-and-such an hour—which made it unhandy for the coachman and his two or three subordinates to put us off with a part of the allotted time and devote the rest of it to a lark of their own.

We were pleasantly situated in a small two-storied inn, in a large empty compound which was surrounded by a mud wall as high as a man's head. The inn was kept by nine Hindu brothers, its owners. They lived, with their families, in a one-storied building within the compound, but off to one side, and there was always a long pile of their little comely brown children loosely stacked in its veranda, and a detachment of the parents wedged among them, smoking the hookah or the howdah, or whatever they call it. By the veranda stood a palm, and a monkey lived in it, and led a lonesome life, and always looked sad and weary, and the crows bothered him a good deal.

The inn cow poked about the compound and emphasized the secluded and country air of the place, and there was a dog of no particular breed, who was always present in the compound, and always asleep, always stretched out baking in the sun and adding to the deep tranquillity and reposeful-ness of the place, when the crows were away on business. White-draperied servants were coming and going all the time, but they seemed only spirits, for their feet were bare and made no sound. Down the lane a piece lived an elephant in the shade of a noble tree, and rocked and rocked, and reached about with his trunk, begging of his brown mistress or fum-bling the children playing at his feet. And there were camels about, but they go on velvet feet, and were proper to the silence and serenity of the surroundings.

The Satan mentioned at the head of this chapter was not our Satan, but the other one. Our Satan was lost to us. In these later days he had passed out of our life—lamented by me, and sincerely. I was missing him; I am missing him yet, after all these months. He was an astonishing creature to fly around and do things. He didn't always do them quite right, but he *did* them, and did them suddenly. There was no time wasted. You would say:

"Pack the trunks and bags, Satan."

"Wair good" (very good).

Then there would be a brief sound of thrashing and

slashing and humming and buzzing, and a spectacle as of a whirlwind spinning gowns and jackets and coats and boots and things through the air, and then—with bow and touch: "Awready, master."

It was wonderful. It made one dizzy. He crumpled dresses a good deal, and he had no particular plan about the work—at first—except to put each article into the trunk it didn't belong in. But he soon reformed, in this matter. Not entirely; for, to the last, he would cram into the satchel sacred to literature any odds and ends of rubbish that he couldn't find a handy place for elsewhere. When threatened with death for this, it did not trouble him; he only looked pleasant, saluted with soldierly grace, said "Wair good," and did it again next day.

He was always busy; kept the rooms tidied up, the boots polished, the clothes brushed, the wash-basin full of clean water, my dress-clothes laid out and ready for the lecture-hall an hour ahead of time; and he dressed me from head to heel in spite of my determination to do it myself, according to my life-long custom.

He was a born boss, and loved to command, and to jaw and dispute with inferiors and harry them and bullyrag them. He was fine at the railway-station—yes, he was at his finest there. He would shoulder and plunge and paw his violent way through the packed multitude of natives with nineteen coolies at his tail, each bearing a trifle of luggage—one a trunk, another a parasol, another a shawl, another a fan, and so on; one article to each, and the longer the procession, the better he was suited—and he was sure to make for some engaged sleeper and begin to hurl the owner's things out of it, swearing that it was ours and that there had been a mistake. Arrived at our own sleeper, he would undo the bedding-bundles and make the beds and put everything to rights and shipshape in two minutes; then put his head out at a window and have a restful good time abusing his gang of coolies and disputing their bill until we arrived and made him pay them and stop his noise.

Speaking of noise, he certainly was the noisiest little devil in India—and that is saying much, very much, indeed. I loved him for his noise, but the family detested him for it. They could not abide it; they could not get reconciled to it. It humiliated them. As a rule, when we got within six hundred yards of one of those big railway-stations, a mighty racket of screaming and shrieking and shouting and storming would break upon us, and I would be happy to myself, and the family would say, with shame:

"There—that's Satan. Why *do* you keep him?"

And, sure enough, there in the whirling midst of fifteen hundred wondering people we would find that little scrap of a creature gesticulating like a spider with the colic, his black eyes snapping, his fez-tassel dancing, his jaws pouring out floods of billingsgate upon his gang of beseeching and astonished coolies.

I loved him; I couldn't help it; but the family—why, they could hardly speak of him with patience. To this day I regret his loss, and wish I had him back; but they—it is different with them. He was a native, and came from Surat. Twenty degrees of latitude lay between his birthplace and Manuel's and fifteen hundred between their ways and characters and dispositions. I only liked Manuel, but I loved Satan. This latter's real name was intensely Indian. I could not quite get the hang of it, but it sounded like Bunder Rao Ram Chunder Clam Chowder. It was too long for handy use, anyway; so I reduced it.

When he had been with us two or three weeks, he began to make mistakes which I had difficulty in patching up for him. Approaching Benares one day, he got out of the train to see if he could get up a misunderstanding with somebody, for it had been a weary, long journey and he wanted to freshen up. He found what he was after, but kept up his pow-wow a shade too long and got left. So there we were in a strange city and no chambermaid. It was awkward for us, and we told him he must not do so any more. He saluted and said in his dear, pleasant way, "Wair good." Then at Lucknow he got drunk. I said it was a fever, and got the family's compassion and solicitude aroused; so they gave him a teaspoonful of liquid quinine and it set his vitals on fire. He made several grimaces which gave me a better idea of the Lisbon earthquake than any I have ever got of it from paintings and descriptions. His drunk was still portentously solid next morning, but I could have pulled him through with the family if he would only have taken another spoonful of that remedy; but no, although he was stupefied, his memory still had flickerings of life; so he smiled a divinely dull smile and said, fumblingly saluting:

"Scoose me, mem Saheb, scoose me, Missy Saheb; Satan not prefer it, please."

Then some instinct revealed to them that he was drunk. They gave him prompt notice that next time this happened he must go. He got out a maudlin and most gentle "Wair good," and saluted indefinitely.

Only one short week later he fell again. And oh, sorrow! not in a hotel this time, but in an English gentleman's private house. And in Agra, of all places. So he had to go. When I told him, he said patiently, "Wair good," and made his parting salute, and went out from us to return no more forever. Dear me! I would rather have lost a hundred angels than that one poor lovely devil. What style he used to put on, in a swell hotel or in a private house—snow-white muslin from his chin to his bare feet, a crimson sash embroidered with gold thread around his waist, and on his head a great sea-green turban like to the turban of the Grand Turk.

He was not a liar, but he will become one if he keeps on. He told me once that he used to crack cocoanuts with his teeth when he was a boy; and when I asked how he got them into his mouth, he said he was upward of six feet high at that time, and had an unusual mouth. And when I followed him up and asked him what had become of that other foot, he said a house fell on him and he was never able to get his stature back again. Swervings like these from the strict line of fact often beguile a truthful man on and on until he eventually becomes a liar.

His successor was a Mohammedan, Sahadat Mohammed Khan; very dark, very tall, very grave. He went always in flowing masses of white, from the top of his big turban down to his bare feet. His voice was low. He glided about in a noiseless way, and looked like a ghost. He was competent and satisfactory. But where he was, it seemed always Sunday. It was not so in Satan's time.

Jeypore is intensely Indian, but it has two or three features which indicate the presence of European science and European interest in the weal of the common public, such as the liberal water-supply furnished by great works built at the state's expense; good sanitation, resulting in a degree of healthfulness unusually high for India; a noble pleasure garden, with privileged days for women; schools for the instruction of native youth in advanced art, both ornamental and utilitarian; and a new and beautiful palace stocked with a museum of extraordinary interest and value. Without the Maharaja's sympathy and purse these beneficences could not have been created; but he is a man of wide views and large generosities, and all such matters find hospitality with him.

We drove often to the city from the hotel Kaiser-i-Hind, a journey which was always full of interest, both night and day, for that country road was never quiet, never empty, but was always India in motion, always a streaming flood of brown people clothed in smouchings from the rainbow, a tossing and moiling flood, happy, noisy, a charming and satisfying confusion of strange human and strange animal life and equally strange and outlandish vehicles.

And the city itself is a curiosity. Any Indian city is that, but this one is not like any other that we saw. It is shut up in a lofty turreted wall; the main body of it is divided into six parts by perfectly straight streets that are more than a hundred feet wide; the blocks of houses exhibit a long frontage of the most taking architectural quaintnesses, the straight lines being broken everywhere by pretty little balconies, pillared and highly ornamented, and other cunning and cozy and inviting perches and projections, and many of the fronts are curiously pictured by the brush, and the whole of them have the soft rich tint of strawberry ice-cream. One cannot look down the far stretch of the chief street and persuade himself that these are real houses, and that it is all out-of-doors—the impression that it is an unreality, a picture, a scene in a theater, is the only one that will take hold.

Then there came a great day when this illusion was more pronounced than ever. A rich Hindu had been spending a fortune upon the manufacture of a crowd of idols and accompanying paraphernalia whose purpose was to illustrate scenes in the life of his especial god or saint, and this fine show was to be brought through the town in processional state at ten in the morning. As we passed through the great public pleasure garden on our way to the city we found it crowded with natives. That was one sight. Then there was another. In the midst of the spacious lawns stands the palace which contains the museum—a beautiful construction of stone which shows arched colonnades, one above another, and receding, terrace-fashion, toward the sky. Every one of these terraces, all the way to the top one, was packed and jammed with natives. One must try to imagine those solid masses of splendid color, one above another, up and up, against the blue sky, and the Indian sun turning them all to beds of fire and flame.

Later, when we reached the city, and glanced down the chief avenue, smoldering in its crushed-strawberry tint, those splendid effects were repeated; for every balcony, and every fanciful bird-cage of a snuggery countersunk in the house-fronts, and all the long lines of roofs, were crowded with people, and each crowd was an explosion of brilliant color.

Then the wide street itself, away down and down and down into the distance, was alive with gorgeously clothed people—not still, but moving, swaying, drifting, eddying, a delirious display of all colors and all shades of color, delicate, lovely, pale, soft, strong, stunning, vivid, brilliant, a sort of storm of sweet-pea blossoms passing on the wings of a hurricane; and presently, through this storm of color, came swaying and swinging the majestic elephants, clothed in their Sunday best of gaudinesses, and the long procession of fanciful trucks freighted with their groups of curious and costly images, and then the long rear-guard of stately camels, with their picturesque riders.

For color, and picturesqueness, and novelty, and outlandishness, and sustained interest and fascination, it was the most satisfying show I had ever seen, and I suppose I shall not have the privilege of looking upon its like again.

Chapter XXV

In the first place God made idiots. This was for practice.
Then He made School Boards.
—Pudd'nhead Wilson's New Calender.

S UPPOSE we applied no more ingenuity to the instruction
of deaf and dumb and blind children than we sometimes
apply in our American public schools to the instruction of
children who are in possession of all their faculties? The result
would be that the deaf and dumb and blind would acquire
nothing. They would live and die as ignorant as bricks and
stones. The methods used in the asylums are rational. The
teacher exactly measures the child's capacity, to begin with;
and from thence onward the tasks imposed are nicely gaged
to the gradual development of that capacity; the tasks keep
pace with the steps of the child's progress, they don't jump
miles and leagues ahead of it by irrational caprice and land in
vacancy—according to the average public-school plan. In the
public school, apparently, they teach the child to spell cat,
then ask it to calculate an eclipse; when it can read words of
two syllables, they require it to explain the circulation of the
blood; when it reaches the head of the infant class they bully

it with conundrums that cover the domain of universal knowledge. This sounds extravagant—and is; yet it goes no great way beyond the facts.

I received a curious letter one day, from the Punjab (you must pronounce it Pun*jawb*). The handwriting was excellent, and the wording was English—English, and yet not exactly English. The style was easy and smooth and flowing, yet there was something subtly foreign about it—something tropically ornate and sentimental and rhetorical. It turned out to be the work of a Hindu youth, the holder of a humble clerical billet in a railway office. He had been educated in one of the numerous colleges of India. Upon inquiry I was told that the country was full of young fellows of his like. They had been educated away up to the snow-summits of learning—and the market for all this elaborate cultivation was minutely out of proportion to the vastness of the product. This market consisted of some thousands of small clerical posts under the government—the supply of material for it was multitudinous. If this youth with the flowing style and the blossoming English was occupying a small railway clerk-ship, it meant that there were hundreds and hundreds as capable as he, or he would be in a high place; and it certainly meant that there were thousands whose education and capacity had fallen a little short, and that they would have to go *without* places. Apparently, then, the colleges of India were doing what our high schools have long been doing—richly oversupplying the market for highly educated service; and thereby doing a damage to the scholar, and through him to the country.

At home I once made a speech deploring the injuries inflicted by the high school in making handicrafts distasteful to boys who would have been willing to make a living at trades and agriculture if they had but had the good luck to stop with the common school. But I made no converts. Not one, in a community overrun with educated idlers who were above following their fathers' mechanical trades, yet could find no market for their book-knowledge. The same mail that brought me the letter from the Punjab, brought also a little book published by Messrs. Thacker, Spink & Co., of Calcutta, which interested me, for both its preface and its contents treated of this matter of over-education. In the preface occurs this paragraph from the Calcutta *Review*. For "government office" read "dry-goods clerkship" and it will fit more than one region of America:

> The education that we give makes the boys a little less clownish in their manners, and more intelligent when spoken to by strangers. On the other hand, it has made them less contented with their lot in life, and less willing to work with their hands. The form which discontent takes in this country is not of a healthy kind; for the Natives of India consider that the only occupation worthy of an educated man is that of a writership in some office, and especially in a government office. The village school-boy goes back to the plow with the greatest reluctance; and the town school-boy carries the same discontent and inefficiency into his father's workshop. Sometimes these ex-students positively refuse at first to work; and more than once parents have openly expressed their regret that they ever allowed their sons to be inveigled to school.

The little book which I am quoting from is called *Indo-Anglian Literature,* and is well stocked with "babu" English— clerkly English, booky English, acquired in the schools. Some of it is very funny—almost as funny, perhaps, as what you and I produce when we try to write in a language not our own; but much of it is surprisingly correct and free. If I were going to quote *good* English—but I am not. India is well stocked with natives who speak it and write it as well as the best of us. I merely wish to show some of the quaint imperfect attempts at the use of our tongue. There are many letters in the book; poverty imploring help—bread, money, kindness, office—generally an office, a clerkship, some way to get food and a rag out of the applicant's unmarketable education; and food not for himself alone, but sometimes for a dozen helpless relations in addition to his own family; for those people are astonishingly unselfish, and admirably faithful to their ties of kinship. Among us I think there is nothing approaching it. Strange as some of these wailing and supplicating letters are, humble and even groveling as some of them are, and quaintly funny and confused as a goodly number of them are, there is still a pathos about them, as a rule, that checks the rising laugh and reproaches it. In the following letter "father" is not to be read literally. In Ceylon a little native beggar-girl embarrassed me by calling me father, although I knew she was mistaken. I was so new that I did not know that she was merely following the custom of the dependent and the supplicant.

> SIR:
>
> I pray please to give me some action (work) for I am very poor boy I have no one to help me even so father for it so it seemed in thy good sight, you give the Telegraph Office, and another work what is your wish I am very poor boy, this understand what is your wish you my father I am your son this understand what is your wish.
>
> Your Sirvent, P.C.B.

Through ages of debasing oppression suffered by these people at the hands of their native rulers, they come legitimately by the attitude and language of fawning and flattery, and one must remember this in mitigation when passing judgment upon the native character. It is common in these letters to find the petitioner furtively trying to get at the white man's soft religious side; even this poor boy baits his hook with a macerated Bible text in the hope that it may catch something if all else fail.

Here is an application for the post of instructor in English to some children:

> My Dear Sir or Gentleman, that your Petitioner has much qualification in the Language of English to instruct the young boys; I was given to understand that your of suitable children has to acquire the knowledge of English language.

As a sample of the flowery Eastern style, I will take a sentence or two from a long letter written by a young native to the Lieutenant-Governor of Bengal—an application for employment:

> HONORED AND MUCH RESPECTED SIR:
> I hope your honor will condescend to hear the tale of this poor creature. I shall overflow with gratitude at this mark of your royal condescension. The birdlike happiness has flown away from my nestlike heart and has not hitherto returned from the period whence the rose of my father's life suffered the autumnal breath of death, in plain English he passed through the gates of Grave, and from that hour the phantom of delight has never danced before me.

It is all school-English, book-English, you see; and good enough, too, all things considered. If the native boy had but that one study he would shine, he would dazzle, no doubt. But that is not the case. He is situated as are our public-school children—loaded down with an over-freightage of other studies; and frequently they are as far beyond the actual point of progress reached by him and suited to the stage of development attained, as could be imagined by the insanest fancy.

Apparently—like our public-school boy—he must work, work, work, in school and out, and play but little. Apparently—like our public-school boy—his "education" consists in learning *things*, not the meaning of them; he is fed upon the husks, not the corn. From several essays written by native school-boys in answer to the question of how they spend their day, I select one—the one which goes most into detail:

> 66. At the break of day I rises from my own bed and finish my daily duty, then I employ myself till 8 o'clock, after which I employ myself to bathe, then take for my body some sweet meat, and just at 9½ I came to school to attend my class duty, then, at 2½ P.M. I returned from school and engage myself to do my natural duty, then I engage for a quarter to take my tiffin, then I study till 5 P.M., after which I began to play anything which comes in my head. After 8½ half pass to eight we are began to sleep, before sleeping I told a constable just 11 o' he came and rose us from half pass eleven we began to read still morning.

It is not perfectly clear, now that I come to cipher upon it. He gets up at about five in the morning, or along there somewhere, and goes to bed about fifteen or sixteen hours afterward—that much of it seems straight; but why he should rise again three hours later and resume his studies till morning is puzzling.

I think it is because he is studying history. History requires a world of time and bitter hard work when your "education" is no further advanced than the cat's; when you are merely stuffing yourself with a mixed-up mess of empty names and random incidents and elusive dates, which no one teaches you how to interpret, and which, uninterpreted, pay you not a farthing's value for your waste of time. Yes, I think he had to get up at half past 11 P.M. in order to be sure to be perfect with his history lesson by noon. With results as follows—from a Calcutta school examination:

Q. *Who was Cardinal Wolsey?*

Cardinal Wolsey was an Editor of a paper named *North Briton*. No. 45 of his publication he charged the King of uttering a lie from the throne. He was arrested and cast into prison; and after releasing went to France.

3. As Bishop of York but died in disentry in a church on his way to be blockheaded.

8. Cardinal Wolsey was the son of Edward IV., after his father's death he himself ascended the throne at the age of (10) ten only, but when he surpassed or when he was fallen in his twenty years of age at that time he wished to make a journey in his countries under him, but he was opposed by his mother to do journey, and according to his mother's example he remained in the home, and then became King. After many times obstacles and many confusion he become King and afterward his brother.

There is probably not a word of truth in that.

Q. *What is the meaning of Ich Dien?*

10. An honor conferred on the first or eldest sons of English Sovereigns. It is nothing more than some feathers.

11. Ich Dien was the word which was written on the feathers of the blind King who came to fight, being interlaced with the bridles of the horse.

13. Ich Dien is a title given to Henry VII. by the Pope of Rome, when he forwarded the Reformation of Cardinal Wolsy to Rome, and for this reason he was called Commander of the faith.

A dozen or so of this kind of insane answers are quoted in the book from that examination. Each answer is sweeping proof, all by itself, that the person uttering it was pushed ahead of where he belonged when he was put into history; proof that he had been put to the task of acquiring history before he had had a single lesson in the *art* of acquiring it, which is the equivalent of dumping a pupil into geometry before he has learned the progressive steps which lead up to it and make its acquirement possible. Those Calcutta novices had no business with history. There was no excuse for examining them in it, no excuse for exposing them and their teachers. They were totally empty; there was nothing to "examine."

Helen Keller has been dumb, stone deaf, and stone blind, ever since she was a little baby a year and a half old; and now at sixteen years of age this miraculous creature, this wonder of all ages, passes the Harvard University examination in Latin, German, French history, *belles-lettres*, and such things, and does it brilliantly, too, not in a commonplace fashion. She doesn't know merely *things*, she is splendidly familiar with the *meanings* of them. When she writes an essay on a Shakespearean character, her English is fine and strong, her grasp of the subject is the grasp of one who *knows*, and her page is electric with light. Has Miss Sullivan taught her by the methods of India and the American public school? No, oh, no; for then she would be deafer and dumber and blinder than she was before. It is a pity that we can't educate all the children in the asylums.

To continue the Calcutta exposure:

What is the meaning of a Sheriff?
25. Sheriff is a post opened in the time of John. The duty of Sheriff here in Calcutta, to look out and catch those carriages which is rashly driven out by the coachman; but it is a high post in England.
26. Sheriff was the English bill of common prayer.

27. The man with whom the accusative persons are placed is called Sheriff.

28. Sheriff—Latin term for "shrub," we called broom, worn by the first earl of Enjue, as an emblem of humility when they went to the pilgrimage, and from this their hairs took their crest and sur name.

29. Sheriff is a kind of titlous sect of people, as Barons, Nobles, etc.

30. *Sheriff*, a tittle given on those persons who were respective and pious in England.

The students were examined in the following bulky matters: Geometry, the Solar Spectrum, the Habeas Corpus Act, the British Parliament, and in Metaphysics they were asked to trace the progress of skepticism from Descartes to Hume. It is within bounds to say that some of the results were astonishing. Without doubt, there were students present who justified their teachers' wisdom in introducing them to these studies; but the fact is also evident that others had been pushed into these studies to waste their time over them when they could have been profitably employed in hunting smaller game. Under the head of Geometry, one of the answers is this:

49. The whole BD = the whole CA, and so-so-so-so-so—so.

To me this is cloudy, but I was never well up in geometry. That was the only effort made among the five students who appeared for examination in geometry; the other four wailed and surrendered without a fight. They are piteous wails, too, wails of despair; and one of them is an eloquent reproach; it comes from a poor fellow who has been laden beyond his strength by a stupid teacher, and is eloquent in spite of the poverty of its English. The poor chap finds himself required to explain riddles which even Sir Isaac Newton was not able to understand.

50. Oh my dear father examiner you my father and you kindly give a number of pass you my great father.

51. I am a poor boy and have no means to support my mother and two brothers who are suffering much for want of food. I get four rupees monthly from charity fund of this place, from which I send two rupees for their support, and keep two for my own support. Father, if I relate the unlucky circumstance under which we are placed, then, I think, you will not be able to suppress the tender tear.

52. Sir which Sir Isaac Newton and other experienced mathematicians cannot understand I being third of Entrance Class can understand these which is too impossible to imagine. And my examiner also has put very tiresome and very heavy propositions to prove.

We must remember that these pupils had to do their thinking in one language, and express themselves in another and alien one. It was a heavy handicap. I have by me *English as She is Taught*—a collection of American examinations made in the public schools of Brooklyn by one of the teachers, Miss Caroline B. Le Row. An extract or two from its pages will show that when the American pupil is using but one language, and that one his own, his performance is no whit better than his Indian brother's:

ON HISTORY

Christopher Columbus was called the father of his Country. Queen Isabella of Spain sold her watch and chain and other millinery so that Columbus could discover America.

The Indian wars were very desecrating to the country.

The Indians pursued their warfare by hiding in the bushes and then scalping them.

Captain John Smith has been styled the father of his country. His life was saved by his daughter Pochahantas.

The Puritans found an insane asylum in the wilds of America.

The Stamp Act was to make everybody stamp all materials so they should be null and void.

Washington died in Spain almost broken-hearted. His remains were taken to the cathedral in Havana.

Gorilla warfare was where men rode on gorillas.

In Brooklyn, as in India, they examine a pupil, and when they find out he doesn't know anything, they put him into literature, or geometry, or astronomy, or government, or something like that, so that he can properly display the assification of the whole system:

On Literature

Bracebridge Hall was written by Henry Irving.

Edgar A. Poe was a very curdling writer.

Beowulf wrote the Scriptures.

Ben Johnson survived Shakespeare in some respects.

In the *Canterbury Tale* it gives account of King Alfred on his way to the shrine of Thomas Bucket.

Chaucer was the father of English pottery.

Chaucer was succeeded by H. Wads. Longfellow.

We will finish with a couple of samples of "literature,"— one from America, the other from India. The first is a Brooklyn public-school boy's attempt to turn a few verses of the *Lady of the Lake* into prose. You will have to concede that he did it:

The man who rode on the horse performed the whip and an instrument made of steel alone with strong ardor not diminishing, for, being tired from the time passed with hard labor overworked with anger and ignorant with weariness, while every breath for labor he drew with cries full of sorrow, the young deer made imperfect who worked hard filtered in sight.

The following paragraph is from a little book which is famous in India—the biography of a distinguished Hindu judge, Onoocool Chunder Mookerjee; it was written by his nephew, and is unintentionally funny—in fact, exceedingly so. I offer here the closing scene. If you would like to sample the rest of the book, it can be had by applying to the publishers, Messrs. Thacker, Spink & Co., Calcutta:

And having said these words he hermetically sealed his lips not to open them again. All the well-known doctors of Calcutta that could be procured for a man of his position and wealth were brought—Doctors Payne, Fayrer, and Nilmadhub Mookerjee and others; they did what they could do, with their puissance and knack of medical knowledge, but it proved after all as if to milk the ram! His wife and children had not the mournful consolation to hear his last words; he remained *sotto voce* for a few hours, and then was taken from us at 6.12 P.M. according to the caprice of God which passeth understanding.

Chapter XXVI

There are no people who are quite so vulgar as the over-refined ones.

—Pudd'nhead Wilson's New Calendar.

WE sailed from Calcutta toward the end of March; stopped a day at Madras; two or three days in Ceylon; then sailed westward on a long flight for Mauritius. From my diary:

April 7. We are far abroad upon the smooth waters of the Indian Ocean, now; it is shady and pleasant and peaceful under the vast spread of the awnings, and life is perfect again—ideal.

The difference between a river and a sea is, that the river looks fluid, and the sea solid—usually looks as if you could step out and walk on it.

The captain has this peculiarity—he cannot tell the truth in a plausible way. In this he is the very opposite of the austere Scot who sits midway of the table; *he* cannot tell a lie in an *un*plausible way. When the captain finishes a statement the passengers glance at each other privately, as who should say, "Do you believe that?" When the Scot finishes one, the look says, "How strange and interesting." The whole secret is in the manner and method of the two men. The captain is a little shy and diffident, and he states the simplest fact as if he were a little afraid of it, while the Scot delivers himself of the most abandoned lie with such an air of stern veracity that one is forced to believe it although one knows it isn't so. For instance, the Scot told about a pet flying-fish he once owned, that lived in a little fountain in his conservatory, and supported itself by catching birds and frogs and rats in the neighboring fields. It was plain that no one at the table doubted this statement.

By and by, in the course of some talk about customhouse annoyances, the captain brought out the following simple every-day incident, but through his infirmity of style managed to tell it in such a way that it got no credence. He said:

> I went ashore at Naples one voyage when I was in that trade, and stood around helping my passengers, for I could speak a little Italian. Two or three times, at intervals, the officer asked me if I had anything dutiable about me, and seemed more and more put out and disappointed every time I told him no. Finally, a passenger whom I had helped through asked me to come out and take something. I thanked him, but excused myself, saying I had taken a whisky just before I came ashore.
>
> It was a fatal admission. The officer at once made me pay sixpence import duty on the whisky—just from ship to shore, you see; and he fined me £5 for not declaring the goods, another £5 for falsely denying that I had anything dutiable about me, also £5 for concealing the goods, and £50 for smuggling, which is the maximum penalty for unlawfully bringing in goods under the value of sevenpence ha'penny. Altogether, sixty-five pounds sixpence for a little thing like that.

The Scot is always believed, yet he never tells anything but lies; whereas the captain is never believed, although he never tells a lie, so far as I can judge. If he should say his uncle was a male person, he would probably say it in such a way that nobody would believe it; at the same time the Scot could claim that he had a female uncle and not stir a doubt in anybody's mind. My own luck has been curious all my literary life; I never could tell a lie that anybody would doubt, nor a truth that anybody would believe.

Lots of pets on board—birds and things. In these far countries the white people do seem to run remarkably to pets. Our host in Cawnpore had a fine collection of birds—the finest we saw in a private house in India. And in Colombo, Dr. Murray's great compound and commodious bungalow were well populated with domesticated company from the woods: frisky little squirrels; a Ceylon mina walking sociably about the house; a small green parrot that whistled a single urgent note of call without motion of its beak, also chuckled; a monkey in a cage on the back veranda, and some more out in the trees; also a number of beautiful macaws in the trees; and various and sundry birds and animals of breeds not known to me. But no cat. Yet a cat would have liked that place.

April 9. Tea-planting is the great business in Ceylon, now. A passenger says it often pays forty per cent. on the investment. Says there is a boom.

April 10. The sea is a Mediterranean blue; and I believe that that is about the divinest color known to nature.

It is strange and fine—Nature's lavish generosities to her creatures. At least to all of them except man. For those that fly she has provided a home that is nobly spacious—a home which is forty miles deep and envelops the whole globe, and has not an obstruction in it. For those that swim she has provided a more than imperial domain—a domain which is miles deep and covers four-fifths of the globe. But as for man, she has cut him off with the mere odds and ends of the creation. She has given him the thin skin, the meager skin which is stretched over the remaining one-fifth—the naked bones stick up through it in most places. On the one-half of this domain he can raise snow, ice, sand, rocks, and nothing else. So the valuable part of his inheritance really consists of but a single fifth of the family estate; and out of it he has to grub hard to get enough to keep him alive and provide kings and soldiers and powder to extend the blessings of civilization with. Yet man, in his simplicity and complacency and inability to cipher, thinks Nature regards him as the important member of the family—in fact, her favorite. Surely, it must occur to even his dull head, sometimes, that she has a curious way of showing it.

Afternoon. The captain has been telling how, in one of his Arctic voyages, it was so cold that the mate's shadow froze fast to the deck and had to be ripped loose by main strength. And even then he got only about two-thirds of it back. Nobody said anything, and the captain went away. I think he is becoming disheartened. . . . Also, to be fair, there is another word of praise due to this ship's library: it contains no copy of the *Vicar of Wakefield*, that strange menagerie of complacent hypocrites and idiots, of theatrical cheap-john heroes and heroines, who are always showing off, of bad people who are not interesting, and good people who are fatiguing. A singular book. Not a sincere line in it, and not a character that invites respect; a book which is one long waste-pipe discharge of goody-goody puerilities and dreary moralities; a book which is full of pathos which revolts, and humor which grieves the heart. There are few things in literature that are more piteous, more pathetic, than the celebrated "humorous" incident of Moses and the spectacles.

Jane Austen's books, too, are absent from this library. Just that one omission alone would make a fairly good library out of a library that hadn't a book in it.

Customs in tropic seas. At five in the morning they pipe to wash down the decks, and at once the ladies who are sleeping there turn out and they and their beds go below. Then one after another the men come up from the bath in their pajamas, and walk the decks an hour or two with bare legs and bare feet. Coffee and fruit served. The ship cat and her kitten now appear and get about their toilets; next the barber comes and flays us on the breezy deck. Breakfast at nine-thirty, and the day begins. I do not know how a day could be more reposeful: no motion; a level blue sea; nothing in sight from horizon to horizon; the speed of the ship furnishes a cooling breeze; there is no mail to read and answer; no newspapers to excite you; no telegrams to fret you or fright you—the world is far, far away; it has ceased to exist for you—seemed a fading dream, along in the first days; has dissolved to an unreality now; it is gone from your mind with all its businesses and ambitions, its prosperities and disasters, its exultations and despairs, its joys and griefs and cares and worries. They are no concern of yours any more; they have gone out of your life; they are a storm which has passed and left a deep calm behind. The people group themselves about the decks in their snowy-white linen, and read, smoke, sew, play cards, talk, nap, and so on. In other ships the passengers are always ciphering about when they are going to arrive; out in these seas it is rare, very rare, to hear that subject broached. In other ships there is always an eager rush to the bulletin-board at noon to find out what the "run" has been; in these seas the bulletin seems to attract no interest; I have seen no one visit it; in thirteen days I have visited it only once. Then I happened to notice the figures of the day's run. On that day there happened to be talk, at dinner, about the speed of modern ships. I was the only passenger present who knew this ship's gait. Necessarily, the Atlantic custom of betting on the ship's run is not a custom here—nobody ever mentions it.

I myself am wholly indifferent as to when we are going to "get in"; if any one else feels interested in the matter he has not indicated it in my hearing. If I had my way we should never get in at all. This sort of sea-life is charged with an indestructible charm. There is no weariness, no fatigue, no worry, no responsibility, no work, no depression of spirits. There is nothing like this serenity, this comfort, this peace, this deep contentment, to be found anywhere on land. If I had my way I would sail on forever and never go to live on the solid ground again.

One of Kipling's ballads has delivered the aspect and sentiment of this bewitching sea correctly:

> The Injian Ocean sets an' smiles
> So sof', so bright, so bloomin' blue;
> There aren't a wave for miles an' miles
> Excep' the jiggle from the screw.

April 14. It turns out that the astronomical apprentice worked off a section of the Milky Way on me for the Magellan Clouds. A man of more experience in the business showed one of them to me last night. It was small and faint and delicate, and looked like the ghost of a bunch of white smoke left floating in the sky by an exploded bombshell.

Wednesday, April 15. Mauritius. Arrived and anchored off Port Louis 2 A.M. Rugged clusters of crags and peaks, green to their summits; from their bases to the sea a green plain with just tilt enough to it to make the water drain off. I believe it is in 56° E. and 22° S.—a hot, tropical country. The green plain has an inviting look; has scattering dwellings nestling among the greenery. Scene of the sentimental adventure of Paul and Virginia.

Island under French control—which means a community which depends upon quarantines, not sanitation, for its health.

Thursday, April 16. Went ashore in the forenoon at Port Louis, a little town, but with the largest variety of nationalities and complexions we have encountered yet. French, English, Chinese, Arabs, Africans with wool, blacks with straight hair, East Indians, half-white, quadroons—and great varieties in costumes and colors.

Took the train for Curepipe at one-thirty—two hours' run, gradually uphill. What a contrast, this frantic luxuriance of vegetation, with the arid plains of India; these architecturally picturesque crags and knobs and miniature mountains, with the monotony of the Indian dead-levels.

A native pointed out a handsome swarthy man of grave and dignified bearing, and said in an awed tone, "That is so-and-so; has held office of one sort or another under this government for thirty-seven years—he is known all over this whole island—and in the other countries of the world perhaps—who knows! One thing is certain; you can speak his name anywhere in this whole island, and you will find not one grown person that has not heard it. It is a wonderful thing to be so celebrated; yet look at him; it makes no change in him; he does not even seem to know it."

Curepipe (means Pincushion or Pegtown, probably). Sixteen miles (two hours) by rail from Port Louis. At each end of every roof and on the apex of every dormer window a wooden peg two feet high stands up; in some cases its top is blunt, in others the peg is sharp and looks like a toothpick. The passion for this humble ornament is universal.

Apparently, there has been only one prominent event in the history of Mauritius, and that one didn't happen. I refer to the romantic sojourn of Paul and Virginia here. It was that story that made Mauritius known to the world, made the name familiar to everybody, the geographical position of it to nobody.

A clergyman was asked to guess what was in a box on a table. It was a vellum fan painted with the shipwreck, and was *"one of Virginia's wedding gifts."*

April 18. This is the only country in the world where the stranger is not asked "How do you like this place?" This is indeed a large distinction. Here the citizen does the talking about the country himself; the stranger is not asked to help. You get all sorts of information. From one citizen you gather the idea that Mauritius was made first, and then heaven; and that heaven was copied after Mauritius. Another one tells you that this is an exaggeration; that the two chief villages, Port Louis and Curepipe, fall short of heavenly perfection; that nobody lives in Port Louis except upon compulsion, and that Curepipe is the wettest and rainiest place in the world. An English citizen said:

> In the early part of this century Mauritius was used by the French as a basis from which to operate against England's Indian merchantmen; so England captured the island and also the neighbor, Bourbon, to stop that annoyance. England gave Bourbon back; the government in London did not want any more possessions "in the West Indies." If the government had had a better quality of geography in stock it would not have wasted Bourbon in that foolish way. A big war will temporarily shut up the Suez Canal some day, and the English ships will have to go to India around the Cape of Good Hope again; then England will have to have Bourbon, and will take it.
>
> Mauritius was a Crown colony until twenty years ago, with a Governor appointed by the Crown and assisted by a Council appointed by himself; but Pope Hennessey came out

as Governor then, and he worked hard to get a part of the Council made elective, and succeeded. So now the whole Council is French, and in all ordinary matters of legislation they vote together and in the French interest, not the English. The English population is very slender; it has not votes enough to elect a legislator. Half a dozen rich French families elect the legislature. Pope Hennessey was an Irishman, a Catholic, a Home Ruler, M.P., a hater of England and the English, a very troublesome person and a serious encumbrance at Westminster; so it was decided to send him out to govern unhealthy countries, in hope that something would happen to him. But nothing did. The first experiment was not merely a failure, it was more than a failure. He proved to be more of a disease himself than any he was sent to encounter. The next experiment was here. The dark scheme failed again. It was an off season and there was nothing but measles here at the time. Pope Hennessey's health was not affected. He worked with the French and for the French and against the English, and he made the English very tired and the French very happy, and lived to have the joy of seeing the flag he served publicly hissed. His memory is held in worshipful reverence and affection by the French.

It is a land of extraordinary quarantine. They quarantine a ship for anything or for nothing; quarantine her for twenty, or even thirty days. They once quarantined a ship because her captain had had the smallpox when he was a boy. That and because he was English.

The population is very small; small to insignificance. The majority is East Indian; then mongrels; then negroes (descendants of the slaves of the French times); then French; then English. There was an American, but he is dead or mislaid. The mongrels are the result of all kinds of mixtures: black and white, mulatto and white, quadroon and white, octoroon and white. And so there is every shade of complexion; ebony, old mahogany, horse-chestnut, sorrel, molasses candy, clouded amber, clear amber, old-ivory white, new-ivory white, fish-belly white—this latter the leprous complexion frequent with the Anglo-Saxon long resident in tropical climates.

You wouldn't expect a person to be proud of being a Mauritian, now, would you? But it is so. The most of them have never been out of the island, and haven't read much or studied much, and they think the world consists of three principal countries—Judæa, France, and Mauritius; so they are very proud of belonging to one of the three grand divisions of the globe. They think that Russia and Germany are in England, and that England does not amount to much. They have heard vaguely about the United States and the equator, but think both of them are monarchies. They think Mount Peter Botte is the highest mountain in the world, and if you show one of them a picture of Milan Cathedral he will swell up with satisfaction and say that the idea of that jungle of spires was stolen from the forest of peg-tops and toothpicks that makes the roofs of Curepipe look so fine and prickly.

There is not much trade in books. The newspapers educate and entertain the people. Mainly the latter. They have two pages of large-print reading-matter—one of them English, the other French. The English page is a translation of the French one. The typography is super-extra primitive; in this quality it has not its equal anywhere. There is no proof-reader now; he is dead.

Where do they get matter to fill up a page in this little island lost in the wastes of the Indian Ocean? Oh, Madagascar. They discuss Madagascar and France. That is the bulk. Then they chock up the rest with advice to the government. Also, slurs upon the English administration. The papers are all owned and edited by creoles—French.

The language of the country is French. Everybody speaks it—has to. You have to know French—particularly mongrel French, the patois spoken by Tom, Dick, and Harry of the multiform complexions—or you can't get along.

This was a flourishing country in former days, for it made then and still makes the best sugar in the world; but first the Suez Canal severed it from the world and left it out in the cold, and next the beet-root sugar, helped by bounties, captured the European markets. Sugar is the life of Mauritius, and it is losing its grip. Its downward course was checked by the depreciation of the rupee—for the planter pays wages in rupees but sells his crop for gold—and the insurrection in Cuba and paralyzation of the sugar industry there have given our prices here a life-saving lift; but the outlook has nothing permanently favorable about it. It takes a year to mature the canes—on the high ground three and six months longer—and there is always a chance that the annual cyclone will rip the profit out of the crop. In recent times a cyclone took the whole crop, as you may say; and the island never saw a finer one. Some of the noblest sugar estates on the island are in deep difficulties. A dozen of them are investments of English capital; and the companies that own them are at work now, trying to settle up and get out with a saving of half the money they put in. You know, in these days, when a country begins to introduce the tea culture, it means that its own specialty has gone back on it. Look at Bengal; look at Ceylon. Well, they've begun to introduce the tea culture *here*.

Many copies of *Paul and Virginia* are sold every year in Mauritius. No other book is so popular here except the Bible. By many it is supposed to be a part of the Bible. All the missionaries work up their French on it when they come here to pervert the Catholic mongrel. It is the greatest story that was ever written about Mauritius, and the only one.

Chapter XXVII

The principal difference between a cat and a lie is that the cat has only nine lives.
—Pudd'nhead Wilson's New Calendar.

*A*PRIL 20.—The cyclone of 1892 killed and crippled hundreds of people; it was accompanied by a deluge of rain, which drowned Port Louis and *produced a water famine*. Quite true; for it burst the reservoir and the water-pipes; and for a time after the flood had disappeared there was much distress from want of water.

This is the only place in the world where *no* breed of matches can stand the damp. Only one match in sixteen will light.

The roads are hard and smooth; some of the compounds are spacious, some of the bungalows commodious, and the roadways are walled by tall bamboo hedges, trim and green and beautiful; and there are azalea hedges, too, both the white and the red; I never saw that before.

As to healthiness: I translate from to-day's (April 20) *Merchants' and Planters' Gazette*, from the article of a regular contributor, "Carminge," concerning the death of the nephew of a prominent citizen:

> Sad and lugubrious existence, this which we lead in Mauritius; I believe there is no other country in the world where one dies more easily than among us. The least indisposition becomes a mortal malady; a simple headache develops into meningitis; a cold into pneumonia, and presently, when we are least expecting it, death is a guest in our home.

This daily paper has a meteorological report which tells you what the weather was day before yesterday.

One is never pestered by a beggar or a peddler in this town, so far as I can see. This is pleasantly different from India.

April 22. To such as believe that the quaint product called French civilization would be an improvement upon the civilization of New Guinea and the like, the snatching of Madagascar and the laying on of French civilization there will be fully justified. But why did the English allow the French to have Madagascar? Did she respect a theft of a couple of centuries ago? Dear me, robbery by European nations of each other's territories has never been a sin, is not a sin to-day. To the several cabinets the several political establishments of the world are clothes-lines; and a large part of the official duty of these cabinets is to keep an eye on each other's wash and grab what they can of it as opportunity offers. All the territorial possessions of all the political establishments in the earth—including America, of course—consist of pilferings from other people's wash. No tribe, howsoever insignificant, and no nation, howsoever mighty, occupies a foot of land that was not stolen. When the English, the French, and the Spaniards reached America, the Indian tribes had been raiding each other's territorial clotheslines for ages, and every acre of ground in the continent had been stolen and restolen five hundred times. The English, the French, and the Spaniards went to work and stole it all over again; and when that was satisfactorily accomplished they went diligently to work and stole it from each other. In Europe and Asia and Africa every acre of ground has been stolen several millions of times. A crime persevered in a thousand centuries ceases to be a crime, and becomes a virtue. This is the law of custom, and custom supersedes all other forms of law. Christian governments are as frank to-day, as open and above-board, in discussing projects for raiding each other's clothes-lines as ever they were before the Golden Rule came smiling into this inhospitable world and couldn't get a night's lodging anywhere. In one hundred and fifty years England has beneficently retired garment after garment from the Indian lines, until there is hardly a rag of the original wash left dangling anywhere. In eight hundred years an obscure tribe of Muscovite savages has risen to the dazzling position of Land-Robber-in-Chief; she found a quarter of the world hanging out to dry on a hundred parallels of latitude, and she scooped in the whole wash. She keeps a sharp eye on a multitude of little lines that stretch along the northern boundaries of India, and every now and then she snatches a hip-rag or a pair of pajamas. It is England's prospective property, and Russia knows it; but Russia cares nothing for that. In fact, in our day, land-robbery, claim-jumping, is become a European governmental frenzy. Some have been hard at it in the borders of China, in Burma, in Siam, and the islands of the sea; and *all* have been at it in Africa. Africa has been as coolly divided up and portioned out among the gang as if they had bought it and paid for it. And now straightway they are beginning the old game again—to steal each other's grabbings. Germany found a vast slice of Central Africa with the English flag and the English missionary and the English trader scattered all over it, but with certain formalities neglected—no signs up, "Keep off the grass," "Trespassers forbidden," etc.—and she stepped in with a cold calm smile and put up the signs herself, and swept those English pioneers promptly out of the country.

There is a tremendous point there. It can be put into the form of a maxim: Get your formalities right—never mind about the moralities.

It was an impudent thing; but England had to put up with it. Now, in the case of Madagascar, the formalities had originally been observed, but by neglect they had fallen into desuetude ages ago. England should have snatched Madagascar from the French clothes-line. Without an effort she could have saved those harmless natives from the calamity of French civilization, and she did not do it. Now it is too late.

The signs of the times show plainly enough what is going to happen. All the savage lands in the world are going to be brought under subjection to the Christian governments of Europe. I am not sorry, but glad. This coming fate might have been a calamity to those savage peoples two hundred years ago; but now it will in some cases be a benefaction. The sooner the seizure is consummated, the better for the savages. The dreary and dragging ages of bloodshed and disorder and oppression will give place to peace and order and the reign of law. When one considers what India was under her Hindu and Mohammedan rulers, and what she is now; when he remembers the miseries of her millions then and the protections and humanities which they enjoy now, he must concede that the most fortunate thing that has ever befallen that empire was the establishment of British supremacy there. The savage lands of the world are to pass to alien possession, their peoples to the mercies of alien rulers. Let us hope and believe that they will all benefit by the change.

April 23. "The first year they gather shells; the second year they gather shells and drink; the third year they do not gather shells." (Said of immigrants to Mauritius.)

Population 375,000. One hundred and twenty sugar factories.

Population 1851, 185,000. The increase is due mainly to the introduction of Indian coolies. They now apparently form the great majority of the population. They are admirable breeders; their homes are always hazy with children. Great savers of money. A British officer told me that in India he paid his servant ten rupees a month, and he had eleven cousins, uncles, parents, etc., dependent upon him, and he supported them on his wages. These thrifty coolies are said to be acquiring land a trifle at a time, and cultivating it; and may own the island by and by.

The Indian women do very hard labor for wages running from forty one-hundredths of a rupee for twelve hours' work, to fifty one-hundredths. They carry mats of sugar on their heads (seventy pounds) all day lading ships, for half a rupee, and work at gardening all day for less.

The camaron is a fresh-water creature like a crayfish. It is regarded here as the world's chiefest delicacy—and certainly it is good. Guards patrol the streams to prevent poaching it. A fine of Rs. 200 or 300 (they say) for poaching. Bait is thrown in the water; the camaron goes for it; the fisher drops his loop in and works it around and about the camaron he has selected, till he gets it over its tail; then there's a jerk or something to certify the camaron that it is his turn now; he suddenly backs away, which moves the loop still further up his person and draws it taut, and his days are ended.

Another dish, called palmiste, is like raw turnip-shavings and tastes like green almonds; is very delicate and good. Costs the life of a palm tree twelve to twenty years old—for it is the pith.

Another dish—looks like greens or a tangle of fine seaweed—is a preparation of the deadly nightshade. Good enough.

The monkeys live in the dense forests on the flanks of the toy mountains, and they flock down nights and raid the sugar-fields. Also on other estates they come down and destroy a sort of bean-crop—just for fun, apparently—tear off the pods and throw them down.

The cyclone of 1892 tore down two great blocks of stone buildings in the center of Port Louis—the chief architectural feature—and left the uncomely and apparently frail blocks standing. Everywhere in its track it annihilated houses, tore off roofs, destroyed trees and crops. The men were in the towns, the women and children at home in the country getting crippled, killed, frightened to insanity; and the rain deluging them, the wind howling, the thunder crashing, the lightning glaring. This for an hour or so. Then a lull and sunshine; many ventured out of safe shelter; then suddenly here it came again from the opposite point and renewed and completed the devastation. It is said the Chinese fed the sufferers for days on free rice.

Whole streets in Port Louis were laid flat—wrecked. During a minute and a half the wind blew one hundred and twenty-three miles an hour; no official record made after that, when it may have reached one hundred and fifty. It cut down an obelisk. It carried an American ship into the woods after breaking the chains of two anchors. They now use four—two forward, two astern. Common report says it killed twelve hundred in Port Louis alone, in half an hour. Then came the lull of the central calm—people did not know the barometer was still going down—then suddenly all perdition broke loose again while people were rushing around seeking friends and rescuing the wounded. The noise was comparable to nothing; there is nothing resembling it but thunder and cannon, and these are feeble in comparison.

What there is of Mauritius is beautiful. You have undulating wide expanses of sugar-cane—a fine, fresh green and very pleasant to the eye; and everywhere else you have a ragged luxuriance of tropic vegetation of vivid greens of varying shades, a wild tangle of underbrush, with graceful tall palms lifting their crippled plumes high above it; and you have stretches of shady dense forest with limpid streams frolicking through them, continually glimpsed and lost and glimpsed again in the pleasantest hide-and-seek fashion; and you have some tiny mountains, some quaint and picturesque groups of toy peaks, and a dainty little vest-pocket Matterhorn; and here and there and now and then a strip of sea with a white ruffle of surf breaks into the view.

That is Mauritius; and pretty enough. The details are few, the massed result is charming, but not imposing; not riotous, not exciting; it is a Sunday landscape. Perspective, and the enchantments wrought by distance, are wanting. There are no distances; there is no perspective, so to speak. Fifteen miles as the crow flies is the usual limit of vision. Mauritius is a garden and a park combined. It affects one's emotions as parks and gardens affect them. The surfaces of one's spiritual deeps are pleasantly played upon, the deeps themselves are not reached, not stirred. Spaciousness, remote altitudes, the sense of mystery which haunts apparently inaccessible mountain domes and summits reposing in the sky— these are the things which exalt the spirit and move it to see visions and dream dreams.

The Sandwich Islands remain my ideal of the perfect thing in the matter of tropical islands. I would add another story to Mauna Loa's sixteen thousand feet if I could, and make it particularly bold and steep and craggy and forbidding and snowy; and I would make the volcano spout its lava-floods out of its summit instead of its sides; but aside from these non-essentials I have no corrections to suggest. I hope these will be attended to; I do not wish to have to speak of it again.

Chapter XXVIII

*When your watch gets out of order you have choice of
two things to do: throw it in the fire or take it to the
watch-tinker. The former is the quickest.*
—Pudd'nhead Wilson's New Calendar.

THE *Arundel Castle* is the finest boat I have seen in these
seas. She is thoroughly modern, and that statement covers a great deal of ground. She has the usual defect, the common defect, the universal defect, the defect that has never
been missing from any ship that ever sailed—she has imperfect beds. Many ships have good beds, but no ship has *very*
good ones. In the matter of beds all ships have been badly
edited, ignorantly edited, from the beginning. The selection of
the beds is given to some hearty, strong-backed, self-made man,
when it ought to be given to a frail woman accustomed from
girlhood to backaches and insomnia. Nothing is so rare, on
either side of the ocean, as a perfect bed; nothing is so difficult
to make. Some of the hotels on both sides provide it, but no
ship ever does or ever did. In Noah's Ark the beds were simply
scandalous. Noah set the fashion, and it will endure in one
degree of modification or another till the next flood.

8 A.M. Passing Isle de Bourbon. Broken-up sky-line of volcanic mountains in the middle. Surely it would not cost much to repair them, and it seems inexcusable neglect to leave them as they are.

It seems stupid to send tired men to Europe to rest. It is no proper rest for the mind to clatter from town to town in the dust and cinders, and examine galleries and architecture, and be always meeting people and lunching and teaing and dining, and receiving worrying cables and letters. And a sea-voyage on the Atlantic is of no use—voyage too short, sea too rough. The peaceful Indian and Pacific Oceans and the long stretches of time are the healing thing.

May 2, A.M. A fair, great ship in sight, almost the first we have seen in these weeks of lonely voyaging. We are now in the Mozambique Channel, between Madagascar and South Africa, sailing straight west for Delagoa Bay.

Last night, the burly chief engineer, middle-aged, was standing telling a spirited seafaring tale, and had reached the most exciting place, where a man overboard was washing swiftly astern on the great seas, and uplifting despairing cries, everybody racing aft in a frenzy of excitement and fading hope, when the band, which had been silent a moment, began impressively its closing piece, the English national anthem. As simply as if he was unconscious of what he was doing, he stopped his story, uncovered, laid his laced cap against his breast, and slightly bent his grizzled head. The few bars finished, he put on his cap and took up his tale again as naturally as if that interjection of music had been a part of it. There was something touching and fine about it, and it was moving to reflect that he was one of a myriad, scattered over every part of the globe, who by turn were doing as he was doing every hour of the twenty-four—those awake doing it while the others slept—those impressive bars forever floating up out of the various climes, never silent and never lacking reverent listeners.

All that I remember about Madagascar is that Thackeray's little Billee went up to the top of the mast and there knelt him upon his knee, saying, "I see

> Jerusalem and Madagascar,
> And North and South Amerikee."

May 3. Sunday. Fifteen or twenty Africanders who will end their voyage to-day and strike for their several homes from Delagoa Bay to-morrow, sat up singing on the after-deck in the moonlight till 3 A.M. Good fun and wholesome. And the songs were clean songs, and some of them were hallowed by tender associations. Finally, in a pause, a man asked, "Have you heard about the fellow that kept a diary crossing the Atlantic?" It was a discord, a wet blanket. The men were not in the mood for humorous dirt. The songs had carried them to their homes, and in spirit they sat by those far hearth-stones, and saw faces and heard voices other than those that were about them. And so this disposition to drag in an old indecent anecdote got no welcome; nobody answered. The poor man hadn't wit enough to see that he had blundered, but asked his question again. Again there was no response. It was embarrassing for him. In his confusion he chose the wrong course, did the wrong thing—began the anecdote. Began it in a deep and hostile stillness, where had been such life and stir and warm comradeship before. He delivered himself of the brief details of the diary's first day, and did it with some confidence and a fair degree of eagerness. It fell flat. There was an awkward pause. The two rows of men sat like statues. There was no movement, no sound. He *had* to go on; there was no other way, at least none that an animal of his caliber could think of. At the close of each day's diary the same dismal silence followed. When at last he finished his tale and sprung the indelicate surprise which is wont to fetch a crash of laughter, not a ripple of sound resulted. It was as if the tale had been told to dead men. After what seemed a long, long time, somebody sighed, somebody else stirred in his seat; presently, the man dropped into a low murmur of confidential talk, each with his neighbor, and the incident was closed. There were indications that that man was fond of his anecdote; that it was his pet, his standby, his shot that never missed, his reputation-maker. But he will never tell it again. No doubt he will think of it sometimes, for that cannot well be helped; and then he will see a picture, and always the same picture—the double rank of dead men; the vacant deck stretching away in dimming perspective beyond them, the wide desert of smooth sea all abroad; the rim of the moon spying from behind a rag of black cloud; the remote top of the mizzenmast shearing a zigzag path through the fields of stars in the deeps of space; and this soft picture will remind him of the time that he sat in the midst of it and told his poor little tale and felt *so* lonesome when he got through.

Fifty Indians and Chinamen asleep in a big tent in the waist of the ship forward; they lie side by side with no space between; the former wrapped up, head and all, as in the Indian streets, the Chinamen uncovered; the lamp and things for opium-smoking in the center.

A passenger said it was ten two-ton truck-loads of dynamite that lately exploded at Johannesburg. Hundreds killed; he doesn't know how many; limbs picked up for miles around. Glass shattered, and roofs swept away or collapsed two hundred yards off; fragment of iron flung three and a half miles.

It occurred at 3 P.M.; at 6, £65,000 had been subscribed. When this passenger left, £35,000 had been voted by city and state governments and £100,000 by citizens and business corporations. When news of the disaster was telephoned to the Exchange £35,000 were subscribed in the first five minutes. Subscribing was still going on when he left; the papers had omitted the names, only the amounts—too many names; not enough room. £100,000 subscribed by companies and citizens; if this is true, it must be what they call in Australia "a record"—the biggest instance of a spontaneous outpour for charity in history, considering the size of the population it was drawn from, $8 or $10 for each white resident, babies at the breast included.

Monday, May 4. Steaming slowly in the stupendous Delagoa Bay, its dim arms stretching far away and disappearing on both sides. It could furnish plenty of room for all the ships in the world, but it is shoal. The lead has given us three and a half fathoms several times, and we are drawing that, lacking six inches.

A bold headland—precipitous wall, one hundred and fifty feet high, very strong, red color, stretching a mile or so. A man said it was Portuguese blood—battle fought here with the natives last year. I think this doubtful. Pretty cluster of houses on the tableland above the red—and rolling stretches of grass and groups of trees, like England.

The Portuguese have the railroad (one passenger-train a day) to the border—seventy miles—then the Netherlands Company have it. Thousands of tons of freight on the shore—no cover. This is Portuguese all over—indolence, piousness, poverty, impotence.

Crews of small boats and tugs, all jet-black woolly heads and very muscular.

Winter. The South African winter is just beginning now, but nobody but an expert can tell it from summer. However, I am tired of summer; we have had it unbroken for eleven months. We spent the afternoon on shore, Delagoa Bay. A small town—no sights. No carriages. Three 'rikishas, but we couldn't get them—apparently private. These Portuguese are a rich brown, like some of the Indians. Some of the blacks have the long horse-heads and very long chins of the negroes of the picture-books; but most of them are exactly like the negroes of our Southern states—round faces, flat noses, good-natured, and easy laughers.

Flocks of black women passed along, carrying outrageously heavy bags of freight on their heads—the quiver of their leg as the foot was planted and the strain exhibited by their bodies showed what a tax upon their strength the load was. They were stevedores, and doing full stevedore's work. They were very erect when unladen—from carrying weights on their heads—just like the Indian women. It gives them a proud, fine carriage.

Sometimes one saw a woman carrying on her head a laden and top-heavy basket the shape of an inverted pyramid—its top the size of a soup-plate, its base the diameter of a teacup. It required nice balancing—and got it.

No bright colors; yet there were a good many Hindus.

The Second Class Passenger came over as usual at "lights out" (eleven) and we lounged along the spacious vague solitudes of the deck and smoked the peaceful pipe and talked. He told me an incident in Mr. Barnum's life which was evidently characteristic of that great showman in several ways:

This was Barnum's purchase of Shakespeare's birthplace, a quarter of a century ago. The Second Class Passenger was in Jamrach's employ at the time and knew Barnum well. He said the thing began in this way. One morning Barnum and Jamrach were in Jamrach's little private snuggery back of the wilderness of caged monkeys and snakes and other commonplaces of Jamrach's stock in trade, refreshing themselves after an arduous stroke of business, Jamrach with something orthodox, Barnum with something heterodox—for Barnum was a teetotaler. The stroke of business was in the elephant line. Jamrach had contracted to deliver to Barnum in New York eighteen elephants for three hundred and sixty thousand dollars in time for the next season's opening. Then it occurred to Mr. Barnum that he needed a "card." He suggested Jumbo. Jamrach said he would have to think of something else— Jumbo couldn't be had; the Zoo wouldn't part with that elephant. Barnum said he was willing to pay a fortune for Jumbo if he could get him. Jamrach said it was no use to think about it; that Jumbo was as popular as the Prince of Wales and the Zoo wouldn't dare to sell him; all England would be outraged at the idea; Jumbo was an English institution; he was part of the national glory; one might as well think of buying the Nelson monument. Barnum spoke up with vivacity and said:

"It's a first-rate idea. *I'll buy the monument.*"

Jamrach was speechless for a second. Then he said, like one ashamed:

"You caught me. I was napping. For a moment I thought you were in earnest."

Barnum said pleasantly:

"I *was* in earnest. I know they won't sell it, but no matter, I will not throw away a good idea for all that. All I want is a big advertisement. I will keep the thing in mind, and if nothing better turns up I will offer to buy it. That will answer every purpose. It will furnish me a couple of columns of gratis advertising in every English and American paper for a couple of months, and give my show the biggest boom a show ever had in this world."

Jamrach started to deliver a burst of admiration, but was interrupted by Barnum, who said:

"Here is a state of things! England ought to blush."

His eye had fallen upon something in the newspaper. He

read it through to himself, then read it aloud. It said that the house that Shakespeare was born in at Stratford-on-Avon was falling gradually to ruin through neglect; that the room where the poet first saw the light was now serving as a butcher's shop; that all appeals to England to contribute money (the requisite sum stated) to buy and repair the house and place it in the care of salaried and trustworthy keepers had fallen resultless. Then Barnum said:

"There's my chance. Let Jumbo and the Monument alone for the present—they'll keep. I'll buy Shakespeare's house. I'll set it up in my Museum in New York and put a glass case around it and make a sacred thing of it; and you'll see all America flock there to worship; yes, and pilgrims from the whole earth; and I'll make them take their hats off, too. In America we know how to value anything that Shakespeare's touch has made holy. You'll see."

In conclusion the S. C. P. said:

"That is the way the thing came about. Barnum did buy Shakespeare's house. He paid the price asked, and received the properly attested documents of sale. Then there was an explosion. I can tell you. England rose! What, the birthplace of the master-genius of all the ages and all the climes—that priceless possession of Britain—to be carted out of the country like so much old lumber and set up for sixpenny desecration in a Yankee show-shop—the idea was not to be tolerated for a moment. England rose in her indignation, and Barnum was glad to relinquish his prize and offer apologies. However, he stood out for a compromise; he claimed a concession— England must let him have Jumbo. And England consented, but not cheerfully."

It shows how, by help of time, a story can grow—even after Barnum has had the first innings in the telling of it. Mr. Barnum told me the story himself, years ago. He said that the permission to buy Jumbo was not a concession; the purchase was made and the animal delivered before the public knew anything about it. Also, that the securing of Jumbo was all the advertisement he needed. It produced many columns of newspaper talk, free of cost, and he was satisfied. He said that if he had failed to get Jumbo he would have caused his notion of buying the Nelson Monument to be treacherously smuggled into print by some trusty friend, and after he had gotten a few hundred pages of gratuitous advertising out of it, he would have come out with a blundering, obtuse, but warm-hearted letter of apology, and in a postscript to it would have naïvely proposed to let the Monument go, and take Stonehenge in place of it at the same price.

It was his opinion that such a letter, written with well-simulated asinine innocence and gush, would have gotten his ignorance and stupidity an amount of newspaper abuse worth six fortunes to him, and not purchasable for twice the money.

I knew Mr. Barnum well, and I placed every confidence in the account which he gave me of the Shakespeare-birthplace episode. He said he found the house neglected and going to decay, and he inquired into the matter and was told that many times earnest efforts had been made to raise money for its proper repair and preservation, but without success. He then proposed to buy it. The proposition was entertained, and a price named—fifty thousand dollars, I think; but whatever it was, Barnum paid the money down, without remark, and the papers were drawn up and executed. He said that it had been his purpose to set up the house in his Museum, keep it in repair, protect it from name-scribblers and other desecrators, and leave it by bequest to the safe and perpetual guardianship of the Smithsonian Institute at Washington.

But as soon as it was found that Shakespeare's house had passed into foreign hands and was going to be carried across the ocean, England was stirred as no appeal from the custodians of the relic had ever stirred England before, and protests came flowing in—and money, too, to stop the outrage. Offers of repurchase were made—offers of double the money that Mr. Barnum had paid for the house. He handed the house back, but took only the sum which it had cost him—but on the condition that an endowment sufficient for the future safe-guarding and maintenance of the sacred relic should be raised. This condition was fulfilled.

That was Barnum's account of the episode; and to the end of his days he claimed with pride and satisfaction that not England, but America—represented by him—saved the birthplace of Shakespeare from destruction.

At 3 P.M., May 6th, the ship slowed down, off the land, and thoughtfully and cautiously picked her way into the snug harbor of Durban, South Africa.

Chapter XXIX

In statesmanship get the formalities right, never mind about the moralities.
                    —*Pudd'nhead Wilson's New Calendar.*

FROM DIARY:

Royal Hotel. Comfortable, good table, good service of natives and Madrasis. Curious jumble of modern and ancient city and village, primitiveness and the other thing. Electric bells, but they don't ring. Asked why they didn't, the watchman in the office said he thought they must be out of order; he thought so because some of them rang, but most of them didn't. Wouldn't it be a good idea to put them in order? He hesitated—like one who isn't quite sure—then conceded the point.

May 7. A bang on the door at six. Did I want my boots cleaned? Fifteen minutes later another bang. Did we want coffee? Fifteen later, bang again, my wife's bath ready; fifteen later, my bath ready. Two other bangs; I forget what they were about. Then lots of shouting back and forth, among the servants, just as in an Indian hotel.

Evening. At 4 P.M. it was unpleasantly warm. Half-hour after sunset one needed a spring overcoat; by eight a winter one.

Durban is a neat and clean town. One notices that without having his attention called to it.

'Rikishas drawn by splendidly built black Zulus, so overflowing with strength, seemingly, that it is a pleasure, not a pain, to see them snatch a 'rikisha along. They smile and laugh and show their teeth—a good-natured lot. Not allowed to drink; 2^s per hour for one person; 3^s for two; 3^d for a course—one person.

The chameleon in the hotel court. He is fat and indolent and contemplative; but is businesslike and capable when a fly comes about—reaches out a tongue like a teaspoon and takes him in. He gums his tongue first. He is always pious, in his looks. And pious and thankful both, when Providence or one of us sends him a fly. He has a froggy head, and a back like a new grave—for shape; and hands like a bird's toes that have been frost-bitten. But his eyes are his exhibition feature. A couple of skinny cones project from the sides of his head, with a wee shiny bead of an eye set in the apex of each; and these cones turn bodily like pivot-guns and point every which way, and they are independent of each other; each has its own exclusive machinery. When I am behind him and C. in front of him, he whirls one eye rearward and the other forward—which gives him a most Congressional expression (one eye on the constituency and one on the swag); and then if something happens above and below him he shoots out one eye upward like a telescope and the other downward—and this changes his expression, but does not improve it.

Natives must not be out after the curfew-bell without a pass. In Natal there are ten blacks to one white.

Sturdy plump creatures are the women. They comb their

wool up to a peak and keep it in position by stiffening it with brown-red clay—half of this tower colored, denotes engagement; the whole of it colored, denotes marriage.

None but heathen Zulus on the police; Christian ones not allowed.

May 9. A drive yesterday with friends over the Berea. Very fine roads and lofty, overlooking the whole town, the harbor, and the sea—beautiful views. Residences all along, set in the midst of green lawns with shrubs and generally one or two intensely red outbursts of poinsettia—the flaming splotch of blinding red a stunning contrast with the world of surrounding green. The cactus tree—candelabrumlike; and one twisted like gray writhing serpents. The "flat-crown" (should be flat-roof)—half a dozen naked branches full of elbows, slant upward like artificial supports, and fling a roof of delicate foliage out in a horizontal platform as flat as a floor; and you look up through this thin floor as through a green cobweb or veil. The branches are japanesic. All about you is a bewildering variety of unfamiliar and beautiful trees; one sort wonderfully dense foliage and very dark green—so dark that you notice it at once, notwithstanding there are so many orange trees. The "flamboyant"—not in flower, now, but when in flower lives up to its name, we are told. Another tree with a lovely upright tassel scattered among its rich greenery, red and glowing as a fire-coal. Here and there a gum tree; half a dozen lofty Norfolk Island pines lifting their fronded arms skyward. Groups of tall bamboo.

Saw one bird. Not many birds here, and *they* have no music—and the flowers not much smell, they grow so fast.

Everything neat and trim and clean like the town. The loveliest trees and the greatest variety I have ever seen anywhere, except approaching Darjeeling. Have not heard any one call Natal the garden of South Africa, but that is what it probably is.

It was when Bishop of Natal that Colenso raised such a storm in the religious world. The concerns of religion are a vital matter here yet. A vigilant eye is kept upon Sunday. Museums and other dangerous resorts are not allowed to be open. You may sail on the Bay, but it is wicked to play cricket. For a while a Sunday concert was tolerated, upon condition that it must be admission free and the money taken by collection. But the collection was alarmingly large and that stopped the matter. They are particular about babies. A clergyman would not bury a child according to the sacred rites because it had not been baptized. The Hindu is more liberal. He burns no child under three, holding that it does not need purifying.

The King of the Zulus, a fine fellow of thirty, was banished six years ago for a term of seven years. He is occupying Napoleon's old stand—St. Helena. The people are a little nervous about having him come back, and they may well be, for Zulu kings have been terrible people sometimes—like Tchaka, Dingaan, and Cetewayo.

There is a large Trappist monastery two hours from Durban, over the country roads, and in company with Mr. Milligan and Mr. Hunter, general manager of the Natal Government railways, who knew the heads of it, we went out to see it.

There it all was, just as one reads about it in books and cannot believe that it is so—I mean the rough hard work, the impossible hours, the scanty food, the coarse raiment, the Maryborough beds, the *tabu* of human speech, of social intercourse, of relaxation, of amusement, of entertainment, of the presence of woman in the men's establishment. There it all was. It was not a dream, it was not a lie. And yet with the fact before one's face it was still incredible. It is such a sweeping suppression of human instincts, such an extinction of the man as an individual.

La Trappe must have known the human race well. The scheme which he invented hunts out everything that a man wants and values—and withholds it from him. Apparently there is no detail that can help make life worth living that has not been carefully ascertained and placed out of the Trappist's reach. La Trappe must have known that there were men who would enjoy this kind of misery, but how did he find it out?

If he had consulted you or me he would have been told that his scheme lacked too many attractions; that it was impossible; that it could never be floated. But there in the monastery was proof that he knew the human race better than it knew itself. He set his foot upon every desire that a man has—yet he floated his project, and it has prospered for two hundred years, and will go on prospering forever, no doubt.

Man likes personal distinction—there in the monastery it is obliterated. He likes delicious food—there he gets beans and bread and tea, and not enough of it. He likes to lie softly—there he lies on a sand mattress, and has a pillow and a blanket, but no sheet. When he is dining, in a great company of friends, he likes to laugh and chat—there a monk reads a holy book aloud during meals, and nobody speaks or laughs. When a man has a hundred friends about him, evenings, he likes to have a good time and run late—there he and the rest go silently to bed at eight; and in the dark, too; there is but a loose brown robe to discard, there are no nightclothes to put on, a light is not needed. Man likes to lie abed late—there he gets up once or twice in the night to perform some religious office, and gets up finally for the day at two in the morning. Man likes light work or none at all—there he labors all day in the field, or in the blacksmith shop or the other shops devoted to the mechanical trades, such as shoemaking, saddlery, carpentry, and so on. Man likes the society of girls and women—there he never has it. He likes to have his children about him, and pet them and play with them—there he has none. He likes billiards—there is no table there. He likes outdoor sports and indoor dramatic and musical and social entertainments—there are none there. He likes to bet on things—I was told that betting is forbidden there. When a man's temper is up he likes to pour it out upon somebody— there this is not allowed. A man likes animals—pets; there are none there. He likes to smoke—there he cannot do it. He likes to read the news—no papers or magazines come there. A man likes to know how his parents and brothers and sisters are getting along when he is away, and if they miss him— there he cannot know. A man likes a pretty house, and pretty furniture, and pretty things, and pretty colors—there he has nothing but naked aridity and somber colors. A man likes— name it yourself: whatever it is, it is absent from that place.

From what I could learn, all that a man gets for this is merely the saving of his soul.

It all seems strange, incredible, impossible. But La Trappe knew the race. He knew the powerful attraction of unattractiveness: he knew that no life could be imagined, howsoever comfortless and forbidding, but somebody would want to try it.

This parent establishment of Germans began its work fifteen years ago, strangers, poor, and unencouraged; it owns fifteen thousand acres of land now, and raises grain and fruit, and makes wines, and manufactures all manner of things, and has native apprentices in its shops, and sends them forth able to read and write, and also well equipped to earn their living by their trades. And this young establishment has set up eleven branches in South Africa, and in them they are Christianizing and educating and teaching wage-yielding mechanical trades to twelve hundred boys and girls. Protestant Missionary work is coldly regarded by the commercial white colonists all over the heathen world, as a rule, and its product is nicknamed "rice-Christians" (occupationless incapables who join the church for revenue only), but I think it would be difficult to pick a flaw in the work of these Catholic monks, and I believe that the disposition to attempt it has not shown itself.

Tuesday, May 12. Transvaal politics in a confused condition. First the sentencing of the Johannesburg Reformers startled England by its severity; on the top of this came Kruger's exposure of the cipher correspondence, which showed that the invasion of the Transvaal, with the design of seizing that country and adding it to the British Empire, was planned by Cecil Rhodes and Beit—which made a revulsion in English feeling, and brought out a storm against Rhodes and the Chartered Company for degrading British honor. For a good while I couldn't seem to get at a clear comprehension of it, it was so tangled. But at last by patient study I have managed it, I believe. As I understand it, the Uitlanders and other Dutchmen were dissatisfied because the English would not allow them to take any part in the government except to pay taxes. Next, as I understand it, Dr. Kruger and Dr. Jameson, not having been able to make the medical business pay, made a raid into Matabeleland with the intention of capturing the capital, Johannesburg, and holding the women and children to ransom until the Uitlanders and the other Boers should grant to them and the Chartered Company the political rights which had been withheld from them. They would have succeeded in this great scheme, as I understand it, but for the interference of Cecil Rhodes and Mr. Beit, and other Chiefs of the Matabele, who persuaded their countrymen to revolt and throw off their allegiance to Germany. This, in turn, as I understand it, provoked the King of Abyssinia to destroy the Italian army and fall back upon Johannesburg; this at the instigation of Rhodes, to bull the stock market.

Chapter XXX

Every one is a moon, and has a dark side which he never shows to anybody.
—Pudd'nhead Wilson's New Calendar.

W HEN I scribbled in my note-book a year ago the paragraph which ends the preceding chapter, it was meant to indicate, in an extravagant form, two things: the conflicting nature of the information conveyed by the citizen to the stranger concerning South African politics, and the resulting confusion created in the stranger's mind thereby.

But it does not seem so very extravagant now. Nothing could in that disturbed and excited time make South African politics clear or quite rational to the citizen of the country because his personal interest and his political prejudices were in his way; and nothing could make those politics clear or rational to the stranger, the sources of his information being such as they were.

I was in South Africa some little time. When I arrived there the political pot was boiling fiercely. Four months previously, Jameson had plunged over the Transvaal border with about six hundred armed horsemen at his back, to go to the "relief of the women and children" of Johannesburg; on the fourth day of his march the Boers had defeated him in battle, and carried him and his men to Pretoria, the capital, as prisoners; the Boer Government had turned Jameson and his officers over to the British Government for trial, and shipped them to England; next, it had arrested sixty-four important citizens of Johannesburg as raid-conspirators, condemned their four leaders to death, then commuted the sentences, and now the sixty-four were waiting, in jail, for further results. Before midsummer they were all out excepting two, who refused to sign the petitions for release; fifty-eight had been fined $10,000 each and enlarged, and the four leaders had gotten off with fines of $125,000 each—with permanent exile added, in one case.

Those were wonderfully interesting days for a stranger, and I was glad to be in the thick of the excitement. Everybody was talking, and I expected to understand the whole of *one side* of it in a very little while.

I was disappointed. There were singularities, perplexities, unaccountabilities about it which I was not able to master. I had no personal access to Boers—their side was a secret to me, aside from what I was able to gather of it from published statements. My sympathies were soon with the Reformers in the Pretoria jail, with their friends, and with their cause. By diligent inquiry in Johannesburg I found out—apparently—all the details of their side of the quarrel except one—*what they expected to accomplish by an armed rising.*

Nobody seemed to know.

The reason why the Reformers were discontented and wanted some changes made, seemed quite clear. In Johannesburg it was claimed that the Uitlanders (strangers, foreigners) paid thirteen-fifteenths of the Transvaal taxes, yet got little or nothing for it. Their city had no charter; it had no municipal government; it could levy no taxes for drainage, water-supply, paving, cleaning, sanitation, policing. There was a police force, but it was composed of Boers; it was furnished by the state government, and the city had no control over it. Mining was very costly; the government enormously increased the cost by putting burdensome taxes upon the mines, the output, the machinery, the buildings; by burdensome imposts upon incoming materials; by burdensome railway-freight charges. Hardest of all to bear, the government reserved to itself a monopoly in that essential thing, dynamite, and burdened it with an extravagant price. The detested Hollander from over the water held all the public offices. The government was rank with corruption. The Uitlander had no vote, and must live in the state ten or twelve years before he could get one. He was not represented in the Raad (legislature) that oppressed him and fleeced him. Religion was not free. There were no schools where the teaching was in English, yet the great majority of the white population of the state knew no tongue but that. The state would not pass a liquor law; but allowed a great trade in cheap vile brandy among the blacks, with the result that twenty-five per cent. of the fifty thousand blacks employed in the mines were usually drunk and incapable of working.

There—it was plain enough that the *reasons* for wanting some changes made were abundant and reasonable, if this statement of the existing grievances was correct.

What the Uitlanders wanted was reform—*under the existing Republic.*

What they proposed to do was to secure these reforms by *prayer, petition, and persuasion.*

They did petition. Also, they issued a Manifesto, whose very first note is a bugle-blast of loyalty: "We want the establishment of this Republic as a true Republic."

Could anything be clearer than the Uitlanders' statement of the grievances and oppressions under which they were suffering? Could anything be more legal and citizenlike and law-respecting than their attitude as expressed by their Manifesto? No. Those things were perfectly clear, perfectly comprehensible.

But at this point the puzzles and riddles and confusions begin to flock in. You have arrived at a place which you cannot quite understand.

For you find that as a preparation for this loyal, lawful, and in every way unexceptionable attempt to persuade the government to right their grievances, the Uitlanders had smuggled a Maxim gun or two and fifteen hundred muskets into the town, concealed in oil-tanks and coal-cars, and had begun to form and drill military companies composed of clerks, merchants, and citizens generally.

What was their idea? Did they suppose that the Boers would attack them for *petitioning for redress!* That could not be.

Did they suppose that the Boers would attack them even for issuing a Manifesto *demanding* relief under the existing government?

Yes, they apparently believed so, because the air was full of talk of *forcing* the government to grant redress if it were not granted peacefully.

The Reformers were men of high intelligence. If they were in earnest, they were taking extraordinary risks. They had enormously valuable properties to defend; their town was full of women and children; their mines and compounds were packed with thousands upon thousands of sturdy blacks. If the Boers attacked, the mines would close, the blacks would swarm out and get drunk; riot and conflagration and the Boers together might lose the Reformers more in a day, in money, blood, and suffering, than the desired political relief could compensate in ten years if they won the fight and secured the reforms.

It is May, 1897, now; a year has gone by, and the confusions of that day have been to a considerable degree cleared away. Mr. Cecil Rhodes, Dr. Jameson, and others responsible for the Raid, have testified before the Parliamentary Committee of Inquiry in London, and so have Mr. Lionel Phillips and other Johannesburg Reformers, monthly-nurses of the Revolution which was born dead. These testimonies have thrown light. Three books have added much to this light: *South Africa As It Is,* by Mr. Statham, an able writer partial to the Boers; *The Story of an African Crisis,* by Mr. Garrett, a brilliant writer partial to Rhodes; and *A Woman's Part in a Revolution,* by Mrs. John Hays Hammond, a vigorous and vivid diarist, partial to the Reformers. By liquefying the evidence of the prejudiced books and of the prejudiced parliamentary witnesses and stirring the whole together and pouring it into my own (prejudiced) molds, I have got at the truth of that puzzling South African situation, which is this:

1. The capitalists and other chief men of Johannesburg were fretting under various political and financial burdens imposed by the state (the South African Republic, sometimes called "the Transvaal") and desired to procure by peaceful means a modification of the laws.

2. Mr. Cecil Rhodes, Premier of the British Cape Colony, millionaire, creator and managing director of the territorially immense and financially unproductive South African Company; projector of vast schemes for the unification and consolidation of all the South African states into one imposing commonwealth or empire under the shadow and general protection of the British flag, thought he saw an opportunity to make profitable use of the Uitlander discontent above mentioned—make the Johannesburg cat help pull out one of his consolidation chestnuts for him. With this view he set himself the task of warming the lawful and legitimate petitions and supplications of the Uitlanders into seditious talk, and their frettings into threatenings—the final outcome to be revolt

and armed rebellion. If he could bring about a bloody collision between those people and the Boer Government, Great Britain would have to interfere; her interference would be resisted by the Boers; she would chastise them and add the Transvaal to her South African possessions. It was not a foolish idea, but a rational and practical one.

After a couple of years of judicious plotting, Mr. Rhodes had his reward; the revolutionary kettle was briskly boiling in Johannesburg, and the Uitlander leaders were backing their appeals to the government—now hardened into demands—by threats of force and bloodshed. By the middle of December, 1895, the explosion seemed imminent. Mr. Rhodes was diligently helping, from his distant post in Cape Town. He was helping to procure arms for Johannesburg; he was also arranging to have Jameson break over the border and come to Johannesburg with six hundred mounted men at his back. Jameson—as per instructions from Rhodes, perhaps—wanted a letter from the Reformers requesting him to come to their aid. It was a good idea. It would throw a considerable share of the responsibility of his invasion upon the Reformers. He got the letter—that famous one urging him to fly to the rescue of the women and children. He got it *two months* before he flew. The Reformers seem to have thought it over and concluded that they had not done wisely; for the next day after giving Jameson the implicating document they wanted to withdraw it and leave the women and children in danger; but they were told that it was too late. The original had gone to Mr. Rhodes at the Cape. Jameson had kept a copy, though.

From that time until the 29th of December, a good deal of the Reformers' time was taken up with energetic efforts to keep Jameson from coming to their assistance. Jameson's invasion had been set for the 26th. The Reformers were not ready. The town was not united. Some wanted a fight, some wanted peace; some wanted a new government, some wanted the existing one reformed; apparently very few wanted the revolution to take place in the interest and under the ultimate shelter of the Imperial flag—British; yet a report began to spread that Mr. Rhodes's embarrassing assistance had for its end this latter object.

Jameson was away on the frontier tugging at his leash, fretting to burst over the border. By hard work the Reformers got his starting-date postponed a little, and wanted to get it postponed eleven days. Apparently, Rhodes's agents were seconding their efforts—in fact wearing out the telegraph-wires trying to hold him back. Rhodes was himself the only man who could have effectively postponed Jameson, but that would have been a disadvantage to his scheme; indeed, it could spoil his whole two years' work.

Jameson endured postponement three days, then resolved to wait no longer. Without any orders—excepting Mr. Rhodes's significant silence—he cut the telegraph-wires on the 29th, and made his plunge that night, to go to the rescue of the women and children, by urgent request of a letter now nine days old—as per date—a couple of months old, in fact. He read the letter to his men, and it affected them. It did not affect all of them alike. Some saw in it a piece of piracy of doubtful wisdom, and were sorry to find that they had been assembled to violate friendly territory instead of to raid native kraals, as they had supposed.

Jameson would have to ride one hundred and fifty miles. He knew that there were suspicions abroad in the Transvaal concerning him, but he expected to get through to Johannesburg before they should become general and obstructive. But a telegraph-wire had been overlooked and not cut. It spread the news of his invasion far and wide, and a few hours after his start the Boer farmers were riding hard from every direction to intercept him.

As soon as it was known in Johannesburg that he was on his way to rescue the women and children, the grateful people put the women and children in a train and rushed them for Australia. In fact, the approach of Johannesburg's savior created panic and consternation there, and a multitude of males of peaceable disposition swept to the trains like a sand-storm. The early ones fared best; they secured seats—by sit-ting in them—eight hours before the first train was timed to leave.

Mr. Rhodes lost no time. He cabled the renowned Johan-nesburg letter of invitation to the London press—the gray-headedest piece of ancient history that ever went over a cable.

The new poet laureate lost no time. He came out with a rousing poem lauding Jameson's prompt and splendid hero-ism in flying to the rescue of the women and children; for the poet could not know that he did not fly until two months after the invitation. He was deceived by the false date of the letter, which was December 20th.

Jameson was intercepted by the Boers on New-year's Day, and on the next day he surrendered. He had carried his copy of the letter along, and if his instructions required him— in case of emergency—to see that it fell into the hands of the Boers, he loyally carried them out. Mrs. Hammond gives him a sharp rap for his supposed carelessness, and emphasizes her feeling about it with burning italics: "It was picked up on the battle-field in a leathern pouch, supposed to be Dr. Jameson's saddle-bag. *Why, in the name of all that is discreet and honorable, didn't he eat it!*"

She requires too much. He was not in the service of the Reformers—excepting ostensibly; he was in the service of Mr. Rhodes. It was the only plain English document, undark-ened by ciphers and mysteries, and responsibly signed and authenticated, which squarely implicated the Reformers in the raid, and it was not to Mr. Rhodes's interest that it should be eaten. Besides, that letter was not the original, it was only a copy. Mr. Rhodes had the original—and didn't eat it. He cabled it to the London press. It had already been read in England and America and all over Europe before Jameson dropped it on the battle-field. If the subordinate's knuckles deserved a rap, the principal's deserved as many as a couple of them.

That letter is a juicily dramatic incident and is entitled to all its celebrity, because of the odd and variegated effects which it produced. All within the space of a single week it had made Jameson an illustrious hero in England, a pirate in Pretoria, and an ass without discretion or honor in Johannesburg; also it had produced a poet-laureatic explosion of colored fireworks which filled the world's sky with giddy splendors, and the knowledge that Jameson was coming with it to rescue the women and children emptied Johannesburg of that detail of the population. For an old letter, this was much. For a letter two months old, it did marvels; if it had been a year old it would have done miracles.

Chapter XXXI

First catch your Boer, then kick him.
   —Pudd'nhead Wilson's New Calendar.

THOSE latter days were days of bitter worry and trouble for the harassed Reformers.

From Mrs. Hammond we learn that on the 31st (the day after Johannesburg heard of the invasion) "the Reform Committee repudiates Dr. Jameson's inroad."

It also publishes its intention to adhere to the Manifesto.

It also earnestly desires that the inhabitants shall refrain from overt acts against the Boer Government.

It also "distributes arms" at the Court House, and furnishes horses "to the newly enrolled volunteers."

It also brings a Transvaal flag into the committee-room, and the entire body swear allegiance to it "with uncovered heads and upraised arms."

Also "one thousand Lee-Metford rifles have been given out"—to rebels.

Also, in a speech, Reformer Lionel Phillips informs the public that the Reform Committee Delegation has "been received with courtesy by the Government Commission," and "been assured that their proposals shall be earnestly considered." That "while the Reform Committee regretted Jameson's precipitate action, they would stand by him."

Also the populace are in a state of "wild enthusiasm," and "can scarcely be restrained; they want to go out to meet Jameson and bring him in with triumphal outcry."

Also the British High Commissioner has issued a damnifying proclamation against Jameson and all British abettors of his game. It arrives January 1st.

It is a difficult position for the Reformers, and full of hindrances and perplexities. Their duty is hard but plain:

1. They have to repudiate the inroad, and stand by the inroad, and stand by the inroader.

2. They have to swear allegiance to the Boer Government, and distribute cavalry horses to the rebels.

3. They have to forbid overt acts against the Boer Government, and distribute arms to its enemies.

4. They have to avoid collision with the British Government, but still stand by Jameson and their new oath of allegiance to the Boer Government, taken, uncovered, in presence of its flag.

They did such of these things as they could; they tried to do them all; in fact, did do them all, but only in turn, not simultaneously. In the nature of things they could not be made to simultane.

In preparing for armed revolution and in talking revolution, were the Reformers "bluffing," or were they in earnest? If they were in earnest, they were taking great risks—as has been already pointed out. A gentleman of high position told me in Johannesburg that he had in his possession a printed document proclaiming a *new* government and naming its president—one of the Reform leaders. He said that this proclamation had been ready for issue, but was suppressed when the raid collapsed. Perhaps I misunderstood him. Indeed, I must have misunderstood him, for I have not seen mention of this large incident in print anywhere.

Besides, I hope I am mistaken; for, if I am, then there is argument that the Reformers were privately not serious, but were only trying to scare the Boer Government into granting the desired reforms.

The Boer Government *was* scared, and it had a right to be. For if Mr. Rhodes's plan was to provoke a collision that would compel the interference of England, that was a serious matter. If it could be shown that that was also the Reformers' plan and purpose, it would prove that they had marked out a feasible project, at any rate, although it was one which could hardly fail to cost them ruinously before England should arrive. But it seems clear that they had no such plan nor desire. If, when the worst should come to the worst, they meant to overthrow the government, they also meant to inherit the assets themselves, no doubt.

This scheme could hardly have succeeded. With an army of Boers at their gates and fifty thousand riotous blacks in their midst, the odds against success would have been too heavy—even if the whole town had been armed. With only twenty-five hundred rifles in the place, they stood really no chance.

To me, the military problems of the situation are of more interest than the political ones, because by disposition I have always been especially fond of war. No, I mean fond of discussing war; and fond of giving military advice. If I had been with Jameson the morning after he started, I should have advised him to turn back. That was Monday; it was then that he received his first warning from a Boer source not to violate the friendly soil of the Transvaal. It showed that his invasion was known. If I had been with him on Tuesday morning and afternoon, when he received further warnings,

I should have repeated my advice. If I had been with him the next morning—New Year's—when he received notice that "a few hundred" Boers were waiting for him a few miles ahead, I should not have advised, but commanded him to go back. And if I had been with him two or three hours later—a thing not conceivable to me—I should have retired him by force; for at that time he learned that the few hundred had now grown to 800; and that meant that the growing would go on growing.

For, by authority of Mr. Garrett, one knows that Jameson's 600 were only 530 at most, when you count out his native drivers, etc.; and that the 530 consisted largely of "green" youths, "raw young fellows," not trained and war-worn British soldiers; and I would have told Jameson that those lads would not be able to shoot effectively from horseback in the scamper and racket of battle, and that there would not be anything for them to shoot at, anyway, but rocks; for the Boers would be behind the rocks, not out in the open. I would have told him that 300 Boer sharp-shooters behind rocks would be an over-match for his 500 raw young fellows on horseback.

If pluck were the only thing essential to battle-winning, the English would lose no battles. But discretion, as well as pluck, is required when one fights Boers and Red Indians. In South Africa the Briton has always insisted upon standing bravely up, unsheltered, before the hidden Boer, and taking the results. Jameson's men would follow the custom. Jameson would not have listened to me—he would have been intent upon repeating history, according to precedent. Americans are not acquainted with the British-Boer war of 1881; but its history is interesting, and could have been instructive to Jameson if he had been receptive. I will cull some details of it from trustworthy sources—mainly from *Russell's Natal*.

Mr. Russell is not a Boer, but a Briton. He is inspector of schools, and his history is a text-book whose purpose is the instruction of the Natal English youth.

After the seizure of the Transvaal and the suppression of the Boer Government by England in 1877, the Boers fretted for three years, and made several appeals to England for a restoration of their liberties, but without result. Then they gathered themselves together in a great mass-meeting at Krugersdorp, talked their troubles over, and resolved to fight for their deliverance from the British yoke. (Krugersdorp—the place where the Boers interrupted the Jameson raid.) The little handful of farmers rose against the strongest empire in the world. They proclaimed martial law and the reestablishment of their Republic. They organized their forces and sent them forward to intercept the British battalions. This, although Sir Garnet Wolseley had but lately made proclamation that "so long as the sun shone in the heavens," the Transvaal would be and remain English territory. And also in spite of the fact that the commander of the Ninety-fourth Regiment—already on the march to suppress this rebellion—had been heard to say that "the Boers would turn tail at the first beat of the big drum."[1]

Four days after the flag-raising, the Boer force which had been sent forward to forbid the invasion of the English troops met them at Bronkhorst Spruit—two hundred and forty-six men of the Ninety-fourth Regiment, in command of a colonel, the big drum beating, the band playing—and the first battle was fought. It lasted ten minutes. Result:

British loss, more than 150 officers and men, out of the 246. Surrender of the remnant.

[1] *South Africa As It Is*, by F. Reginald Statham, page 82. London: T. Fisher Unwin, 1897.

Boer loss—if any—not stated.

They are fine marksmen, the Boers. From the cradle up, they live on horseback and hunt wild animals with the rifle. They have a passion for liberty and the Bible, and care for nothing else.

"General Sir George Colley, Lieutenant-Governor and Commander-in-Chief in Natal, felt it his duty to proceed at once to the relief of the loyalists and soldiers beleaguered in the different towns of the Transvaal." He moved out with one thousand men and some artillery. He found the Boers encamped in a strong and sheltered position on high ground at Laing's Nek—every Boer behind a rock. Early in the morning of the 28th of January, 1881, he moved to the attack "with the Fifty-eighth Regiment, commanded by Colonel Deane, a mounted squadron of seventy men, the Sixtieth Rifles, the Naval Brigade with three rocket tubes, and the Artillery with six guns." He shelled the Boers for twenty minutes, then the assault was delivered, the Fifty-eighth marching up the slope *in solid column*. The battle was soon finished, with this result, according to Russell:

British loss in killed and wounded, 174.

Boer loss, "trifling."

Colonel Deane was killed, and apparently every officer above the grade of lieutenant was killed or wounded, for the Fifty-eighth retreated to its camp *in command of a lieutenant.* (*Africa As It Is.*)

That ended the second battle.

On the 7th of February General Colley discovered that the Boers were flanking his position. The next morning he left his camp at Mount Pleasant and marched out and crossed the Ingogo River with two hundred and seventy men, started up the Ingogo heights, and there fought a battle which lasted from noon till nightfall. He then retreated, leaving his wounded with his military chaplain, and in recrossing the now swollen river lost some of his men by drowning. That was the third Boer victory. Result, according to Mr. Russell:

British loss, 150 out of 270 engaged.
Boer loss, 8 killed, 9 wounded—17.

There was a season of quiet, now, but at the end of about three weeks Sir George Colley conceived the idea of climbing, with an infantry and artillery force, the steep and rugged mountain of Amajuba in the night—a bitter hard task, but he accomplished it. On the way he left about two hundred men to guard a strategic point, and took about four hundred up the mountain with him. When the sun rose in the morning, there was an unpleasant surprise for the Boers; yonder were the English troops visible on top of the mountain two or three miles away, and now their own position was at the mercy of the English artillery. The Boer chief resolved to retreat—up that mountain. He asked for volunteers, and got them.

The storming party crossed the swale and began to creep up the steeps, "and from behind rocks and bushes they shot at the soldiers on the sky-line as if they were stalking deer," says Mr. Russell. There was "continuous musketry fire, steady and fatal on the one side, wild and ineffectual on the other." The Boers reached the top, and began to put in their ruinous work. Presently the British "broke and fled for their lives down the rugged steep." The Boers had won the battle. Result in killed and wounded, including among the killed the British general:

British loss, 226 out of 400 engaged.
Boer loss, 1 killed, 5 wounded.

That ended the war. England listened to reason, and recognized the Boer Republic—a government which has never been in any really awful danger since, until Jameson started after it with his five hundred "raw young fellows." To recapitulate:

The Boer farmers and British soldiers fought four battles, and the Boers won them all. Result of the four, in killed and wounded:

British loss, 700 men.

Boer loss, so far as known, 23 men.

It is interesting, now, to note how loyally Jameson and his several trained British military officers tried to make their battles conform to precedent. Mr. Garrett's account of the Raid is much the best one I have met with, and my impressions of the raid are drawn from that.

When Jameson learned that near Krugersdorp he would find eight hundred Boers waiting to dispute his passage, he was not in the least disturbed. He was feeling as he had felt two or three days before, when he had opened his campaign with a historic remark to the same purport as the one with which the commander of the Ninety-fourth had opened the Boer-British war of fourteen years before. That Commander's remark was, that the Boers "would turn tail at the first beat of the big drum." Jameson's was, that with his "raw young fellows" he could kick the (persons) of the Boers "all round the Transvaal." He was keeping close to historic precedent.

Jameson arrived in the presence of the Boers. They—according to precedent—were not visible. It was a country of ridges, depressions, rocks, ditches, moraines of mining-tailings—not even as favorable for cavalry work as Laing's Nek had been in the former disastrous days. Jameson shot at the ridges and rocks with his artillery, just as General Colley had done at the Nek; and did them no damage and persuaded no Boer to show himself. Then about a hundred of his men formed up to charge the ridge—according to the Fifty-eighth's precedent at the Nek; but as they dashed forward they opened out in a long line, which was a considerable improvement on the Fifty-eighth's tactics; when they had gotten to within two hundred yards of the ridge the concealed Boers opened out on them and emptied twenty saddles. The unwounded dismounted and fired at the rocks over the backs of their horses; but the return fire was too hot, and they mounted again, "and galloped back or crawled away into a clump of reeds for cover, where they were shortly afterward taken prisoners as they lay among the reeds. Some thirty prisoners were so taken, and during the night which followed the Boers carried away another thirty killed and wounded— the wounded to Krugersdorp hospital." Sixty per cent. of the assaulting force disposed of—according to Mr. Garrett's estimate.

It was according to Amajuba precedent, where the British loss was 226 out of about 400 engaged.

Also, in Jameson's camp, that night, "there lay about 30 wounded or otherwise disabled" men. Also during the night "some 30 or 40 young fellows got separated from the command and straggled through into Johannesburg." Altogether a possible 150 men gone, out of his 530. His lads had fought valorously, but had not been able to get near enough to a Boer to kick him around the Transvaal.

At dawn the next morning the column of something short of 400 whites resumed its march. Jameson's grit was stubbornly good; indeed, it was always that. He still had hopes. There was a long and tedious zigzagging march through broken ground, with constant harassment from the Boers; and at last the column "walked into a sort of trap," and the Boers "closed in upon it." "Men and horses dropped on all sides. In the column the feeling grew that unless it could burst through the Boer lines at this point it was done for. The Maxims were fired until they grew too hot, and, water failing for the cool jacket, five of them jammed and went out of action. The seven-pounder was fired until only half an hour's ammunition was left to fire with. One last rush was made, and failed, and then the Staats Artillery came up on the left flank, and the game was up."

Jameson hoisted a white flag and surrendered.

There is a story, which may not be true, about an ignorant Boer farmer there who thought that this white flag was the national flag of England. He had been at Bronkhorst, and Laing's Nek, and Ingogo and Amajuba, and supposed that the English did not run up their flag excepting at the end of a fight.

The following is (as I understand it) Mr. Garrett's estimate of Jameson's total loss in killed and wounded for the two days:

"When they gave in they were minus some 20 per cent. of combatants. There were 76 casualties. There were 30 men hurt or sick in the wagons. There were 27 killed on the spot or mortally wounded." Total, 133, out of the original 530. It is just 25 per cent.[1] This is a large improvement upon the precedents established at Bronkhorst, Laing's Nek, Ingogo, and Amajuba, and seems to indicate that Boer marksmanship is not so good now as it was in those days. But there is one detail in which the Raid episode exactly repeats history. By surrender at Bronkhorst, the whole British force disappeared from the theater of war; this was the case with Jameson's force.

In the Boer loss, also, historical precedent is followed with sufficient fidelity. In the four battles named above, the Boer loss, so far as known, was an average of six men per battle, to the British average loss of one hundred and seventy-

---

[1] However, I judge that the total was really 150; for the number of wounded carried to Krugersdorp hospital was 53; not 30, as Mr. Garrett reports it. The lady whose guest I was in Krugersdorp gave me the figures. She was head nurse from the beginning of hostilities (Jan. 1st) until the professional nurses arrived, Jan. 8th. Of the 53, "Three or four were Boers"; I quote her words.

five. In Jameson's battles, as per Boer official report, the Boer loss in killed was four. Two of these were killed by the Boers themselves, by accident, the others by Jameson's army—one of them intentionally, the other by a pathetic mischance. "A young Boer named Jacobz was moving forward to give a drink to one of the wounded troopers (Jameson's) after the first charge, when another wounded man, mistaking his intention, shot him." There were three or four wounded Boers in the Krugersdorp hospital, and apparently no others have been reported. Mr. Garrett, "on a balance of probabilities, fully accepts the official version, and thanks Heaven the killed was not larger."

As a military man, I wish to point out what seems to me to be military errors in the conduct of the campaign which we have just been considering. I have seen active service in the field, and it was in the actualities of war that I acquired my training and my right to speak. I served two weeks in the beginning of our Civil War, and during all that time commanded a battery of infantry composed of twelve men. General Grant knew the history of my campaign, for I told it him. I also told him the principle upon which I had conducted it; which was, to tire the enemy. I tried out and disqualified many battalions, yet never had a casualty myself nor lost a man. General Grant was not given to paying compliments, yet he said frankly that if I had conducted the whole war much bloodshed would have been spared, and that what the army might have lost through the inspiriting results of collision in the field would have been amply made up by the liberalizing influences of travel. Further endorsement does not seem to me to be necessary.

Let us now examine history, and see what it teaches. In the four battles fought in 1881 and the two fought by Jameson, the British loss in killed, wounded, and prisoners, was substantially thirteen hundred men; the Boer loss, as far as is ascertainable, was about thirty men. These figures show that there was a defect somewhere. It was not in the absence of courage. I think it lay in the absence of discretion. The Briton should have done one thing or the other: discarded British methods and fought the Boer with Boer methods, or augmented his own force until—using British methods—it should be large enough to equalize results with the Boer.

To retain the British method requires certain things, determinable by arithmetic. If, for argument's sake, we allow that the aggregate of 1,716 British soldiers engaged in the four early battles was opposed by the same aggregate of Boers, we have this result: the British loss of 700 and the Boer loss of 23 argues that in order to equalize results in future battles you must make the British force thirty times as strong as the Boer force. Mr. Garrett shows that the Boer force immediately opposed to Jameson was 2,000 and that there were 6,000 more on hand by the evening of the second day. Arithmetic shows that in order to make himself the equal of the 8,000 Boers, Jameson should have had 240,000 men, whereas he merely had 530 boys. From a military point of view, backed by the facts of history, I conceive that Jameson's military judgment was at fault.

Another thing. Jameson was encumbered by artillery, ammunition, and rifles. The facts of the battle show that he should have had none of those things along. They were heavy, they were in his way, they impeded his march. There was nothing to shoot at but rocks—he knew quite well that there would be nothing to shoot at but rocks—and he knew that artillery and rifles have no effect upon rocks. He was badly overloaded with unessentials. He had eight Maxims— a Maxim is a kind of Galting, I believe, and shoots about 500 bullets per minute; he had one 12½-pounder cannon and two 7-pounders; also, 145,000 rounds of ammunition. He worked the Maxims so hard upon the rocks that five of them became disabled—five of the Maxims, not the rocks. It is believed that upward of 100,000 rounds of ammunition of the various kinds were fired during the twenty-one hours that the battle lasted. *One man killed.* He must have been much mutilated. It was a pity to bring those futile Maxims along. Jameson should have furnished himself with a battery of Pudd'nhead Wilson maxims instead. They are much more deadly than those others, and they are easily carried, because they have no weight.

Mr. Garrett—not very carefully concealing a smile—excuses the presence of the Maxims by saying that they were of very substantial use because their sputtering disordered the aim of the Boers, and in that way saved lives.

Three cannon, eight Maxims, and five hundred rifles yielded a result which emphasized a fact which had already been established—that the British system of standing out in the open to fight Boers who are behind rocks is not wise, not excusable, and ought to be abandoned for something more efficacious. For the purpose of war is to kill, not merely to waste ammunition.

If I could get the management of one of those campaigns, I would know what to do, for I have studied the Boer. He values the Bible above every other thing. The most delicious edible in South Africa is "biltong." You will have seen it mentioned in Olive Schreiner's books. It is what our plainsmen call "jerked beef." It is the Boer's main standby. He has a passion for it, and he is right.

If I had the command of the campaign I would go with rifles only, no cumbersome Maxims and cannon to spoil good rocks with. I would move surreptitiously by night to a point about a quarter of a mile from the Boer camp, and there I would build up a pyramid of biltong and Bibles fifty feet high, and then conceal my men all about. In the morning the Boers would send out spies, and then the rest would come with a rush. I would surround them, and they would have to fight my men on equal terms, in the open. There wouldn't be any Amajuba results.[1]

[1] Just as I am finishing this book an unfortunate dispute has sprung up between Dr. Jameson and his officers, on the one hand, and Colonel Rhodes on the other, concerning the wording of a note which Colonel Rhodes sent from Johannesburg by a cyclist to Jameson just before hostilities began on the memorable New-year's Day. Some of the fragments of this note were found on the battlefield after the fight, and these have been pieced together; the dispute is as to what words the lacking fragments contained. Jameson says the note promised him a reinforcement of three hundred men from Johannesburg. Colonel Rhodes denies this, and says he merely promised to send out "some" men "to meet you."

It seems a pity that these friends should fall out over so little a thing. If the 300 had been sent, what good would it have done? In twenty-one hours of industrious fighting, Jameson's 530 men, with 8 Maxims, 3 cannon, and 145,000 rounds of ammunition, killed an aggregate of one Boer. These statistics show that a reinforcement of 300 Johannesburgers, armed merely with muskets, would have killed, at the outside, only a little over a half of another Boer. This would not have saved the day. It would not even have seriously affected the general result. The figures show clearly, and with mathematical violence, that the only way to save Jameson, or even give him a fair and equal chance with the enemy, was for Johannesburg to send him 240 Maxims, 90 cannon, 600 car-loads of ammunition, and 240,000 men. Johannesburg was not in a position to do this. Johannesburg has been called very hard names for not reinforcing Jameson. But in every instance this has been done by two classes of persons—people who do not read history, and people, like Jameson, who do not understand what it means after they have read it.

Chapter XXXII

None of us can have as many virtues as the fountain-pen, or half its cursedness; but we can try.
—*Pudd'nhead Wilson's New Calendar.*

The Duke of Fife has borne testimony that Mr. Rhodes deceived him. That is also what Mr. Rhodes did with the Reformers. He got them into trouble, and then stayed out himself. A judicious man. He has always been that. As to this there was a moment of doubt, once. It was when he was out on his last pirating expedition in the Matabele country. The cable shouted out that he had gone unarmed, to visit a party of hostile chiefs. It was true, too; and this daredevil thing came near fetching another indiscretion out of the poet laureate. It would have been too bad, for when the facts were all in, it turned out that there was a lady along, too, and she also was unarmed.

In the opinion of many people Mr. Rhodes is South Africa; others think he is only a large part of it. These latter consider that South Africa consists of Table Mountain, the diamond-mines, the Johannesburg gold-fields, and Cecil Rhodes. The gold-fields are wonderful in every way. In seven or eight years they built up, in a desert, a city of a hundred thousand inhabitants, counting white and black together; and not the ordinary mining city of wooden shanties, but a city made out of lasting material. Nowhere in the world is there such a concentration of rich mines as at Johannesburg. Mr. Bonamici, my manager there, gave me a small gold brick with some statistics engraved upon it which record the output of gold from the early days to July, 1895, and exhibit the strides which have been made in the development of the industry; in 1888 the output was $4,162,440; the output of the next five and a half years was (total) $17,585,894; for the single year ending with June, 1895, it was $45,553,700.

The capital which has developed the mines came from England, the mining engineers from America. This is the case with the diamond-mines also. South Africa seems to be the heaven of the American scientific mining engineer. He gets the choicest places, and keeps them. His salary is not based upon what he would get in America, but apparently upon what a whole family of him would get there.

The successful mines pay great dividends, yet the rock is not rich, from a California point of view. Rock which yields ten or twelve dollars a ton is considered plenty rich enough. It is troubled with base metals to such a degree that twenty years ago it would have been only about half as valuable as it is now; for at that time there was no paying way of getting anything out of such rock but the coarser-grained "free" gold; but the new cyanide process has changed all that, and the gold-fields of the world now deliver up fifty million dollars' worth of gold per year which would have gone into the tailing-pile under the former conditions.

The cyanide process was new to me, and full of interest; and among the costly and elaborate mining machinery there were fine things which were new to me, but I was already familiar with the rest of the details of the gold-mining industry. I had been a gold-miner myself, in my day, and knew substantially everything that those people knew about it, except how to make money at it. But I learned a good deal about the Boers there, and that was a fresh subject. What I heard there was afterward repeated to me in other parts of South Africa. Summed up—according to the information thus gained—this is the Boer:

He is deeply religious, profoundly ignorant, dull, obstinate, bigoted, uncleanly in his habits, hospitable, honest in his dealings with the whites, a hard master to his black servant, lazy, a good shot, good horseman, addicted to the chase, a lover of political independence, a good husband and father, not fond of herding together in towns, but liking the seclusion and remoteness and solitude and empty vastness and silence of the veldt; a man of a mighty appetite, and not delicate about what he appeases it with—well satisfied with pork and Indian corn and biltong, requiring only that the quantity shall not be stinted; willing to ride a long journey to take a hand in a rude all-night dance interspersed with vigorous feeding and boisterous jollity, but ready to ride twice as far for a prayer-meeting; proud of his Dutch and Huguenot origin and its religious and military history; proud of his race's achievements in South Africa, its bold plunges into hostile and uncharted deserts in search of free solitudes unvexed by the pestering and detested English, also its victories over the natives and the British; proudest of all, of the direct and effusive personal interest which the Deity has always taken in its affairs. He cannot read, he cannot write; he has one or two newspapers, but he is apparently not aware of it; until latterly he had no schools, and taught his children nothing; news is a term which has no meaning to him, and the thing itself he cares nothing about. He hates to be taxed and resents it. He has stood stock-still in South Africa for two centuries and a half, and would like to stand still till the end of time, for he has no sympathy with Uitlander notions of progress. He is hungry to be rich, for he is human; but his preference has been for riches in cattle, not in fine clothes and fine houses and gold and diamonds. The gold and the diamonds have brought the godless stranger within his gates, also contamination and broken repose, and he wishes that they had never been discovered.

I think that the bulk of those details can be found in Olive Schreiner's books, and she would not be accused of sketching the Boer's portrait with an unfair hand.

Now what would you expect from that unpromising material? What ought you to expect from it? Laws inimical to religious liberty? Yes. Laws denying representation and suffrage to the intruder? Yes. Laws unfriendly to educational institutions? Yes. Laws obstructive of gold production? Yes. Discouragement of railway expansion? Yes. Laws heavily taxing the intruder and overlooking the Boer? Yes.

The Uitlander seems to have expected something very different from all that. I do not know why. Nothing different from it was rationally to be expected. A round man cannot be expected to fit a square hole right away. He must have time to modify his shape. The modification had begun in a detail or two, before the Raid, and was making some progress. It has made further progress since. There are wise men in the Boer Government, and that accounts for the modification; the modification of the Boer mass has probably not begun yet. If the heads of the Boer Government had not been wise men they would have hanged Jameson, and thus turned a very commonplace pirate into a holy martyr. But even their wisdom has its limits, and they will hang Mr. Rhodes if they ever catch him. That will round him and complete him and make him a saint. He has already been called by all other titles that symbolize human grandeur, and he ought to rise to this one, the grandest of all. It will be a dizzy jump from where he is now, but that is nothing, it will land him in good company and be a pleasant change for him.

Some of the things demanded by the Johannesburgers' Manifesto have been conceded since the days of the Raid, and the others will follow in time, no doubt. It was most fortunate for the miners of Johannesburg that the taxes which distressed them so much were levied by the Boer Government, instead of by their friend Rhodes and his Chartered Company of highwaymen, for these latter take *half* of whatever their mining victims find, they do not stop at a mere percentage. If the Johannesburg miners were under their jurisdiction they would be in the poor-house in twelve months.

I have been under the impression all along that I had an unpleasant paragraph about the Boers somewhere in my note-book, and also a pleasant one. I have found them now. The unpleasant one is datet at an interior village, and says:

> Mr. Z called. He is an English Afrikander; is an old resident, and has a Boer wife. He speaks the language, and his professional business is with the Boers exclusively. He told me that the ancient Boer families in the great region of which this village is the commercial center are falling victims to their inherited indolence and dullness in the materialistic latter-day race and struggle, and are dropping one by one into the grip of the usurer—getting hopelessly in debt—and are losing their high place and retiring to second and lower. The Boer's farm does not go to another Boer when he loses it, but to a foreigner. Some have fallen so low that they sell their daughters to the blacks.

Under date of another South African town I find the note which is creditable to the Boers:

> Dr. X told me that in the Kafir war fifteen hundred Kafirs took refuge in a great cave in the mountains about ninety miles

north of Johannesburg, and the Boers blocked up the entrance and smoked them to death. Dr. X has been in there and seen the great array of bleached skeletons—one a woman with the skeleton of a child hugged to her breast.

The great bulk of the savages must go. The white man wants their lands, and all must go excepting such percentage of them as he will need to do his work for him upon terms to be determined by himself. Since history has removed the element of guesswork from this matter and made it certainty, the humanest way of diminishing the black population should be adopted, not the old cruel ways of the past. Mr. Rhodes and his gang have been following the old ways. They are chartered to rob and slay, and they lawfully do it, but not in a compassionate and Christian spirit. They rob the Mashonas and the Matabeles of a portion of their territories in the hallowed old style of "purchase" for a song, and then they force a quarrel and take the rest by the strong hand. They rob the natives of their cattle under the pretext that all the cattle in the country belonged to the king whom they have tricked and assassinated. They issue "regulations" requiring the incensed and harassed natives to work for the white settlers, and neglect their own affairs to do it. This is slavery, and is several times worse than was the American slavery which used to pain England so much; for when this Rhodesian slave is sick, superannuated, or otherwise disabled, he must support himself or starve—his master is under no obligation to support him.

The reduction of the population by Rhodesian methods to the desired limit is a return to the old-time slow-misery and lingering-death system of a discredited time and a crude "civilization." We humanely reduce an overplus of dogs by swift chloroform; the Boer humanely reduced an overplus of blacks by swift suffocation; the nameless but right-hearted Australian pioneer humanely reduced his overplus of aboriginal neighbors by a sweetened swift death concealed in a poisoned pudding. All these are admirable, and worthy of praise; you and I would rather suffer either of these deaths thirty times over in thirty successive days than linger out one of the Rhodesian twenty-year deaths, with its daily burden of insult, humiliation, and forced labor for a man whose entire race the victim hates. Rhodesia is a happy name for that land of piracy and pillage, and puts the right stain upon it.

Several long journeys gave us experience of the Cape Colony railways; easy-riding, fine cars; all the conveniences; thorough cleanliness; comfortable beds furnished for the night trains. It was in the first days of June, and winter; the daytime was pleasant, the night-time nice and cold. Spinning along all day in the cars it was ecstasy to breathe the bracing air and gaze out over the vast brown solitudes of the velvet plains, soft and lovely near by, still softer and lovelier further away, softest and loveliest of all in the remote distances, where dim island-hills seemed afloat, as in a sea—a sea made of dream-stuff and flushed with colors faint and rich; and dear me, the depth of the sky, and the beauty of the strange new cloud-forms, and the glory of the sunshine, the lavishness, the wastefulness of it! The vigor and freshness and inspiration of the air and the sun—well, it was all just as Olive Schreiner had made it in her books.

To me the veldt, in its sober winter garb, was surpassingly beautiful. There were unlevel stretches where it was rolling and swelling, and rising and subsiding, and sweeping superbly on and on, and still on and on like an ocean, toward the far-away horizon, its pale brown deepening by delicately graduated shades of rich orange, and finally to purple and crimson where it washed against the wooded hills and naked red crags at the base of the sky.

Everywhere, from Cape Town to Kimberley, and from Kimberley to Port Elizabeth and East London, the towns were well populated with tamed blacks; tamed and Christianized too, I suppose, for they wore the dowdy clothes of our Christian civilization. But for that, many of them would have been remarkably handsome. These fiendish clothes, together with the proper lounging gait, good-natured face, happy air, and easy laugh, made them precise counterparts of our American blacks; often where all the other aspects were strikingly and harmoniously and thrillingly African, a flock of these natives would intrude, looking wholly out of place, and spoil it all, making the thing a grating discord, half African and half American.

One Sunday in King William's Town a score of colored women came mincing across the great barren square dressed—oh, in the last perfection of fashion, and newness, and expensiveness, and showy mixture of unrelated colors— all just as I had seen it so often at home; and in their faces and their gait was that languishing, aristocratic, divine delight in their finery which was so familiar to me, and had always been such a satisfaction to my eye and my heart. I seemed among old, old friends; friends of fifty years, and I stopped and cordially greeted them. They broke into a good-fellowship laugh, flashing their white teeth upon me, and all answered at once. I did not understand a word they said. I was astonished; I was not dreaming that they would answer in anything but American.

The voices, too, of the African women, were familiar to me—sweet and musical, just like those of the slave-women of my early days. I followed a couple of them all over the Orange Free State—no, over its capital, Bloemfontein—to hear their liquid voices and the happy ripple of their laughter.

Their language was a large improvement upon American. Also upon the Zulu. It had no Zulu click in it; and it seemed to have no angles or corners, no roughness, no vile *s's* or other hissing sounds, but was very, very mellow and rounded and flowing.

In moving about the country in the trains, I had opportunity to see a good many Boers of the veldt. One day at a village station a hundred of them got out of the third-class cars to feed. Their clothes were very interesting. For ugliness of shapes, and for miracles of ugly colors inharmoniously associated, they were a record.

The effect was nearly as exciting and interesting as that produced by the brilliant and beautiful clothes and perfect taste always on view at the Indian railway-stations. One man had corduroy trousers of a faded chewing-gum tint. And they were new—showing that this tint did not come by calamity, but was intentional; the very ugliest color I have ever seen. A gaunt, shackly country lout six feet high, in battered gray slouched hat with wide brim, and old resin-colored breeches, had on a hideous brand-new woolen coat which was imitation tiger-skin—wavy broad stripes of dazzling yellow and deep brown. I thought he ought to be hanged, and asked the station-master if it could be arranged. He said no; and not only that, but said it rudely; said it with a quite unnecessary show of feeling. Then he muttered something about my being a jackass, and walked away and pointed me out to people, and did everything he could to turn public sentiment against me. It is what one gets for trying to do good.

In the train that day a passenger told me some more about Boer life out in the lonely veldt. He said the Boer gets up early and sets his "niggers" at their tasks (pasturing the cattle, and watching them); eats, smokes, drowses, sleeps; toward evening superintends the milking, etc.; eats, smokes, drowses; goes to bed at early candle-light in the fragrant clothes he (and she) have worn all day and every week-day for years. I remember that last detail, in Olive Schreiner's *Story of an African Farm*. And the passenger told me that the Boers were justly noted for their hospitality. He told me a story about it. He said that his grace the Bishop of a certain See was once making a business progress through the tavernless veldt, and one night he stopped with a Boer; after supper was shown to bed; he undressed, weary and worn out, and was soon sound asleep; in the night he woke up feeling crowded and suffocated, and found the old Boer and his fat wife in bed with him, one on each side, with all their clothes on, and snoring. He had to stay there and stand it—awake and suffering—until toward dawn, when sleep again fell upon him for an hour. Then he woke again. The Boer was gone, but the wife was still at his side.

Those Reformers detested that Boer prison; they were not used to cramped quarters and tedious hours, and weary idleness, and early to bed, and limited movement, and arbitrary and irritating rules, and the absence of the luxuries which wealth comforts the day and the night with. The confinement told upon their bodies and their spirits; still, they were superior men, and they made the best that was to be made of the circumstances. Their wives smuggled delicacies to them, which helped to smooth the way down for the prison fare.

In the train Mr. B. told me that the Boer jail-guards treated the black prisoners—even political ones—mercilessly. An African chief and his following had been kept there nine months without trial, and during all that time they had been without shelter from rain and sun. He said that one day the guards put a big black in the stocks for dashing his soup on the ground; they stretched his legs painfully wide apart, and set him with his back downhill; he could not endure it, and put back his hands upon the slope for a support. The guard ordered him to withdraw the support—and kicked him in the back. "Then," said Mr. B. "the powerful black wrenched the stocks asunder and went for the guard; a Reform prisoner pulled him off, and thrashed the guard himself."

Chapter XXXIII

The very ink with which all history is written is merely fluid prejudice.
　　　　　—Pudd'nhead Wilson's New Calendar.

There isn't a Parallel of Latitude but thinks it would have been the Equator if it had had its rights.
　　　　　—Pudd'nhead Wilson's New Calendar.

NEXT to Mr. Rhodes, to me the most interesting convulsion of nature in South Africa was the diamond-crater. The Rand gold-fields are a stupendous marvel, and they make all other gold-fields small, but I was not a stranger to gold-mining; the veldt was a noble thing to see, but it was only another and lovelier variety of our Great Plains; the natives were very far from being uninteresting, but they were not new; and as for the towns, I could find my way without a guide through the most of them because I had learned the streets, under other names, in towns just like them in other lands; but the diamond-mine was a wholly fresh thing, a splendid and absorbing novelty. Very few people in the world have seen the diamond in its home. It has but three or four homes in the world, whereas gold has a million. It is worth while to journey around the globe to see anything which can truthfully be called a novelty, and the diamond-mine is the greatest and most select and restricted novelty which the globe has in stock.

The Kimberley diamond deposits were discovered about 1869, I think. When everything is taken into consideration, the wonder is that they were not discovered five thousand years ago and made familiar to the African world for the rest of time. For this reason the first diamonds were found on the surface of the ground. They were smooth and limpid, and in the sunlight they vomited fire. They were the very things which an African savage of any era would value above every other thing in the world excepting a glass bead. For two or three centuries we have been buying his lands, his cattle, his neighbor, and any other thing he had for sale, for glass beads: and so it is strange that he was indifferent to the diamonds— for he must have picked them up many and many a time. It would not occur to him to try to sell them to whites, of course, since the whites already had plenty of glass beads, and more fashionably shaped, too, than these; but one would think that the poorer sort of black, who could not afford real glass, would have been humbly content to decorate himself with the imitation, and that presently the white trader would notice the things, and dimly suspect, and carry some of them home, and find out what they were, and at once empty a multitude of fortune-hunters into Africa. There are many strange things in human history; one of the strangest is that the sparkling diamonds lay there so long without exciting any one's interest.

The revelation came at last by accident. In a Boer's hut out in the wide solitude of the plains, a traveling stranger noticed a child playing with a bright object, and was told it was a piece of glass which had been found in the veldt. The stranger bought it for a trifle and carried it away; and being without honor, made another stranger believe it was a diamond, and so got $125 out of him for it, and was as pleased with himself as if he had done a righteous thing. In Paris the wronged stranger sold it to a pawnshop for $10,000, who sold it to a countess for $90,000, who sold it to a brewer for $800,000, who traded it to a king for a dukedom and a pedigree, and the king "put it up the spout."† I know these particulars to be correct.

The news flew around, and the South African diamond boom began. The original traveler—the dishonest one—now remembered that he had once seen a Boer teamster chocking his wagon-wheel on a steep grade with a diamond as large as a football, and he laid aside his occupations and started out to hunt for it, but not with the intention of cheating anybody out of $125 with it, for he had reformed.

We now come to matters more didactic. Diamonds are not embedded in rock ledges fifty miles long, like the Johannesburg gold, but are distributed through the rubbish of a filled-up well, so to speak. The well is rich, its walls are sharply defined; outside of the walls are no diamonds. The well is a crater, and a large one. Before it had been meddled with, its surface was even with the level plain, and there was no sign to suggest that it was there. The pasturage covering the surface of the Kimberley crater was sufficient for the support of a cow, and the pasturage underneath was sufficient for the support of a kingdom; but the cow did not know it, and lost her chance.

The Kimberley crater is roomy enough to admit the

† From the Greek *δ̓ς δ̔ς* meaning "pawned it."

Roman Coliseum; the bottom of the crater has not been reached, and no one can tell how far down in the bowels of the earth it goes. Originally, it was a perpendicular hole packed solidly full of blue rock or cement, and scattered through that blue mass, like raisins in a pudding, were the diamonds. As deep down in the earth as the blue stuff extends, so deep will the diamonds be found.

There are three or four other celebrated craters near by—a circle three miles in diameter would inclose them all. They are owned by the De Beers Company, a consolidation of diamond properties arranged by Mr. Rhodes twelve or fourteen years ago. The De Beers owns other craters; they are under the grass, but the De Beers knows where they are, and will open them some day, if the market should require it.

Originally, the diamond deposits were the property of the Orange Free State; but a judicious "rectification" of the boundary line shifted them over into the British territory of Cape Colony. A high official of the Free State told me that the sum of $400,000 was handed to his commonwealth as a compromise, or indemnity, or something of the sort, and that he thought his commonwealth did wisely to take the money and keep out of a dispute, since the power was all on the one side and the weakness all on the other. The De Beers Company dig out $400,000 worth of diamonds per week, now. The Cape got the territory, but no profit; for Mr. Rhodes and the Rothschilds and the other De Beers people own the mines, and they pay no taxes.

In our day the mines are worked upon scientific principles, under the guidance of the ablest mining-engineering talent procurable in America. There are elaborate works for reducing the blue rock and passing it through one process after another until every diamond it contains has been hunted down and secured. I watched the "concentrators" at work—big tanks containing mud and water and invisible diamonds—and was told that each could stir and churn and properly treat three hundred car-loads of mud per day—sixteen hundred pounds to the car-load—and reduce it to three car-loads of slush. I saw the three car-loads of slush taken to the "pulsators" and there reduced to a quarter of a load of nice clean dark-colored sand. Then I followed it to the sorting-tables and saw the men deftly and swiftly spread it out and brush it about and seize the diamonds as they showed up. I assisted, and once I found a diamond half as large as an almond. It is an exciting kind of fishing, and you feel a fine thrill of pleasure every time you detect the glow of one of those limpid pebbles through the veil of dark sand. I would like to spend my Saturday holidays in that charming sport every now and then. Of course there are disappointments. Sometimes you find a diamond which is not a diamond; it is only a quartz crystal or some such worthless thing. The expert can generally distinguish it from the precious stone which it is counterfeiting; but if he is in doubt he lays it on a flatiron and hits it with a sledge-hammer. If it is a diamond it holds its own; if it is anything else, it is reduced to powder. I liked that experiment very much, and did not tire of repetitions of it. It was full of enjoyable apprehensions, unmarred by any personal sense of risk. The De Beers concern treats 8,000 car-loads—about 6,000 tons—of blue rock per day, and the result is three pounds of diamonds. Value, uncut, $50,000 to $70,000. After cutting, they will weigh considerably less than a pound, but will be worth four or five times as much as they were before.

All the plain around that region is spread over, a foot deep, with blue rock, placed there by the company, and looks like a plowed field. Exposure for a length of time makes the rock easier to work than it is when it comes out of the mine. If mining should cease now, the supply of rock spread over those fields would furnish the usual eight thousand car-loads per day to the separating-works during three years. The fields are fenced and watched; and at night they are under the constant inspection of lofty electric searchlight. They contain fifty or sixty million dollars' worth of diamonds, and there is an abundance of enterprising thieves around.

In the dirt of the Kimberley streets there is much hidden wealth. Some time ago the people were granted the privilege of a free wash-up. There was a general rush, the work was done with thoroughness, and a good harvest of diamonds was gathered.

The deep mining is done by natives. There are many hundreds of them. They live in quarters built around the inside of a great compound. They are a jolly and good-natured lot, and accommodating. They performed a war-dance for us, which was the wildest exhibition I have ever seen. They are not allowed outside of the compound during their term of service—three months, I think it is, as a rule. They go down the shaft, stand their watch, come up again, are searched, and go to bed or to their amusements in the compound; and this routine they repeat, day in and day out.

It is thought that they do not now steal many diamonds—successfully. They used to swallow them, and find other ways of concealing them, but the white man found ways of beating their various games. One man cut his leg and shoved a diamond into the wound, but even that project did not succeed. When they find a fine large diamond they are more likely to report it than to steal it, for in the former case they get a reward, and in the latter they are quite apt to merely get into trouble. Some years ago, in a mine not owned by the De Beers, a black found what has been claimed to be the largest diamond known to the world's history; and as a reward he was released from service and given a blanket, a horse, and five hundred dollars. It made him a Vanderbilt. He could buy four wives, and have money left. Four wives are an ample support for a native. With four wives he is wholly independent, and need never do a stroke of work again.

That great diamond weighs 971 carats. Some say it is as big as a piece of alum, others say it is as large as a bite of rock-candy, but the best authorities agree that it is almost exactly the size of a chunk of ice. But those details are not important; and in my opinion not trustworthy. It has a flaw in it, otherwise it would be of incredible value. As it is, it is held to be worth $2,000,000. After cutting it ought to be worth from $5,000,000 to $8,000,000, therefore persons desiring to save money should buy it now. It is owned by a syndicate, and apparently there is no satisfactory market for it. It is earning nothing; it is eating its head off. Up to this time it had made nobody rich but the native who found it.

He found it in a mine which was being worked by contract. That is to say, a company had bought the privilege of taking from the mine 5,000,000 car-loads of blue rock, for a sum down and a royalty. Their speculation had not paid; but on the very day that their privilege ran out that native found the two-million-dollar diamond and handed it over to them. Even the diamond culture is not without its romantic episodes.

The Koh-i-Noor is a large diamond, and valuable; but it cannot compete in these matters with three which—according to legend—are among the crown trinkets of Portugal and Russia. One of these is held to be worth $20,000,000; another, $25,000,000; and the third something over $28,000,000.

Those are truly wonderful diamonds, whether they exist or not; and yet they are of but little importance by comparison with the one wherewith the Boer wagoner chocked his wheel on that steep grade as heretofore referred to. In Kimberley I had some conversation with the man who saw the Boer do that—an incident which had occurred twenty-seven or twenty-eight years before I had my talk with him. He assured me that that diamond's value could have been over a billion dollars, but not under it. I believed him, because he had devoted twenty-seven years to hunting for it, and was in a position to know.

A fitting and interesting finish to an examination of the tedious and laborious and costly processes whereby the diamonds are gotten out of the deeps of the earth and freed from the base stuffs which imprison them is the visit to the De Beers offices in the town of Kimberley, where the result of each day's mining is brought every day, and weighed, assorted, valued, and deposited in safes against shipping-day. An unknown and unaccredited person cannot get into that place; and it seemed apparent from the generous supply of warning and protective and prohibitory signs that were posted all about that not even the known and accredited can steal diamonds there without inconvenience.

We saw the day's output—shining little nests of diamonds, distributed a foot apart, along a counter, each nest reposing upon a sheet of white paper. That day's catch was about $70,000 worth. In the course of a year half a ton of diamonds pass under the scales there and sleep on that counter; the resulting money is $18,000,000 or $20,000,000. Profit, about $12,000,000.

Young girls were doing the sorting—a nice, clean, dainty, and probably distressing employment. Every day ducal incomes sift and sparkle through the fingers of those young girls; yet they go to bed at night as poor as they were when they got up in the morning. The same thing next day, and all the days.

They are beautiful things, those diamonds, in their native state. They are of various shapes; they have flat surfaces, rounded borders, and never a sharp edge. They are of all colors and shades of color, from dew-drop white to actual black; and their smooth and rounded surfaces and contours, variety of color, and transparent limpidity, make them look like piles of assorted candies. A very light straw color is their commonest tint. It seemed to me that these uncut gems must be more beautiful than any cut ones could be; but when a collection of cut ones was brought out, I saw my mistake. Nothing is so beautiful as a rose diamond with the light playing through it, except that uncostly thing which is just like it—wavy sea-water with the sunlight playing through it and striking a white-sand bottom.

Before the middle of July we reached Cape Town, and the end of our African journeyings. And well satisfied; for, towering above us was Table Mountain—a reminder that we had now seen each and all of the great features of South Africa except Mr. Cecil Rhodes. I realize that that is a large exception. I know quite well that whether Mr. Rhodes is the lofty and worshipful patriot and statesman that multitudes believe him to be, or Satan come again, as the rest of the world account him, he is still the most imposing figure in the British Empire outside of England. When he stands on the Cape of Good Hope, his shadow falls to the Zambesi. He is the only colonial in the British dominions whose goings and comings are chronicled and discussed under all the globe's meridians, and whose speeches, unclipped, are cabled from the ends of the earth; and he is the only unroyal outsider whose arrival in London can compete for attention with an eclipse.

That he is an extraordinary man, and not an accident of fortune, not even his dearest South African enemies were willing to deny, so far as I heard them testify. The whole South African world seemed to stand in a kind of shuddering awe of him, friend and enemy alike. It was as if he were deputy God on the one side, deputy Satan on the other, proprietor of the people, able to make them or ruin them by his breath, worshiped by many, hated by many, but blasphemed by none among the judicious, and even by the indiscreet in guarded whispers only.

What is the secret of his formidable supremacy? One says it is his prodigious wealth—a wealth whose drippings in salaries and in other ways support multitudes and make them his interested and loyal vassals; another says it is his personal magnetism and his persuasive tongue, and that these hypnotize and make happy slaves of all that drift within the circle of their influence; another says it is his majestic ideas, his vast schemes for the territorial aggrandizement of England, his patriotic and unselfish ambition to spread her beneficent protection and her just rule over the pagan wastes of Africa and make luminous the African darkness with the glory of her name; and another says he wants the earth and wants it for his own, and that the belief that he will get it and let his friends in on the ground floor is *the* secret that rivets so many eyes upon him and keeps him in the zenith where the view is unobstructed.

One may take his choice. They are all the same price. One fact is sure: he keeps his prominence and a vast following, no matter what he does. He "deceives" the Duke of Fife—it is the Duke's word—but that does not destroy the Duke's loyalty to him. He tricks the Reformers into immense trouble with his Raid, but the most of them believe he meant well. He weeps over the harshly taxed Johannesburgers and makes them his friends; at the same time he taxes his Charter settlers fifty per cent., and so wins their affection and their confidence that they are squelched with despair at every rumor that the Charter is to be annulled. He raids and robs and slays and enslaves the Matabele and gets worlds of Charter-Christian applause for it. He has beguiled England into buying Charter waste-paper for Bank of England notes, ton for ton, and the ravished still burn incense to him as the Eventual God of Plenty. He has done everything he could think of to pull himself down to the ground; he had done more than enough to pull sixteen common-run great men down; yet there he stands, to this day, upon his dizzy summit under the dome of the sky, an apparent permanency, the marvel of the time, the mystery of the age, an Archangel with wings to half the world, Satan with a tail to the other half.

I admire him, I frankly confess it; and when his time comes I shall buy a piece of the rope for a keepsake.

Conclusion

I have traveled more than any one else, and I have noticed that even the angels speak English with an accent.
                    —Pudd'nhead Wilson's New Calendar.

I SAW Table Rock, anyway—a majestic pile. It is three thousand feet high. It is also seventeen thousand feet high. These figures may be relied upon. I got them in Cape Town from the two best-informed citizens, men who had made Table Rock the study of their lives. And I saw Table Bay, so named for its levelness. I saw the Castle—built by the Dutch East India Company three hundred years ago—where the Commanding General lives; I saw St. Simon's Bay, where the Admiral lives. I saw the Government, also the Parliament, where they quarreled in two languages when I was there, and agreed in none. I saw the club. I saw and explored the beautiful sea-girt drives that wind about the mountains and through the paradise where the villas are. Also I saw some of the fine old Dutch mansions, pleasant homes of the early times, pleasant homes to-day, and enjoyed the privilege of their hospitalities.

And just before I sailed I saw in one of them a quaint old

picture which was a link in a curious romance—a picture of
a pale, intellectual young man in a pink coat with a high black
collar. It was a portrait of Dr. James Barry, a military surgeon
who came out to the Cape fifty years ago with his regiment.
He was a wild young fellow, and was guilty of various kinds
of misbehavior. He was several times reported to headquarters in England, and it was in each case expected that orders
would come out to deal with him promptly and severely, but
for some mysterious reason no orders of any kind ever came
back—nothing came but just an impressive silence. This
made him an imposing and uncanny wonder to the town.

Next, he was promoted—away up. He was made Medical Superintendent General, and transferred to India. Presently he was back at the Cape again and at his escapades once
more. There were plenty of pretty girls, but none of them
caught him, none of them could get hold of his heart; evidently he was not a marrying man. And that was another
marvel, another puzzle, and made no end of perplexed talk.
Once he was called in the night, an obstetric service, to do
what he could for a woman who was believed to be dying.
He was prompt and scientific, and saved both mother and
child. There are other instances of record which testify to his
mastership of his profession; and many which testify to his
love of it and his devotion to it. Among other adventures of
his was a duel of a desperate sort, fought with swords, at the
Castle. He killed his man.

The child heretofore mentioned as having been saved by
Dr. Barry so long ago, was named for him, and still lives in
Cape Town. He had Dr. Barry's portrait painted, and gave
it to the gentleman in whose old Dutch house I saw it—the
quaint figure in pink coat and high black collar.

The story seems to be arriving nowhere. But that is
because I have not finished. Dr. Barry died in Cape Town
thirty years ago. It was then discovered that he was *a woman.*

The legend goes that inquiries—soon silenced—developed the fact that she was a daughter of a great English house, and that that was why her Cape wildnesses brought no punishment and got no notice when reported to the government at home. Her name was an *alias*. She had disgraced herself with her people; so she chose to change her name and her sex and take a new start in the world.

We sailed on the 15th of July in the *Norman,* a beautiful ship, perfectly appointed. The voyage to England occupied a short fortnight, without a stop except at Madeira. A good and restful voyage for tired people, and there were several of us. I seemed to have been lecturing a thousand years, though it was only a twelvemonth, and a considerable number of the others were Reformers who were fagged out with their five months of seclusion in the Pretoria prison.

Our trip around the earth ended at the Southampton pier, where we embarked thirteen months before. It seemed a fine and large thing to have accomplished—the circumnavigation of this great globe in that little time, and I was privately proud of it. For a moment. Then came one of those vanity-snubbing astronomical reports from the Observatory people, whereby it appeared that another great body of light had lately flamed up in the remotenesses of space which was traveling at a gait which would enable it to do all that I had done in *a minute and a half.* Human pride is not worth while; there is always something lying in wait to take the wind out of it.

THE END